26 MILES
TO BOSTON

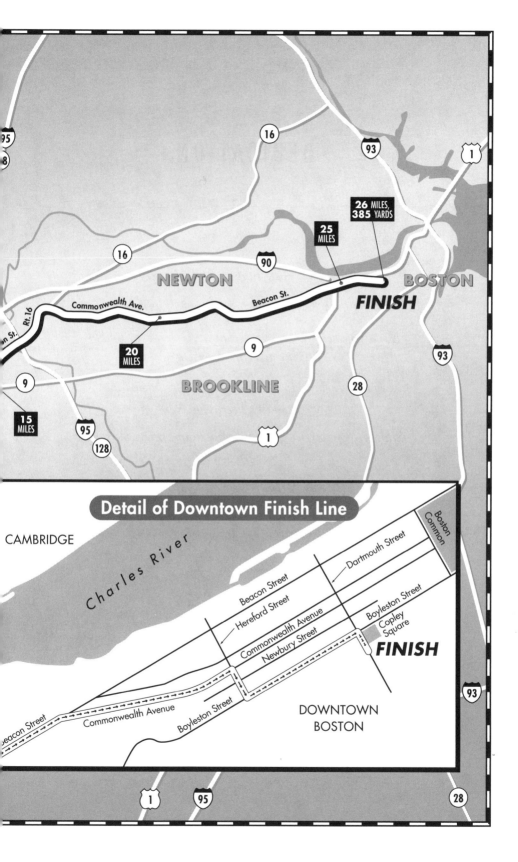

Detail of Downtown Finish Line

DEDICATION

– – – –

To my . . .

Friends for their support and friendship

Nana Kenny, who inspired me to write

*Nana Connelly, whose perpetual smile made a Sunday
lunch a radiant experience*

*Father-in-law, Tom Concannon, who showed me
courage through a simple walk*

*Siblings, who aren't just my brothers and sisters but also
my friends*

Parents, for their love and guidance

*Wife, Noreen, and my son Ryan, for filling my life with
love and purpose*

26 MILES
TO BOSTON

The Boston Marathon Experience from
Hopkinton to Copley Square

MICHAEL CONNELLY

– – – –

Forewords by
John Kelley, Bill Rodgers and Uta Pippig

THE LYONS PRESS

Guilford, Connecticut

An imprint of The Globe Pequot Press

The Lyons Press is an imprint of The Globe Pequot Press

10 9 8 7 6 5 4 3 2

Printed in the United States of America

Designed by Claire Zoghb

Library of Congress Cataloging-in-Publication Data

Connelly, Michael.
  26 Miles to Boston : the Boston Marathon Experience from Hopkinton to Copley Square / by Michael Connelly.
      p. cm.
Includes index.
  ISBN 1-58574-828-5 (pb : alk. paper)
  1. Boston Marathon. 2. Marathon running--Massachussets--Boston. I. Title.
  GV1065.22.B67C66 2003
  796.42'52'0974461--dc21

CONTENTS

– – – –

FOREWORD

By John "the Elder" Kelley

— — — —

The Boston Marathon in its present form is the greatest marathon in the world, due to the guidance of the Boston Athletic Association (Guy Morse, Gloria Ratti and the other members of the BAA) and the John Hancock Financial Services Company (major sponsor) who now is a great help to the BAA.

No other marathon in the world can match the race for its color, longevity, glamour, prestige and history. This is the race that the best runners in the world want to win even above the Olympic Marathon (incidentally first prize is a lot more).

During the past twenty-five years or so the women runners have been added to the race, who in my opinion are just as great. A good female runner can train for two or three years and run a 2:40 marathon. Joan Benoit is a good example. She is the two-time champion in the Women's Division. There are many other fine women runners. I must not forget the Wellesley College girls. Someone once told me that the administration would not allow the girls to watch the runners go by. How things have changed!

In 1921, at the age of 12, my father took me to see my first Boston Marathon. At that race I saw Frank Zuna from New York come down Commonwealth Avenue and my father said, "Look at the all the pep he has." I guess I fell in love with it then. I found out in later years that my parents used to go and watch the marathons and my mother said, "I never, ever dreamed that I would have a son who would run the marathon."

The following pages enabled me to relive the race and its history. *26 Miles to Boston* and its different voices speak to both runners and fans. The book is unique in its ability to capture the Boston Marathon and marathoning itself. Through each chapter the reader can appreciate and feel the challenge of the athletic event while also getting a sense of the celebration over the course of the route.

As a spectator, two-time champion, 61-time participant and Grand Marshall of the race, I truly appreciate the number of perspectives represented in *26 Miles to Boston*. While reading the book, I reflected upon many wonderful experiences and found great pride in the fact that I have been part of something of such character and quality.

I'm proud to be able to participate in this book. I feel it truly captures the spirit, history and strategy of this wonderful event. I hope you enjoy the book as much as I did.

FOREWORD

By Bill Rodgers

— — — —

When Michael Connelly contacted me to write a bit about his book, *26 Miles to Boston*, I wasn't overly enthusiastic. It seemed to me that the race had received enough attention as it was. Was I wrong! Connelly writes about the old race from many new and interesting angles. You can't help but be seduced by this book. The stories flow one after another like a marathon runner's footsteps. Each story adds to the razzle-dazzle of the race's long and colorful history.

Of course that's exactly what the Boston Marathon has to offer – lots of colorful history over the 100 plus years of the race. But no one has told the other stories of the race beyond those of the top runners. Connelly does give the other perspectives and thoughts, and I salute him for doing so, as it is only in recent days (as you'll see from reading the book) that the top runners have received respect as world class athletes. As recently as my win in 1975, a well-known Boston sports commentator indicated that the runners at the Boston Marathon weren't athletes at all.

Because of my own background as a competitive runner, I've always been interested in reading about the top runners at the Boston Marathon and enjoyed the accounts of the race. People like Clarence DeMar, Johnny Kelley and Joan Benoit Samuelson have told of their exploits as champions at Boston. The top racers of the 90's have been of interest too, but what I truly enjoyed reading in *26 Miles to Boston* were the stories that are never told – accounts of volunteers, police officers, medical personnel, merchants in stores along the route, spectators, officials and of course the "average runner," such as Michael Connelly's account of his own race experience as an amateur runner fulfilling a promise to himself to run the Boston Marathon. The athlete's challenge is what the Boston Marathon is all about. The athlete's heart beats away inside all of us. Connelly writes, as he ran up Heartbreak Hill, "I noticed a man running with a prosthesis on one of his legs, thus causing me to be both inspired and proud to be part of an event where courage is just as important as athletic ability."

Having run the race 13 times, won four and dropped out of the race twice, I know what it feels like to take on the challenge of running the Boston Marathon. Michael Connelly does too, but he goes on to explore why a simple foot race has the impact it has on runners and non-runners alike. Some overly intellectual sedentary fellow once observed that runners never seem to smile as they run. Surely he was never at the Boston Marathon. Had he been, he would have seen the real smiles, the ones with really deep satisfaction behind them.

To run the Boston Marathon is not an easy thing. To write well about it and explain its charisma is even harder. Michael Connelly's *26 Miles to Boston* is a winner in this regard. The reason I say this is that not many sports books have the capacity to make you feel as though the event was happening only ten feet away. This one does do that. Connelly has exposed the special qualities of the Boston Marathon foot race and why it is more than an ordinary sporting event.

FOREWORD

By Uta Pippig

— — — —

For more than a century, the Boston Marathon has been a great race. No marathon in the world, including the Olympics, has the tradition, charm and character of Boston. The Boston Marathon is special because its history is so tangible. Because the original course and many great runners are still a part of the race, you can see and live a century of running. Each race adds to this legacy and enhances the allure of this wonderful event.

When I was a citizen of East Germany, I dreamed of running just one race –The Boston Marathon. I dreamed of just being a part of the race; to win seemed beyond my greatest expectations. I feel very fortunate to have been victorious in this great old marathon and rank my win in the 100th running as my most satisfying running achievement.

Many people make this race possible. The Boston Athletic Association does a wonderful job managing such a difficult event. Every runner is treated as an equal and each is able to run on the finely tuned course. John Hancock Financial Services, the race's primary sponsor, provides the Boston Marathon the necessary financial support and guidance to continue into the next century. It is through the efforts of many that those involved in the event are made to feel like a family and a team.

Boston and the Boston Marathon complement each other well. The city contributes immeasurable support while the marathon furnishes Boston with an event of exceptional quality. Both the city and race are very special to me. I just love Boston! I feel as though the people of

Boston have taken me in as one of their own. It's like my home away from home!

The fans that line the course have a wonderful understanding of the race and warm and sincere support for each runner. This is very special—they are as much a part of the race as the runners. I often wonder if other runners also feel a special connection with the spectators. Their overwhelming energy and support carry into other aspects of my life and draw me back to Boston. When I visit in the summer or in the autumn, I enjoy driving out to Hopkinton and Ashland, or running through Newton, or just walking the streets of Boston. I can feel the Boston Marathon even though the race is months away.

The history and important qualities of the Boston Marathon are chronicled well in *26 Miles to Boston*. The many opinions and stories provide a great perspective of the race. For those who are new to Boston, the book is an invitation to the race and its history. It is like a runner's personal handbook, providing a recipe on how to run a marathon. For race veterans, it serves as a memento, a reminder of Boston's great moments and extraordinary history.

In reading *26 Miles to Boston*, you will come to appreciate why this race is so loved around the world. Perhaps it will also give you a good feeling because it shows the Boston Marathon as a wonderful way for people to come together in peace and happiness, and in doing so, help to create another important chapter in the long and illustrious history of this great event.

INTRODUCTION

To capture the essence of the Boston Marathon experience, one must live it, watch it, drink it and run it. Each perspective provides a unique and special look at why a simple road race has taken on the mantle of a legendary event.

The Boston Marathon is life itself. For a hundred years the Mecca of all running events, it is a metaphor for the world around it. As the world has evolved, the Boston Marathon has evolved with it.

Each April, people from every corner of the world travel thousands of miles to run twenty-six. Nowhere on the face of the earth do more people from more diverse backgrounds gather for a one-day event. The Boston Marathon is a celebration of tradition, a celebration of health-and-fitness, a celebration of life. From Hopkinton to Boston, the spectators and runners are provided a stage to act out a play that stretches the gamut from Shakespeare to Pee Wee Herman. Tragedy, triumph, love, frustration and comedy are all components of this road race.

The twenty-six miles of roads, sidewalks, and bridges are nothing more than a backdrop for athletic conquests, athletic failures, weddings, inebriated college students and overpriced vendors—all of whom play an intricate role in molding this race and its legacy.

The Boston Marathon's ultimate purpose is as distinct as the people who embrace it. Whether your goal is to run, to barbecue, to say hello to your neighbor, to gather with your family or to delay studying for college finals, the race is a willing partner for all who come to celebrate.

– – – –

When I contemplated the practicality of writing a book about the Boston Marathon, I became concerned with how many doors I could open considering the fact that I run ten-minute miles.

But thankfully, my concern dissipated the more I focused on the theme of the book. *26 Miles to Boston* is about the entire Boston Marathon experience. It's not a knockdown, black-and-white running book that lectures you about carbohydrates, glycogen, and running form. This book is written so that spectator, runner (amateur or professional), worker, and volunteer can all appreciate their contribution to the race while at the same time getting a better understanding for the different perspectives they have yet to experience.

With that in mind, I realized that my diverse experiences involving the Boston Marathon made me a worthy candidate to write a book of this sort. For almost a third of the race's history, I have had the pleasurable opportunity of witnessing the race from almost every angle possible. In the early years, I saw the race from my father's shoulders; in college, I watched the race from a keg party in an apartment overlooking Cleveland Circle; after college, I cautiously stood on a rooftop just past Kenmore Square; years later, I took the baton from my father, and provided shoulders for my own son; and finally for the 100th running of the Boston Marathon, I celebrated the event by witnessing the race from the inside out as a competitor—fulfilling my annual pledge that someday I would run Boston.

— — — —

The following pages represent my attempt to capture the soul of the race. My ultimate goal is to bring the reader on a marathon odyssey that captures the uniqueness of each mile and each experience of the event. Throughout the book, you'll find four distinct perspectives of the race and its history:

- A narrative description of my experiences both as a runner and as a spectator.
- Historical anecdotes of the race, arranged by mile.
- Comments from the great runners of the race—their thoughts,

remembrances, and running strategies. (The list of past champions represents over forty Boston Marathon championships.)

- The fourth angle is a product of the insights of the many spectators, officials and business owners who line the course including mayors and selectmen, fire chiefs, police chiefs, real estate agents, historians, store owners and representatives from the three colleges, two country clubs and one hospital along the route. These viewpoints provide a thorough look at the race from the outside-in.

━ ━ ━ ━

In my attempt to provide the reader with the quintessential look at the Boston Marathon experience, my labors would have been for naught if it weren't for a number of friends and associates whom helped to make it all possible. I would like to acknowledge their efforts with an insufficient mention of their name: my wife, Noreen Connelly, who was stuck driving the route, listening to me whine and providing encouragement for her spouse no matter how slow he ran or wrote; my son, Ryan, who inspires me everyday; my mother, Marilyn Connelly, who has spent her life reading term papers, book reports and now manuscripts; my father, John Connelly Jr. who provides the ideal devil's advocate; Thomas McCarthy, senior editor of Lyons Press, who took a chance on me; Uta Pippig, whose grace, courage and athletic accomplishment all qualify her as the ideal person to introduce this book and thus honor these pages with her thoughtful words; Johnny "the Elder" Kelley whose two championships, seven second place finishes, eighteen top ten finishes and fifty-eight overall finishes makes him not only the patriarch of the race but also the perfect individual to help christen the book; Bill Rodgers, arguably the greatest marathoner of all time and four time winner of Boston blesses this book with his thoughtful reflections. Also Chris Mongillo, pre-press coordinator for the Lyons Press, Dr. Maureen Connelly, Kevin Connelly, Esquire Jack Fleming (special thanks), Gloria Ratti, Julia Beeson and Lars Dietrich of the Boston Athletic Association, Anthony Catalano (computer savior), Debbie Nocella, Maria Mello,

Mariellen Gipson, Charlie Gaffney, Martin Duffy, Bruce Shaw, Angela Heffernan, Tom McLaughlin, Richard Twombly, Jack Radley, Pat Williams, Tom Ratcliffe, John Cronin at the Boston Herald, Roy Clark, Al Larkin, Chris Young, Dan Shaughnessy, Dorothy Dolongschamps of the Natick Historical Society, Dick Fannon of the Ashland Historical Society, Carolyn McGuire of the Framingham Historical Society, Susan Abele of the Newton Historical Society, Laura Nelson of the Wellesley Historical Society, Bob Sullivan of the Brookline Library, Doe Coover, Becky Saletan, Aaron Schmidt and Charles Longley of the Boston Public Library, Tracey & Jeff McEvoy, Dr. Diane English (Orthopedic Surgeon), Dr. Caroline Foote (Cardiologist), Jennifer Worden and Sandra Southworth—physical therapists at the Prescription Orthopedic Sports Therapy clinic—and a host of others whose ideas, input and suggestions have all been incorporated into this project.

Thank you all for making this project a reality.

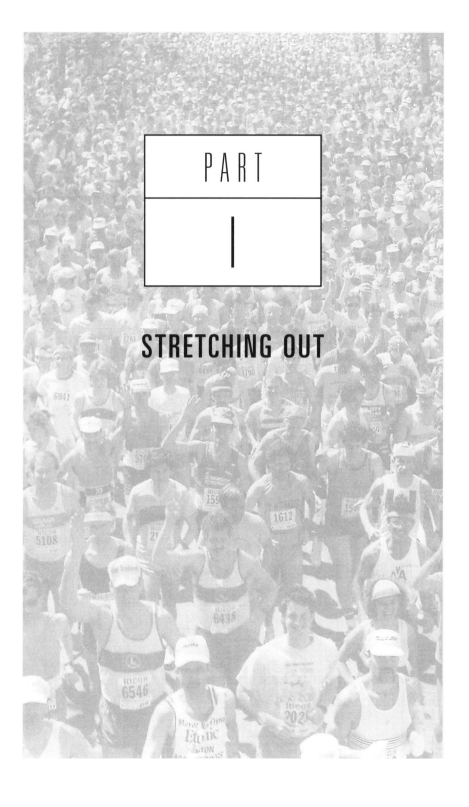

PART

I

STRETCHING OUT

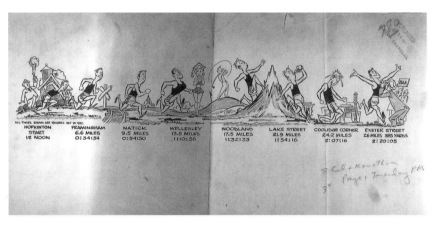

THE GENESIS

Five-time wheelchair champion, Jim Knaub: "The Boston Marathon is a race that is not competed against other athletes but raced against a supreme being. The Boston Marathon is bigger than life. It's a feeling like no other."

— — — —

Every April, runners line up in Hopkinton, Massachusetts, for the honor of participating in the world's greatest race. For over a hundred years, athletes have tested themselves against the most demanding twenty-six miles and 385 yards in the running world. Across eight towns, the runners will be asked to call upon muscle and will in order to be granted the privilege of entering Boston. Down slopes and up mountains, around corners and through crowds, the runners will run their own chapters in the long history of the Boston Marathon. The fight will be individual yet collective; the motivations are diverse but essentially the same. The competitors will run east, tracing the steps of a century of forerunners, leaving their own tracks for those who follow.

Some might ask why so many would subject themselves to such a challenge. Perhaps these people with sneakers on their feet and numbers on their chests are cursed with an excessive level of adrenaline and must run to release the beast within. Or maybe it's the unusually large heart of the typical marathoner—both literally and figuratively—that drives him ahead while others are left behind, curious and unfulfilled.

I'm still not exactly sure why I was drawn to Hopkinton on that third Monday in April of 1996. For three decades, I had cheered from the sidewalks of Newton and was content, although my curiosity had always been aroused. As runner after runner passed before my eyes, I found myself wondering why these athletes moved forward in such contradictory states of discomfort and joy. I guess this annual wonderment evolved into a warped quest to discover the answer. Little by little I was seduced by the race.

The seduction, however, was gradual. It took thirty-two years for my heart to veto my brain's impulse to remain stationary and safe. Why did I do it? It was not simply because the race "was there," like Mt. Everest. There must have been some deeper motive that prompted me to attempt athletic suicide. It is closer to the truth to say that, by the age of thirty-two, I was starting a process of review. I had entered a stage in which life and its offerings were no longer taken for granted; I was beginning to grapple with mortality. Now the lessons that bored me in philosophy class years ago started to have relevance. Now Socrates' famous warning that "the unexamined life is not worth living" took on meaning. The purpose of my mission was clearer and clearer each time I went out for a run.

When I agreed to run Boston, I didn't realize that my life would change. I didn't realize that, beyond eating up miles, part of the process is taking an inventory of life. During my first three decades, I had lived a life devoid of discovery. Now nature was telling me to endeavor outside of my element and test my limitations, because if I didn't now I would always wonder. I would always ask the questions, but I would never have the answers. So I went to Hopkinton that year to explore while I still could climb. I ran to write a new chapter in my life. I ran from Hopkinton to Boston both to run a race and to prove myself worthy of my gift of life.

— — — —

The first train left the Boston & Albany Station at 7:00 A.M., and the second at 9:12 A.M. on the morning of April 19, 1897. In all, fifteen runners made the trip to Ashland to attempt the implausible—a twenty-four and a half mile run back to Boston.

The trains dropped the runners and their attendants off in Ashland. From there, they proceeded to the Central House Hotel for a pre-race dinner. The banquet hall was divided between two groups: the New York contingent on one side and the Boston and Cambridge runners on the other. *The Boston Globe* reported on the morning of the race, "some of the runners are cracks from New York," and "these men are a fast set."

After dinner, a doctor examined the runners to verify their capacity to withstand the demanding journey. Upon receiving a clean bill of health, the runners were then taken by a horse-drawn barge a mile up the road to the starting line. There, Tom Burke organized the fifteen runners on a makeshift starting line, which he drew by dragging his heel across the dusty road, raised his hand, and yelled GO!

The idea for the Boston Marathon was born in 1896. John Graham, coach of the Harvard track team and the U.S. Olympic team and a member of the Boston Athletic Association (B.A.A.), ventured across the ocean to watch the 1896 Olympic Games in Athens, Greece, with his friend Herbert Holton, a Boston financial agent. There the two men witnessed a running event that pushed the limits of human performance. The event was a footrace of endurance to honor the legendary trek of Pheidippides, the Greek soldier who ran from Marathon (Greece) to Athens in 490 B.C. to deliver the message that the Athenian army had conquered the Persians.

Graham and Holton were so awestruck by the race that upon their return to Boston they pledged to bring a similar event to their city. After much discussion, they mapped out a route to honor an American messenger worthy of comparison with Pheidippides—Paul Revere. The designed course traveled the same route as Revere's famous ride in 1775, in which he rode from Boston to Concord to warn the colonists of Massachusetts of the impending attack by the British.

Fortunately the road was clear in 1775, but it was not in 1896 when Holton and Graham attempted to trace the historic gallop. Their efforts were thwarted by the discovery that the bridge from Boston to Cambridge was closed for repairs (the nineteenth century's version of the Big Dig, Boston's current eternal bridge-and-tunnel project). Consequently, the two originators amended their plans and decided to follow the breezes of the Atlantic to their destination. They bicycled out the gate of the Irvington Oval race track onto Huntington Avenue in Boston, each man holding a Veeder cyclometer. The pair headed down Exeter Street, past the B.A.A. clubhouse, and onto Commonwealth Avenue and then rode alongside the Boston-Albany train tracks, which they used as a guide. (The tracks were an ideal escort because at the time railroad engineers used the best technology to map routes and track distances.)

They pedaled and pedaled through town after town: through Boston, into Brookline, past Boston College, over the hills of Newton, through Wellesley, past Natick, over the train tracks of Framingham, and into Ashland. At this point Graham's cyclometer read twenty-five miles, while Holton's read twenty-four and a half. Here they dismounted, grabbed two rocks, and declared the spot the start of the first marathon—a quiet dirt road called Pleasant Street, across from Metcalf's Mill, one mile from Ashland Center.

From 1887 to 1923 Ashland hosted the start of the race, a fact not commonly advertised by the people of Hopkinton. Eventually the starting line was moved down the street to Hopkinton in 1924 to adhere to the accepted Olympic distance: The marathon had been lengthened during the 1908 Olympic Games in England to twenty-six miles, three hundred and eighty-five yards. This was done to appease the sedentary and spoiled King Edward VII, who wanted the race to start at Windsor Castle and to finish in front of his royal box in the Olympic Stadium. The king did what a king does: He issued a proclamation. In the future, the start and finish lines would be moved intermittently to placate other voices—such as sponsors, municipal planners, and the swelling ranks of runners.

Thus, for over a century, the Boston Marathon has been cultivated, shaped, and accommodated by the likes of John Graham, Herbert Holton, King Edward VII, and John Hancock Financial Services, with the ultimate aim of creating and operating a sporting event that respects the needs of the city and the runners—as they honor the first marathoner, Pheidippides. With the train tracks on one side and Boston due east, the runners continue to toe the line in solidarity with their many bothers and sisters, past and present, who have come to pay homage to the Mecca of all marathons.

SIX MONTHS TO GLORY

Pat Williams, president of the Orlando Magic, on why he runs marathons: "It's practice at not quitting."

— — — —

Six months before the 100th running of the Boston Marathon, my exercise regime was limited to a run up and down a basketball court and the occasional fifteen-footer between turnovers. During a break after one of those pickup games, my friends Michael Radley (Rad) and Rich Twombly (Richie) and I were casually discussing our aspiration to run a marathon someday.

The tone of the conversation was more consistent with a throwaway line like, "I'd love to parachute someday," or, "Would you ever bungee jump?" But for some reason, this throwaway line snowballed, and the next thing you know I found myself stretching out on the front porch in preparation for my first step toward the finish line in Boston. One mile later, I gratefully arrived back at my house with tight hamstrings, a cramp in my side, and expanded lungs. It wasn't going to be easy.

But I was in: I gave Richie and Rad my word that I'd do it. And just in case I got an inclination to forgo the jaunt for a more dormant Patriot's Day, I made a point of telling every friend and family member I could that I was running the 100th in April. There was no turning back now, I was stuck. Despite the fact that we lacked official numbers, we vowed that one way or another, we would get ourselves into that race.

To commit to such an undertaking you have to have both feet in. In my heart, there was no doubt that I would see this adventure to its

conclusion. I was determined, as were my running partners, to reach the summit of Boston, with or without Sherpas.

My family on the other hand, for good reason, did not recognize my resolve. When the subject of "running Boston" was forced into a conversation (as it often was), they would respond with halfhearted words of encouragement like, "That's good, Michael. Have fun." It was like a toddler telling his parents that he was going to be an astronaut or a professional baseball player—when a goal is that unrealistic, the best response is probably a vague, loving indulgence. They assumed that I would go out and train for a couple of weeks and then be shocked into submission. My wife and parents guessed that running was so alien to my being that it would be impossible for me to evolve in six short months from trotting a half mile with cramps to running twenty-six miles. They also remembered that my lone road-racing experience had ended ingloriously and almost tragically.

It was twelve years previous on Thanksgiving morning. My family had coerced me into lacing up the sneakers for the annual five-mile Turkey Trot sponsored by Jordan Marsh in Boston. (Considering that I had not run in years, you could say I entered the race completely "cold turkey.") At the sound of the gun, my brother John sprinted off with the real athletes while my sisters, my brother Kevin, and I were left in the back of the pack casually jogging while we laughed and joked. But soon the humor left the race. Each mile seemed to defy science. I was convinced that some practical joker was hiding in the Boston Common, moving mile markers, sending us down the wrong roads, like Wile E. Coyote's attempts to catch the Roadrunner. But there were no Looney Tunes characters on the streets of Boston that day—it was just me, sucking wind in and out of my realm.

By the end of the race, my laughing and jocularity was a distant memory. Just after crossing the finish line, I teetered on the verge of unconsciousness, leading my parents to prop me on the sidewalk against the Jordan Marsh store, where street vendors toil and homeless slumber. Feeling nauseous and weak, I waited for the episode to run its course.

In the past, a simple bout of dizziness or fainting would not have overly concerned my parents, but things were different now. My tendency to keel over in church or after a hot day in the sun could no longer be shrugged off as a simple spell, because these spells now had an identified medical source: heart disease. When I was eighteen, my doctor decided that it would be prudent to investigate the cause of my blackouts. Like Frankenstein, I found myself lying on doctors' tables being tested and prodded. The neurological results were pristine but the same could not be said for the cardiology readings. After digesting the test results, the doctor announced that my echocardiogram showed rhythms that were consistent with a heart disease known as Wolff-Parkinson-White (WPW) Syndrome, an arrhythmia in which the heart beats in a volatile and potentially life-threatening fashion. While the electronics of a normal heart run from ventricle to ventricle, hearts with WPW are outfitted with an extra wire that sends the beat outside the heart, causing it to pulse with

9

an irregular rhythm during an episode. According to doctors, a danger exists when the heart is slowing down from top speeds of 200-plus beats a minute, which could be fatal.

Now I sat on the sidewalk trying to relax and slow my pulse. Meanwhile my father had retrieved the trusty station wagon and backed it up over the race route with his probation officer's badge sticking out the window. By the time he arrived, I had recovered sufficiently to put an end to the scare, but needless to say my days of being pressured into running races were over. My family learned their lesson: on Thanksgiving mornings, it's best to let me sleep late and then proceed over to my high school's football field to watch Catholic Memorial in their annual victory over Boston College High School.

Over the next decade or so, I suffered a number of episodes, most of which turned out to be your basic rapid-heartbeat spells. I coped with these episodes by slowing my breathing and relaxing my body; eventually my pulse would revert to normal. The exception was an attack I had during a baseball game. Playing for Bentley College, I took a ball off the inside of my knee, causing my pulse to spike. I made my way back to the bench and sat down next to my friend Jimmy Delaney, sweating profusely. Soon thereafter, I lost consciousness and collapsed onto his shoulder. The trainer ministered to me while an ambulance was called. Later that day, my coach showed up in the emergency room of the local hospital. Satisfied that I had returned to good health, he joked, "Thank God, you didn't die—I don't know where we would have bought black armbands for tomorrow's game." Episodes such as these kept my loved ones on high alert.

The years went by. I aged, receded, and gained a wife and child. In the medical field, they were busy developing a procedure, called radiofrequency catheter ablation, that promised to rid me of my disease permanently. In the procedure, a catheter is guided into the heart and used to destroy the tissue that is interfering with the heart's normal electrical function. For fourteen years, I had been reporting to my cardiologist for my quarterly EKG exam: I took off my shirt, they connected me to some wires to confirm that my rhythm hadn't changed, and I went on my way. It was an inconvenience, but I was hesitant to have any kind of intrusive procedure—call me crazy, but I'm not too wild about having foreign objects traveling through my body.

Now I had no choice. My training had progressed and I was running five miles every other day, over the objections of my parents and my wife Noreen, who is a nurse. I had called their bluff. Now they called my bluff and joined forces to give me an ultimatum: If I was going to continue this tomfoolery, I would have to concede to surgery.

In late October 1995, I arrived at New England Medical Center and changed from my street clothes into a johnny. The procedure could take anywhere from one to twelve hours. In the hands of the very competent Dr. Caroline Foote, my mood was one of confident apprehension. During the operation, minuscule catheters equipped with lasers were inserted into the femoral artery at the top of my legs. Once inside, the lasers were carefully maneuvered to the epicenter of the disease. After identifying the infamous extra wire, Dr. Foote burned the extraneous pathway in half, hopefully ridding me of heart disease. I no longer had an excuse not to shovel snow or carry groceries up stairs—my physical being was whole again.

One hour later, my wife joined me in the recovery room. As the sedatives wore off, she stroked my hair and we joked about the wasted worry. It all seemed for naught. That was until my heart went blank and forgot to beat. The steady beep on my heart monitor alerted the medical staff that I just gone flat-line. Quickly, they hustled my wife to the hallway—things could get ugly.

They sat her down and left her to her thoughts. Around her people passed and went about their business while she pondered life as a widow and a single mother. She wondered if this was really happening. Down the hall walked my father. Anxious to hear the results of the surgery, he was horrified to see the look in Noreen's eyes. Together they sat in the hall, hoping for the best and fearing the worst.

On the table, I existed. I don't remember much. My life didn't pass before my eyes, and I didn't hover over my body in some out-of-body experience. There was no light calling me (I hope that's not a bad sign). I sat on the precipice of life, sliding maybe toward death. I don't know quite what went on during that period, or how long it lasted. Eventually

I regained consciousness choking on the intubation tube they had shoved down my throat. Above me on the gurney a doctor straddled my chest, while nurses hustled to the bedside with a defibrillator. Thankfully my heartbeat returned before my chest was burnt and my ribs were broken.

My wife, along with my father, was allowed to rejoin me in the recovery room. Not knowing whether to laugh or cry or kiss me, they did all three.

— — — —

The following day was a beautiful Indian summer day. My wife took me by the arm and we moved slowly around our block at home. I couldn't help but think what a great day it would be to run. But I was thankful to be walking.

Ten days later, I ran two miles and I was back on my way to Hopkinton. My running continued and I was more motivated than ever. Already, my mission to run Boston had paid dividends: as a result of my decision to compete, I no longer had heart disease. Two miles became four miles, and then six.

Ever since I was diagnosed with heart disease in the early 1980s, I had been preoccupied with the tragic, sudden deaths of athletes in the prime of their lives, such as Jim Fixx, Reggie Lewis, Hank Gathers, and Sergei Grinkov. I still thought I was bulletproof—I still dove for loose balls on the basketball court and played extra sets of tennis—but in the back of my mind, I wondered sometimes if my athletic endeavors were putting me in harm's way. As my chest pounded and my breath shortened, I wondered if this was how Gathers felt before falling to the ground. My ailment didn't interrupt my life, but it was a wild card.

Now there was no more ambivalence. Boston would be my opportunity to put all fears and concerns to rest. I would train and succeed to prove to my parents, my wife, and mostly myself that my heart was my greatest asset.

MARATHON YEAR

Kathy Switzer, eight-time competitor and television commentator, sees the Boston Marathon as a spiritual-athletic experience: "To push yourself, and consider yourself a runner, you must make the pilgrimage to Mecca. That's how important Boston is to runners. It's a religious experience."

— — — —

The Boston Marathon, originally called the American Marathon of the Boston Athletic Association, is known throughout the world as the granddaddy of all marathons. Runners come from all corners of the world for the privilege of running Boston. Over the last century, the number of racers has grown from fifteen to over 40,000. This explosion in the field has forced the organizer of the race, the Boston Athletic Association (B.A.A.), to evolve from a small group with a shoebox office to an army of professionals with the awesome responsibility of governing the greatest race of all.

The Boston Athletic Association was founded in 1887. Its original clubhouse was located on Exeter Street, on the present-day site of the Boston Public Library's Johnson Building. The finish line of the marathon was placed here from 1899 until 1964, when it was moved to Boylston Street. Men like John Graham, George Brown, Walter Brown, Jock Semple, Will Cloney, Jack Fleming, Guy Morse, and David McGillivray

were all worthy representatives of the B.A.A. and the club's famous race.

Each year, the B.A.A. begins planning the next year's race as soon as the last runner crosses the finish line. It takes 364 days to organize an event that will be won in a couple of hours. Committees from Hopkinton to Boston negotiate, coordinate, bang heads, and fine-tune until the night before the race, which they spend tossing through sweaty nightmares about six-foot snowfalls and burst water pipes the following morning. (Eighteen inches of snow fell on Hopkinton just days before the 1996 race.)

It is the distinctiveness of the marathon course that makes the race so special for the runners and so difficult for the organizers. With the race winding its way through eight different towns from start to finish, the coordination of logistics and the appeasement of the many voices is a major undertaking. Each town has different concerns and singular needs, which must be resolved sometime before April. If one town backed out of the marathon, the continuity of the world's oldest race would be disturbed forever.

The costs to a town of managing and administering such an event can be significant. Limited money and tried patience have many times caused town officials to ask the B.A.A. to exercise restraint. In 1966 the fine people of Hopkinton implored race officials to control the growing number of runners by issuing invitations to a select list only. The previous year's field of 540 had so overtaxed the town that this request evolved into a petition, ultimately unsuccessful, demanding that the B.A.A. move the starting line out of Hopkinton.

Playing host to tens of thousands of runners and officials is a Herculean task for some of these small towns. Consider that, for the 100th running of the race in 1996, 45,000 numbered and non-numbered (bandit) runners from over seventy countries lined up in Hopkinton. Add to the mix spectators, race officials, and fried dough salesmen, and the town population had swelled from about 13,350 to over 75,000 in one day.

Through compromise and concession, the towns and the B.A.A. come to a consensus each April allowing the event to proceed. Following

NON-QUALIFYING APPLICANTS FOR THE BOSTON MARATHON TRIED TO INFLUENCE THE BOSTON ATHLETIC ASSOCIATION BY SENDING LETTERS, PICTURES, AND EVEN A METAL ROD THAT WAS REMOVED FROM A RUNNER'S LEG DURING SURGERY. PHOTO COURTESY OF THE *BOSTON HERALD.*

the onslaught of 1996, Race Director Guy Morse pledged to restrict the size of future races: "We made commitments to the communities of Hopkinton and Boston that we would go back to a reasonable field size."

1915 **The Boston Globe wrote, "Throughout the forenoon the little square in the town resembled a scene in the country on a main railroad line that had been honored by a circus."**

For decades, the B.A.A. had been besieged with requests from runners and townsfolk alike to improve the quality of the event by providing the funding and amenities needed for officials to run the world's greatest race properly. Often these concerns fell upon deaf ears. Arrogant race officials were well aware that the Boston Marathon was the only race around—apart from the Olympics, distance runners had no other place to showcase their skills. Consequently, the repeated complaints about the lack of crowd control, scarce water stops, irregular checkpoints, and the absence of timing devices evolved into frustration that eventually compromised the image of the race in the minds of the world's greatest runners. Inevitably this dissatisfaction resulted in declining numbers at the starting line in Hopkinton and on the sidewalks of the eight towns along the route.

1927 **Because the water stops had been little used in the previous year's race, the B.A.A. decided to cut costs by eliminating them in the 1927 marathon. In that year's race, temperatures climbed into the mid-eighties, and many runners were stricken with dehydration.**

1933 **The B.A.A. criticized their own race, calling for sponsors to assist them in planning and funding. They threatened to end the marathon unless they got help from the newspapers and the local Chamber of Commerce.**

Finally B.A.A. director and past race director Will Cloney heeded the protests. In 1981, the B.A.A. crossed a self-imposed line of "purity" and sought financial support from the corporate world. To accomplish this task, the B.A.A. brought in a local attorney by the name of Marshall Medoff who assumed the role of sponsor broker. Throughout Boston and the running community, Medoff's methods—which rankled many traditionalists—created much animosity. Eventually the role of middleman for the race's sponsorship was placed in the capable hands of race sponsor John Hancock Financial Services in 1986.

In the years leading up to 1986, the quality of the race and the runners was beginning to slip. Elite runners were turning to the many alternative marathons that had sprung up over the years to promote themselves and their sneakers. They needed a reason to return to Boston. John Hancock gave them that reason in the form of prize money and appearance fees for attending running clinics on the Saturday and Sunday before the race.

Boston Marathon guru Tom Leonard described a pre-1986 running of the race as only he could: "The Boston Marathon is a vintage wine which should have a delicate bouquet. The race has a million-dollar audience and a twenty-five cent field."

The world-class runners did return to Boston, extending its legacy as a top venue into the next century. The organizers of rival marathons, like Chicago's, took issue with this approach, arguing in particular that the use of appearance money caused the runners to "lose the fire in their bellies" to win on race day. Whether or not these charges were a case of sour grapes, there is no question that the Boston Marathon had sacrificed some of its innocence with the injection of corporate money and the shift toward professionalism. The race was now in the real world, competing in a dog-eat-dog market in order to stay alive.

But from many points of view, the marriage between the B.A.A. and John Hancock has been a great success. Funding from John Hancock has revitalized the race with a new spirit and high quality competition and organization. The problems and concerns that nagged the race throughout its existence have been virtually eliminated as a result of corporate sponsorship. Financial subsidies have provided the necessary monetary support for the race to survive and prosper. Under the new arrangements, each town is provided with a stipend to help defray a large percentage of the costs incurred in hosting the race. This greatly improves relations between the towns and the B.A.A., and between the towns' budget committees and their selectmen. John Hancock is currently signed on into the twenty-first century with a long-term commitment of $18 million.

With the money received by the town of Hopkinton for hosting the 100th race and the pre-race activities, the local school built a new track and installed lights on their field hockey, soccer, and baseball fields. Hopkintonites also initiated their own fund-raisers. Prior to the race, the town sold marathon quilts, auctioned off the pace car, built a corporate box at the starting line, and even created a special wine for the event, which *The Boston Globe* compared to the marathon itself: "Aroma of sneakers, might give you the runs, and starts strong but wilts."

Four-time Boston Marathon winner Bill Rodgers: "The marriage between John Hancock and the Boston Marathon is the most significant event since the origin of the race. This sponsorship allows the race to head into its second century while maintaining the highest regard for quality and sportsmanship possible."

1996 Contributions from sponsors totaled $3.6 million. This income, plus $1.9 million from entry fees and $400,000 from royalties, was used to offset the cost of the race, $5.9 million.

— — — —

BELOW IS A LIST OF THE SPONSORS OF THE 1996 RACE AND THE RESPECTIVE VALUE OF THEIR SERVICES OR DONATIONS:

$1.4 million
John Hancock Financial Services, Inc.

$400,000 to $500,000
Adidas of America, Inc.

Citgo Petroleum Corporation

$100,000 to $200,000
Belmont Springs Water Company, Inc.

Digital Equipment Corporation

Gatorade/Quaker Oats Company, Inc.

Northwest Airlines

Pontiac

Ronzoni/Hershey Pasta

Tylenol

$30,000 to $75,000
AT&T

Boston Gas

Boston Phoenix

CellularOne

CVS

Filene's

Longs Jewelers/RJC Company

Ocean Spray Cranberries, Inc.

Offtech, Inc.

PowerBar/Powerfood, Inc.

Sunshine Biscuits

Sponsors see the Boston Marathon as a perfect marketing vehicle for their products, services, and brands. For instance, Adidas of America felt fortunate to be involved with an event such as the Boston Marathon. "To be able to link yourself with an event like the Boston Marathon provides our company with instant credibility," said one executive. "To formulate a relationship with a health and fitness celebration of this magnitude, which is held in such high regard throughout the world for its tradition, class, and quality, is a marketing dream. The exposure our company receives is national and international. Events like this are few and far between."

1905 It cost the B.A.A. a total of $1,326 to organize and run the ninth Boston Marathon. In following years, the B.A.A. would annually divert $2,500 from the proceeds of a popular indoor track event to fund the race.

1981 The budget for the 1981 marathon was $45,000.

1996 The 100th race cost $5.9 million.

While committees, sponsors, athletic associations, and residents stomp their feet and iron out differences of opinion, fire chiefs, police chiefs, and package-store owners from the eight towns also gather to coordinate their own song and dance. Safety rules, alternate routes, overtime pay, and price increases on kegs of beer are all important issues that must be settled long before the starter's gun is fired.

Back in Boston, the B.A.A. continues to put out fires and move the race toward fruition. In addition to the central task of coordinating the logistics on the course, a daunting array of responsibilities confronts the organizers of a modern marquee marathon. From housing the elite runners, to organizing publicity runs with the president of the United States, to accommodating the press, to fielding applications from non-qualifying runners—the B.A.A.'s tasks are all-consuming. To get an idea of the undertaking, consider that more press credentials are issued for the Boston Marathon than for any other one-day event in the world, with the exception of the Super Bowl.

1928 WEEI provided radio coverage of the Boston Marathon for the first time, including musical interludes from the Daily Maide.

1941 Runners lined up on the starting line and ran a mock start before the race to provide footage for Movietone cameras.

1949 Television coverage was provided for the first time, with live shots from Kenmore Square and the finish line transmitted into American living rooms.

1979 The Public Broadcasting System (PBS) covered the race in its entirety for the first time, although the event was shown in tape delay. Kathy Switzer, past competitor and one of the commentators that day, recalls the pioneering coverage: "We drove the course in golf carts in the freezing cold. After a half hour of footage, we would take the tape and throw it from the course over the crowd of spectators to a waiting PBS employee. He would then deliver it to the press truck for showing."

1996 The B.A.A. handed out press credentials to over 1,500 journalists from 350 organizations.

— — — —

QUALIFYING TIMES

Age	Male	Female
18 – 34	3:10	3:40
35 – 39	3:15	3:45
40 – 44	3:20	3:50
45 – 49	3:30	4:00
50 – 54	3:35	4:05
55 – 59	3:45	4:15
60 – 64	4:00	4:30
65 – 69	4:15	4:45
70 – 74	4:30	5:00
75 – 79	4:45	5:15
80 +	5:00	5:30

— — — —

Fielding requests from applicants who have failed to run a qualifying time is one of the major tasks facing the B.A.A. The duty is both heart-wrenching and time-consuming: for the 1996 race there were roughly 30,000 rejections. Each year the requests increase in both number and creativity. Some applicants have self-diagnosed diseases, while others claim to have suffered some type of ailment or misfortune while running a qualifying marathon earlier in the year.

One such request arrived at B.A.A. headquarters in 1976. Dennis Rainear had always dreamed of running the Boston Marathon. To qualify for the race, Rainear needed to run the Grand Valley Marathon in Allendale, Michigan, in a time of three hours or better. His previous best had been 3:00:31.

As he passed the ten-mile mark, on pace to qualify, Dennis experienced a painful sensation in the side of his head, as if he had been struck by a brick. He looked around to see who might have attacked him but was unable to identify the source. Dazed but mindful of the clock, Rainear pushed on to a disappointing finishing time of 3:09.

Still disheartened hours later, Rainear also continued to suffer pains in his head where he had been hit during the race. Concerned, he admitted himself to the local hospital with a pounding headache resembling a migraine. There a doctor discovered that the runner had in fact been shot in the head by some nut with a twenty-two-caliber rifle. Luckily, Rainear was treated and released with no long-term repercussions. His effort and resilience did not go unnoticed either by the press or by the B.A.A., which awarded him the treasured number despite his failure to break three hours.

Mind you though, pardons like this are rare. But that doesn't discourage non-qualifying candidates from applying with all kinds of explanations. This plea came from the exasperated wife of a runner: "Either you give my husband a number, or I'll be divorced or widowed—because if he doesn't run, I won't be able to live with him!"

MARATHON WEEK

A week before the 1976 marathon, Jack Fultz wrote to his friend Jerry, "I just have this good feeling. Something big is going to happen next week." One week later, Jack Fultz was crowned champion of the Boston Marathon.

— — — —

How much should I run in the week prior to the race? When should I start carbo-loading? Water or Gatorade? Why am I doing this?

Heading into the final week before the Boston Marathon is like getting on the school bus for your first day of preschool. You are plucked from a comfortable, controlled environment (like a nest, or a fortress) and conveyed forward inexorably into a new world that will surely find your weaknesses and flaws. When we get on that school bus, or count down to Patriot's Day Monday, the barriers that normally protect us break down, exposing our wavering resolve and our fragile self-esteem to the shining light of the unknown.

Soon we will stand out in Hopkinton, half-hoping that the starter's gun is broken and half-wishing that he would fire already and release us from the nervous anticipation. Quitting an unsatisfying job, beginning a family, running the Boston Marathon, climbing Mt. Everest— all of these acts evict us from our bunkers and test both our limits and our potential.

With a week to go before the race, I decided to ingest one more relaxed ten-mile run. Part of me wanted to log the extra miles to add

MEMBERS OF THE KOREAN CONTINGENT (LEFT TO RIGHT, MANAGER SOHN KEE CHUNG, SONG KIL YOON, HANN KIL YONG, AND CHOI YAN CHIL) ARRIVE AT LOGAN AIRPORT FOR THE 1950 BOSTON MARATHON. PHOTO COURTESY OF THE *BOSTON HERALD*.

to the suspect foundation I had built up over the last six months; the other part of me just wanted to get out of the house and burn off some nervous energy.

As I had done throughout my training, I picked the brain of anyone with sneakers on his feet. The general consensus about the last week was to take it easy. If you didn't have your road work in by now, you were toast anyway.

Over the last hundred years, the marathon has blossomed from a half-day event into an entire week of Marathon Madness. Sometimes the week prior to the race is more of a marathon than the event itself. Bars and restaurants busy themselves with marathon-related activities and extra staff, while the B.A.A. prepares the course and ties up loose ends.

At Logan Airport, the terminals are thronged with slight travelers arriving in sweat suits, carrying water. Among them are the elite runners, who begin to arrive from around the world. To have a fighting chance at the laurel wreath, these superhuman athletes must reach the starting line in peak condition. That means arriving in Boston as early as possible to get acclimated to the city and its time zone, climate and topography.

Prior to the days of corporate sponsorship, runners interested in racing Boston were left to their own means to get from their homes to the hub of the universe. Some would hobo from train to train, while others hitchhiked. In 1913, the working-class marathoner William "Bricklayer Bill" Kennedy migrated from Chicago to Boston over a five-day period. Just months after recovering from typhoid fever, Kennedy bounced from horse-drawn carriages to unsuspecting freight trains to motor cars, demonstrating how far a serious runner would go to participate in the world's greatest race. Four years later, Bricklayer Bill reaped the fruits of his efforts by conquering the race and his competitors in 1917.

1998 After negotiating for months to secure an exit visa, Russian marathoner Andrey Kuznetov was finally granted the document, but was only allowed to travel with the sweat suit on his back and the sneakers on his feet. His journey to Boston started on Wednesday from his home in the Central Russian village of Havarovsk. To travel just from his village to Moscow took the elite Masters competitor (age 40 and over) eight hours. From there he hopped on a flight to Helsinki, where he connected to New York and then bused to Boston.

He arrived in Boston Sunday night and had to resort to napping in a chair in the lobby of the Fairmount Copley Plaza because there were no vacancies. On Monday morning he made the odyssey worthwhile by winning the Masters race with a time of 2:15:27.

Before the 1980s, elite runners were still unable to accept prize money or appearance fees without jeopardizing their amateur status.

With the growth of the marathon, however, rich benefactors began to creep in from the shadows to associate themselves with the top runners—to sponsor the winner of the Boston Marathon could have a tangible impact on the business interests of the patron, not to mention his ego. So the issue of amateur status was finessed with respect to travel: Arrangements were made such that top runners would arrive "safely." Officials turned a blind eye to practices like this, knowing that such sponsorship would promote the attendance of elite runners and thereby maintain the lofty image of the race. When the Olympic marathon champion Frank Shorter threatened to skip the 1977 race, complaining that he was "not going to hitchhike to Boston," race coordinator Will Cloney retorted, "He knows there is a little 'angel'"—a silent financial patron—"available to provide the trip to Boston."

1939 When Ellison "Tarzan" Brown showed up at the starting line he was penniless. Consequently, BAA patriarch Walter Brown quietly paid the $1 fee. Tarzan went on to win the race.

Ever since 1986, when corporate sponsorship was officially blessed by the B.A.A., elite athletes have received the gamut of benefits available for those who ran fast. From the moment they arrive in Boston, elite runners enjoy the advantages that are usually bestowed upon people who dominate a trade. They are picked up at the airport by assigned volunteers and delivered to their home away from home, a makeshift Olympic Village at the John Hancock Conference Center, located just yards from the finish line. Sixty-four suites and a recreation room, normally reserved for the captains of industry, are set aside for the harriers, decorated appropriately with the paintings of John "Elder" Kelley—the two-time winner, sixty-one-time participant, and universally acknowledged patriarch of the race.

Here the runners eat what they want, when they want. Ethiopian specialty dishes? They have it, as they have beef stroganoff, knockwurst, and anything else you can imagine, all prepared as ordered and served according to the native time zones of the runners. In addition to the private chefs, top runners are also provided with in-house masseuses, a movie room with a full video library (comedies are the most requested films) and tickets for the Celtics, Bruins, and Red Sox—all an attempt to provide your basic Boston hospitality.

Three-time champion Cosmas Ndeti acts as his own chef when he arrives on the Thursday before the race. Cosmas concocts his favorite meal, Ugaali, which consists of white corn meal complemented with a souplike mixture of chicken, onions, tomatoes, greens, and carrots.

Runners who are new to the race are always anxious to the see the route prior to Monday, and especially "Heartbreak Hill." For years their fellow runners have arrived home from Boston with war stories about the three protrusions that rise from the pavement on Commonwealth Avenue in Newton—stories which only heighten the legends already surrounding "the hills." Thus the rookies often scout out this arduous stretch, if only to confirm that these mountains are truly as high as the Himalayas.

The elite runners can arrange with their dedicated volunteer to drive out to see the race route. The more average runners can travel the course on one of the many shuttles operated by Marathon Tours, which provides sightseeing trips over the length of the course. During the tour, there are quizzes, prizes, and photo opportunities at famous landmarks along the route.

1929 Two-time champion Johnny Miles was asked by the press if he was going to drive the course before the race. He answered, "Why? I'll see enough of it tomorrow."

When the rookies finally set eyes on the hills, it can be a bit of a let-down: They look like three inclines, sitting somewhere between the starting line and the finish. Apparently, no crampons will be required. But don't be fooled—Niagara Falls doesn't look too bad either, until you're in the barrel.

Some runners don't feel comfortable simply viewing the course. In 1949, Swedish runner Karl Gosta Leandersson ran the entire course to familiarize himself with the route. As he finished the training run, he realized that his time was faster than the current record for the course; he also realized that he had injured his Achilles tendon in the process. On race day, the Swede ignored the pain and won the race by over three minutes. However, preparation like Leandersson's is not recommended for average runners so soon before Monday's undertaking.

A more typical pre-race ritual used to occur at the Eliot Lounge, where runners would join bartender Tommy Leonard to kick off Marathon Weekend by raising the flags of the participating countries and partaking in some early liquid carbo-loading. Tommy Leonard has been described as the Archbishop of the Boston Marathon, the Official Greeter, or simply the Guru, but whatever he is called, Tommy is passionate about the Boston Marathon. Leonard's love affair with the race compels him to wax poetic at every opportunity about the event. His side job is to draw beers for thirsty runners, but Tommy's true vocation is to provide a metaphorical, analytical history-and-sermon on the beauty and meaning of the race that he holds so close to his heart (and which he has conquered over twenty times himself, with a personal record of 3:17 in 1975).

Sadly, in the autumn of 1996 the Eliot Lounge was closed, forcing the veteran bartender to find another home for himself and the thousands of marathoners who consider the Eliot Lounge to be as much a part of the race as Heartbreak Hill. After twenty-five years, Leonard could only say, "I'm laughing on the outside but crying on the inside."

1988 On the Thursday night before the race, John Treacy of Ireland, then one of the world's premier marathon runners, rolled over in bed and told his wife that he had decided to run Boston. After leading the race in Mile 21, he fell back to finish third in a time of 2:09:15.

"I was convinced I could win the Boston Marathon," he recalled. "I had a great week of running and felt I was as prepared as I could be. It just so happens that [Ibrahim] Hussein and [Juma] Ikangaa pulled away and then worked

**together, leaving me alone to work by myself. I knew I'd run
well; sometimes that's enough."**

By the time the weekend arrives, every hotel within fifty miles of the course has a NO VACANCY sign hung in front. The lobbies are filled with tourists who stretch their quads and glance nervously at their watches. Local restaurants like the steakhouse Abe and Louie's, not far from the finish line, serve more dinners in the three-day span around the race than during any other period in the year. It was estimated that the 100th running of the Boston Marathon generated $140 million for the Boston-area economy.

HERE IS A BREAKDOWN OF THE ESTIMATED REVENUE GENERATED BY THE 1996 BOSTON MARATHON, IN TOTAL ABOUT $140 MILLION:

Massachusetts runners:	**$1.5 million**
U.S. runners from other states and their guests:	**$49.3 million**
International runners and their guests:	**$28.1 million**
Visitors and spectators along the course:	**$42.8 million**
Media fees:	**$1.3 million**
Transportation:	**$11.7 million**
Prize money:	**$600,000**
Maintenance of course:	**$900,000**
Sports and Fitness Expo:	**$3.9 million**

With the city flooded with runners and spectators, there are not enough hotel rooms to go around. To fill the lodging gap, a number of Massachusetts families have traditionally hosted runners in their homes, creating goodwill and adding a personal touch to the experience. One resident of Hopkinton, a veteran of Fort Bragg in North Carolina, gives back to his old fort by hosting runners currently stationed at the base. Bob Nichol, a wheelchair competitor from Sharon, Massachusetts, has hosted a fellow wheelchair racer from South Africa for the last couple of years. This veteran of the wars in South Africa travels halfway across the world to visit a friend, compete in a race, fulfill a dream, and overcome his disability.

In 1996, hundreds of Hopkinton families were called upon to open their homes to the thousands of homeless runners who arrived in Boston with nothing but sneakers and a number. Such acts of neighborly kindness add greatly to the special nature of the race. In today's world of locked doors and locked hearts, these gestures serve notice to runners from every corner of the world that there is still a 26.2-mile stretch of the universe where the Golden Rule is in effect.

Seventy-two hours prior to running the 2002 Boston Marathon, seventeen British soldiers ran 26.2 miles in London wearing combat boots and army fatigues while dragging a 2,000-pound Royal Navy field gun; they finished in a time of 4:58. Three days later, they arrived in Hopkinton and conquered their second marathon in a time of 5:15, this time carrying the Union Jack and the American flag together as a symbol of unity between the two countries. Their feat was undertaken to pay homage to their fallen comrade, Simon Turner, who died in the attacks of September 11th. Their efforts brought great honor to their contingent, the Honourable Artillery Company, the oldest regiment in the British Army, formed in 1537 by King Henry VIII.

Eighty-four years before the Englishmen's run, in the middle of World War I, the American armed forces ran their own Boston marathon to demonstrate the fitness of the U.S. soldier and his garb. As a contribution to the war effort, the B.A.A. helped to organize a relay race from Ashland to Boston consisting of ten legs of two and a half miles each. Competing teams of U.S. servicemen representing different branches of the military ran the marathon in their uniforms and boots. The Fort Devens Divisional Team won the race with a time of 2:24:53.

With housing procured, the average runner can now focus on the weekend's annual events, which include the Sports and Fitness Expo and the marathon-eve pasta dinner. Many partake in classic Boston activities such as shopping on Newbury Street, taking in a baseball game at Fenway Park, or touring the city—including the Charles River—in a restored World War II amphibious landing vehicle, courtesy of Boston Duck Tours.

The race favorites, however, are not blessed with this period of reflection and relaxation. From the moment they arrive, their time is spoken for. After meeting the demands of training, they must lead clinics; after clinics, they must make appearances; and after appearances, they must attend press conferences. Questioners question, translators translate, and the runners attempt to answer the same question, over and over again.

1984 Elite runner Tom Fleming was unhappy with the press that Englishman Geoff Smith was receiving. "I just don't think Geoff Smith is as great as he thinks he is. I know this marathon too well. Geoff Smith went out at New York fast, he then tired, fell down and was lying on the finish line like a dead dog." Geoff Smith went on to win the 1984 race.

1995 Cosmas Ndeti was upset to read that *USA Today* reported that he wasn't capable of winning the race that year. At the pre-race press conference, Cosmas made a brief statement: "I will give my interview on the course." He carried the *USA Today* story to the starting line with him and went on to win his third Boston Marathon.

1997 One of the women's favorites, Fatuma Roba of Ethiopia, was asked at the pre-race press conference if she was going to view the course before the race. "I don't like to see the race place," she answered. She went on: "I am very sure I will win. You have an American girl, a German girl

who is good, a Russian—all these are my competitors. But I know I will beat them." Roba was proved correct.

Saturday and Sunday are the big days for the Sports and Fitness Expo at the John Hynes Convention Center, located on Boylston Street just down from the finish line. The marathon exhibition started in the late 1970s on a folding table at the local YWCA and has grown with the race. The first order of business is to pick up your official number, which also happens at the Convention Center. One clerical error could send a runner to the back of the line in Hopkinton with the numberless, so most marathoners will not relax and start browsing until the coveted bib is secured.

Number in hand, the runners move across the hall to sample hundreds of exhibits—a running smorgasbord. Here you can buy running shoes that do everything but move themselves: Some flash, some pump, some caress, but they all look better at the exhibit booth than they will at Mile 26. Along with the many promotional booths (which cost upwards of $50,000 to rent), there are several running and health clinics with titles like The Boys of Boston, Running Your Best, The Future of Running Shoes, and Medical Q&A.

Thousands of running buffs attend the Expo each year and are treated to a runners' paradise. Two of the more visible exhibitors each year are Adidas and Nike. The two sneaker monsters fight for prime space and struggle to catch the eyes of the consumers just as they do at your local sports shop, pushing free posters, $200 coats, sweat suits, socks, and gloves, all in an effort to move product and grab a larger percentage of the runners' discretionary income.

While some search for answers at the Expo, others seek guidance at the annual Marathon Mass at the church Our Lady of Victories in Boston. In 2002 Father Philip Laplante had special words for the extraordinarily fit congregation before him: "We've had many groups in our church over the years. But nobody, I mean nobody, as noble as you runners. Tomorrow is your day. I wish you well. I hope all of you have a great day."

2000 While racing around lap 138 in fourth position of the Talladega Die Hard, Michael Waltrip fell victim to a multi-car accident. Forced to retire for the day, Waltrip decided to take a break from his hectic and dangerous vocation and flew to Boston Sunday night, where he entered his first marathon, finishing with a time of 4:32.

Out in the towns along the route, the respective municipalities gear up for the marathon throughout the day by staging races and race-related events for their townspeople. On Sunday morning, Boston hosts the International Friendship Run and the parade of former marathon champions. In the afternoon, the town of Newton holds a similar event called the Heartbreak Hill International Youth Race, which includes a family fun walk. And Wellesley throws its own party, called the Wellesley Community Children's Center Fun Run.

By nighttime, the runners may feel like they have already completed a marathon. It is now time to get serious and start satisfying those cravings for carbohydrates, the prime fuel for endurance athletes. All along the race route, runners are treated to pasta dinners worthy of a marathon of this stature. The first pasta dinner for runners was started back at the Eliot Lounge some fifteen years ago. For a dollar you could stuff yourself sick. Today countless restaurants and hotels in the vicinity of the course throw miniature versions of the pasta festival held at City Hall Plaza in Boston.

Image Impact, a New York–based company that organizes corporate and sporting events, first started coming to Boston in 1985 to organize the pre- and post-race activities. The company looks forward each year to the good-natured Boston racing crowd and the family atmosphere of the race. For the 100th running, it was estimated that the crowd at the annual pasta dinner was in excess of 20,000 runners and family members—the largest pasta dinner ever held, another record to add to a record Marathon Weekend. To

feed such a large family, Image Impact must do some serious shopping. Here is a peek at their shopping list:

3,000 pounds of pasta
2,500 pounds of lasagna noodles
350 gallons of sauce
1,500 pounds of salad
12,000 rolls

Any leftovers are donated to the local food banks for the hungry.

On the Saturday before the 1996 race, I traveled to Philadelphia with my running partners for the wedding of two friends, Tim and Cathy Mahoney. It was a wonderful ceremony followed by a spectacular reception—exquisite food, festive dancing, and an open bar.

Rad, Richie, and I, conscious of our six-month investment in Monday's race, spent the day drinking water. (I wonder what odds Las Vegas would have put on the prospect of us three drinking water at an open bar?) On the dance floor we were certainly busting a move, but also doing our best not to deplete our built-up glycogen reserves.

Throughout the day, friends and strangers alike wished us luck in the pending race. Even the band made an announcement conveying their regards. It reminded me of the scene in the movie *The Deer Hunter* when Michael and his cohorts celebrate their friends' wedding just before being shipped out to Vietnam. It almost made me nervous like, What do these people know that we don't? Were we getting ourselves into something that was beyond us?

During the trip back to Boston, we dissected and discussed our game plan for the looming event. It was now less than twenty-four hours to the gun, and the pressure was mounting. By the time we arrived back in Boston, you might have thought that we had solved world hunger for all the talking, but we had only succeeded in tightening our nerves.

That night, my running partners—Rad, Rad's brother Jack, and Richie—joined my wife and me for a pasta dinner: The Last Supper.

Spaghetti, some sauce, bread, and tons of water. Between bites we blamed each other for getting us into the mess and tried to recall the exact genesis of the brainstorm. After dinner we continued to work the phones in search of a number for the race. We had left no stone unturned in our efforts to obtain an official number for the 100th running of the marathon. We called race sponsors, the B.A.A., politicians in each town, and running clubs. We offered money, pathetic excuses, and every sob story the four of us could think of, but we still came up empty. We would be forced to run as bandits.

As bandits, we had no choice but to procure lodging in Hopkinton the night before the race, because the roads into town were to be closed to the public at 6:30 A.M. on Monday. Luckily, family friends Jeff and Tracey McEvoy opened their door to the four of us.

After cleaning up dinner, we kissed our loved ones and drove out to Hopkinton around 10:00 P.M. Sunday night. It was intimidating to drive out the marathon route in a car: It took us nearly an hour to cover the distance to the starting line. Tracing almost the exact route that Holton and Graham had followed almost exactly a century ago, we again felt the awesome continuity and beauty of the Boston Marathon. We traveled away from Boston in hopes of making it back.

By the time we reached Hopkinton, the air was electric with a strange, surreal feeling. Marathon signs hung from the houses, campers squatted on the side of road, and there was a quiet so loud that it caused the adrenaline to flow. We felt like children on Christmas Eve night, while at the same time feeling like convicts awaiting execution at dawn. In fourteen hours, we would discover the magic of the Boston Marathon.

Uta Pippig works her way through the Congregational Church cemetery toward the starting line in 1996. Photo courtesy of Tim DeFrisco.

MARATHON DAY

**1982 Boston Marathon champion Alberto Salazar:
"Standing on the starting line, we are all cowards."**

— — — —

Helicopters hover overhead, officials bark into two-way radios, trucks capped with satellite dishes fight for parking space, and the National Guard take position. Hopkinton is about to host the start of another Boston Marathon. As the clock approaches high noon, thousands of athletes will toe the line one century after the original starting line was drawn in the dirt just down the road in Ashland.

For 364 days of the year, the sleepy colonial town of Hopkinton slowly rises to welcome each new morning. But today is the 365th day, and no matter how hard Hopkinton tries to hide her head under the pillow, it is impossible. Today is a day like no other: Today is the Boston Marathon.

On this morning, the sounds of chirping birds are drowned out by a parade of shuttle buses; the smell of fresh coffee is overpowered by the aroma of muscle-soothing liniment; the knock on the door is not the morning paper but a total stranger requesting the use of your bathroom; the town green is abandoned by the squirrels to thousands upon thousands of carbo-crazed contortionists with bursting bladders.

For decade after decade, athletes of the highest caliber, if not the greatest common sense, have ventured west of Boston in search of their Holy Grail. On this day, they will struggle and conquer, or they will sadly realize their limits, both physical and mental. They will abuse their bodies over the next two to six hours until they approach the gates of Boston or the gates of St. Peter. The race is irresistible, like a drug. The runners understand the pain and anguish that will soon find them, but they can't turn away from the light. Through the suburbs of Boston and at last on the streets of the city, the runners will throw themselves forward, drawn on by the awesome possibility of pushing oneself to the physical and psychological zenith. The pasta has been eaten, the *Cheers* T-shirts have been bought, and the runners are sick of trying on sneakers—it's time to go out and run.

The Boston Marathon is run each year on the Massachusetts holiday of Patriot's Day, which commemorates the famous ride of Paul Revere and the battles in Lexington and Concord, which ignited the American Revolution. Patriot's Day is widely celebrated throughout the state with many events, including reenactments of battles, replays of Paul Revere's ride, Boston Red Sox games at Fenway Park, and of course the Boston Marathon.

Beginning at 4:00 A.M., residents of Hopkinton begin arriving in pajamas and old sweats to stake out the town center—the best vantage point for the start—with blankets and lawn chairs. By 6:00 A.M., the Hopkinton Lion's Club has served the first sitting at their annual pancake breakfast. Proceeds go to college scholarships for local residents. Head pancake flipper Jimmy Dumas has been known to cook over 3,000 pancakes in a single morning.

While the people of Hopkinton were bustling around the common, my stomach was tied in knots. I had tossed and turned throughout the night, and my REM sleep wasn't as sound as it usually is. As each hour ticked away and the sun began to rise, I felt more and more the pressure to sleep, knowing my reserves would be called upon later in the day. Eventually, I surrendered and made my way to the kitchen. No one else was awake, so I was left alone with my thoughts. Had I trained enough? Would we be able to enter the race, even though we didn't have numbers? Would my knee hold up? I felt like Admiral James Stockdale in the 1992 vice-presidential debate asking, "Who am I? And why am I here?" The longest race I had ever run was a 10K, less than a quarter of what I would attempt on this day. Everything about this day was foreign to me. I was out of my element and I knew it.

For almost an hour I sat at the kitchen table and contemplated my fate. My ultimate fear was failure and all that surrounds it. Six months of commitment, pain, and energy would be wasted if I pulled up on the sidewalk somewhere in Newton or Brookline waving a white flag. Sure people would pat me on the back, and my family would tell me that I was a "winner in their book." But in the back of my mind, I worried about the subtler, more pervasive effects of failure on a person's life. If I caved in today, would my confidence be undermined? Would I attack future challenges, or approach them with doubt and hesitation?

When Uta Pippig, three-time Boston Marathon champion, sits down to breakfast on race day, the menu doesn't differ much from any other morning. "I want this day to be like any other day. Maybe I'll increase my carbohydrates slightly, but the more this day begins like any other day, the more likely I'll be relaxed and ready to run at my peak."

By 7:00 A.M., the first shuttle leaves Copley Square carrying runners to Hopkinton. The trip, which can last from an hour to an hour and a half, is filled with anxiety and apprehension. Some of the competitors chatter nervously among themselves while others, like eight-time winner of the wheelchair division Jean Driscoll, put on headphones and withdraw into a shell to focus on the task ahead. Still others, like Jim Knaub, bundle up and take a nap. By this hour back in the old days, the Tebeau family, who hosted the start of the race at their Hopkinton farm from 1924 to 1965, would have the cows milked and locked up to prevent injury to the livestock or the runners.

1962 Four B.A.A. officials were involved in a serious car crash while driving out to the start. Their beach wagon flipped over two times before the car settled. One man was

hospitalized with a head injury, but the other three were released in time to watch the finish, back brace and eye patch included.

By the time the first shuttle bus arrives in Hopkinton, Mugs Away Pub, at the seven-mile mark in Framingham, has served their first beer of the day in a race of another kind. All along the route, restaurants and pubs are readying themselves for a flood of customers. Hopkinton already contains its full ration of fans and consumers, since the town is closed to all vehicle traffic except for shuttle buses and vendors at 6:30 A.M.

One by one, the buses unload their cargo of competitors, who are then wrangled up to Hopkinton High School, some 1,000 yards from the start, where they find their assigned corral for the start, dress, and simply try to stay warm. The B.A.A. tries to keep the athletes occupied with slide shows, music, and massages. For the 100th running, the Japanese contingent requested their own tent to cater to their 1,355 runners. The largest international representation in that race was actually from Canada, with 1,982 numbered competitors. California had the largest showing from any state outside of Massachusetts with 2,828.

In past races, runners assembled at various sites, including the Central House, the Columbia House, the Ashland Hotel, the Tebeau family farm, and finally the Hopkinton Community Center building, before ending up at the high school.

These early gathering points also served as makeshift doctor's offices, where runners could receive physical exams prior to the race to prove their ability to withstand the ordeal. From 1931 to 1973, Dr. Thomas Kelley oversaw the pre-race checkups. After the running craze exploded in the late 1970s, it was impossible to administer the tests because of the size of the field. As a result, runners sign a release that states: "You acknowledge that the BAA does not assume responsibility for your health, safety, security, or support."

1903 After receiving his physical, John Lorden was told by his doctor, "If you run, your bowel problems could kill you." When Lorden arrived at the starting line, he hid the doctor's

note in his pocket and told the doctor on the scene that his physical was all set. They handed him his number and he ended up winning the race.

1908 Doctors issued a statement prior to the race: "Rain, wind, race, and the proper handling of stimulants will all be factors in the race."

1958 Runners John Lafferty, Ted Corbitt, and Al Confalone, all veterans of the race, were ruled ineligible to run because doctors diagnosed each with heart murmurs. All three runners ran the race anyway, starting twenty-five yards behind the other competitors. They ended up finishing sixth, seventh, and ninth, respectively, but the results were not recognized by the B.A.A.

By 10:00 A.M. the last shuttle leaves Boston. If you miss that one, you better start running. As the clock rolls toward the witching hour, the athletes start meandering down to the town common to stretch out. On the bandstand sits the middle and high school band, helping you concentrate with every high note.

Running crazily around the common, Rob Phipps of the Hopkinton Athletic Association keeps an eye on one of his many responsibilities: the positioning of the valuable portable bathrooms. Over the year, many issues have been addressed, but none is more serious than the placement of these facilities because of two important facility factors: spillage and tonnage. In 1996 the B.A.A. erected the world's largest urinal, with over five hundred portable potties standing at attention to provide ample depositories for the hordes of bladder-strained runners. With this in mind, the town has put great emphasis on the installation of these receptacles in areas of flat topography, downwind of the better parts of town.

While the toilets awaited the onslaught of thousands, we were busy finishing our stay at the house of our hosts. The clock couldn't move fast enough or slow enough. With the sun outside rising toward its pinnacle,

we knew that it was time for us to finish breakfast and start getting dressed. For breakfast, we feasted on toast with jam or peanut butter, bagels, oranges, and bananas. While slugging down the first of many liters of fluid, it came to my attention that I hadn't drank with such passion since my final week in college. (Little did I know that at the end of this event I would feel quite similar to the way I felt at the conclusion of my college career.) One by one, each of us took his turn in the bathroom while the others surrounded the television to watch the pre-race festivities and the shuttle buses arriving at the high school to drop off loads of tired and cramped runners. As the cameras scanned the Woodstock-like scene on the school grounds, we heaved a collective sigh of relief that we were warm and dry in the house of friends.

Surfing the channels to find race-related news, we stopped at WCVB TV, Channel 5 in Boston. Mike Lynch, the head sportscaster, was in the middle of a live shot from Hopkinton when he introduced their race analyst, Marty Liquori, the famed miler from the 1960s and 1970s. Liquori took advantage of his airtime to castigate the dreaded bandits expected to jump into the 100th running. His tirade reached its climax:

"You've had ninety-nine years to qualify. If you haven't done it by now, then stay home!"

I was outraged! Who was he to tell me that I didn't deserve the opportunity to run this race? I was forced to undergo corrective heart surgery in order to run this event. I took a cortisone shot in my left knee and struggled through months of physical therapy. I trained through the worst winter in the history of Boston—110 inches of snow. I ran through fifteen-inch snowstorms and eight-degree mornings. All this in order to fulfill a childhood dream. Besides, not everyone with a number had run a fast time. Was some other back-of-the-pack runner more welcome than I, just because he had a political connection, or was part of a foreign tour group, or had enough money to make a large contribution to the right charity, or was lucky enough to have his name pulled out of a hat? This is as much my race as theirs. For thirty years I had watched the race: with cheek-pinching aunts in Newton, with inebriated college friends at Cleveland Circle, or at the twenty-mile mark with my wife and newborn son. How many times did Marty Liquori stand in the rain or under the beating sun to cheer on some ten-minute miler just because he or she dared to try?

Listen Marty, you're our guest. So mind your manners, pick up your check, and watch the race. When I cross that finish line some twenty-six miles down the road, not with a number but with the storied history of the Boston Marathon in my blood, then I will consider myself qualified! (By the way, Marty, a little fun fact for you: You and I are tied with the same number of Boston Marathon championships.)

Galvanized by the scolding, we went about our business, our determination to line up in Hopkinton only deepened. As we prepared it seemed like we were embarking on a CIA survival mission instead of a road race: In the kitchen, we spread out our rations of pretzels, sour balls, oranges, and a special mixture of water (80%) and Gatorade (20%)—not too sweet but a little bit of kick. We packed our provisions in Ziploc bags and stuffed our pockets. We each made one last visit to the bathroom, thanked Tracey for her hospitality, and jumped in Jeff's car for the short ride to the course. When he had taken us as far as he could, we disembarked and thanked him profusely.

Now we were faced with the reality of finding a way to get into the race. This subject had been discussed over and over among the four of us. It was my intention to work my way down the route and at some point jump into the race after the start. But luckily, Richie talked me into filing to the back of the line so that we could experience the thrill of crossing over the starting line. Some bandits, concerned that race officials would block their entry into the course, opted to meet at 8:00 A.M. and run the race uninhibited. But we chose to partake in the actual event. We snuck past policemen, race officials, and National Guardsmen, with our chests covered to hide the lack of a number, feeling a little like members of the French underground in occupied France.

Even as we maneuvered through enemy territory, we tried to stay in the moment and appreciate the carnival atmosphere of pre-race Hopkinton. Across from the town common, runners Os and Bev Oskam of Vancouver, Canada, were exchanging wedding vows at the Hopkinton First Congregational Church, in front of the church's trademark sign which reads AT HEARTBREAK HILL, YOU CAN DO IT THROUGH JESUS CHRIST WHO GIVES YOU STRENGTH. The bride wore a customized gown for running, while the groom looked equally dapper in his tux and sneakers.

Up at the runners' village at the high school, shuttle bus after shuttle bus arrived with their human cargoes: in all 700 buses delivered 35,000 runners. One by one the runners emerged and unfolded themselves after the uncomfortable ride, reporting that the traffic jam on the road from Boston had forced many fluid-filled runners to use their empty water bottles as makeshift porta-potties.

Once off the bus, the athletes soon discovered that the blizzard that had hit Massachusetts earlier in the week had left the town of Hopkinton swimming in mud. The town had placed Astroturf over the athletic fields in an attempt to save the grounds and the runners' gear. A number of runners wore plastic bags over their sneakers to keep them dry. I wish we had thought of that.

As we walked, we sought out other bandits in the hopes of hearing news about our prospects or learning strategies for getting into the race. To spot fellow bandits, we looked for a computer microchip tied up in the laces of our competitors' running shoes. The B.A.A. was using these chips to record the times of the numbered runners via satellite, so a runner with no chip was one of us. Opinions were bountiful and answers were scarce. We decided to sit on the sidewalk of a side street and wait. Just one hour to go.

– – – –

With the shuttle buses moving in and out from all over the state, B.A.A. officials are biting their fingernails down. Dave McGillivray, the race director, starts to connect with officials and police chiefs in each town along the route. Soon he will poll all the town officials over the same channel on a two-way radio, praying that each one will give him the "all clear." Until that transaction is made, organized chaos reigns. Across the street from the starting line, the church takes advantage of the unusual assembly. As the runners prepare for the gun, they are treated to sermons from the green and renditions of "Amazing Grace."

Runners spend the last minutes before the race in one of two ways: Either they banter nervously or they slip into a cocoon. Winner of the 1957 race, John "Younger" Kelley—not to be confused with the better-known John "Elder" Kelley who won in 1935 and 1945—used to concentrate on anything other than the race: "It was important to put the race in perspective. If you didn't you would go crazy. I remember trying to focus on the fields and woods of Hopkinton while at the same time ignoring all the talk around me. I often thought that my friends and peers must have thought I was a jerk, but that's just the way I was on race day." By contrast, 1976 winner Jack Fultz preferred to talk with the runners around him before the race: "It's important to have relaxed concentration. It's not like being a sprinter, who needs to be hyper-focused. A marathoner who is obsessed with concentration will not be able to relax sufficiently enough to run to his or her potential."

– – – –

The minute hand is climbing toward the promised hour. The starter's gun is loaded. By now the runners have made peace with the Lord or

Yahweh or Mohammed or the Golden Sneaker God. Minutes slowly tick off the digital watches of the runners just as surely as it dripped off the timepieces of derby-donned gentlemen in years gone by. The last-minute stretching, the faraway stares, the nervous babble—the last rituals all seem to speed the clock forward. The officials are preparing the 11:45 start of the wheelchair competition.

Upon the call for the runners, the competitors make their way to the starting line, which runs across the road between a cemetery and the Dough Boy statue, a World War I infantry soldier who has presided over the start for decades, with a gun on his shoulder and a concerned look on his bronze face. The Dough Boy was sculpted to honor the 115 Hopkinton residents who fought in World War I. Please note the ominous fact that the statue marches in the opposite direction of the race.

Prior to the start of the race, the elite runners find refuge in a church fifty yards from the starting line. At 11:45, they are marched through the neighboring cemetery in order to gain unmolested access to the starting line. This strange and rapid change in scenery has always created a wide range of emotions in Uta Pippig: "One moment I'm sitting in a church, where you are supposed to be quiet and respectful. Before you know it, you're walking through a cemetery over graves and by tombstones. In a different way, I feel a quiet connection with the people who might lie beneath my feet. Then, after quickly reflecting upon the lives of people who are no longer with us, I walk out on the street and there stand thousands of people who are waiting to start the most alive competition in the world. In the span of five minutes, I passed through every facet of life."

Now the band baptizes the largest one-day sporting event in the world with a Rockwellian rendition of "The Star Spangled Banner." With the national anthem reverberating in the air, race officials begin to hyperventilate while the runners contemplate their mission and try to control their emotions. Over the last year, these competitors have logged

thousands of miles in an effort to reach their respective goals. Whether the goal is to win, to break a time barrier, or simply to finish, each is of equal importance and each provides for great thought in these last seconds before the gun.

All of those long runs—in the dark of night, through the slippery streets of a New England winter, on a monotonous treadmill in Oslo, in the early morning streets of Tokyo before work, or sneaking back to your desk before your boss realizes that your split time has exceeded your lunch hour. All that you have endured—the sore muscles and knees, the blisters, the dog bites, that game of chicken with the pickup truck with the Yodel wrappers on the dashboard. All those nightmares of forgetting your sneakers. All of these commitments you have made, all of these trials you have faced, in order to stand on this line.

The course ahead holds many peaks and valleys, both mental and physical. There is good reason for doubt. But now is not the time to decide that you didn't train properly, or that you ate too much pasta last night, or that you should have gone to the bathroom again. There is no turning back now. Your year of commitment is about to face the test. Truth is just a few ticks of the clock away.

In the months leading up to the marathon I had several dreams about the race. In some of these visions I ran the last yards of the race jubilantly, while in others I missed the start for various reasons. Apparently my subconscious was quite aware of the magnitude of this event and the significance that it played in my life. After a number of these dreams, I became concerned that I was getting too preoccupied with the race. So I was glad to learn that other runners had suffered through similar hallucinations. After her 1983 win, two-time Boston champion and Olympic Marathon gold medalist Joan Benoit confessed that she had had a nightmare just before the race. She was window-shopping in one of Hopkinton's boutiques when the gun sounded. She sprinted out of the shop and had to join the race in the back of the pack. She was relieved when she woke up.

Though sometimes this nightmare comes to fruition. One of the pioneers of women's running, Kathy Switzer, lived through a real-life running nightmare prior to the 1976 race. With the running boom in full swing, a traffic jam approaching the starting line brought cars to a standstill. Switzer was forced to draw her number with a magic marker on the back of a newspaper and jump from the car. She raced to the starting line, only to find that no one was there. Remembering that the start had been moved, she sprinted up and around the Hopkinton Common. She reached the starting line one minute before the gun was shot.

Because of the huge field running the 100th Boston Marathon in 1996, the B.A.A. organized corrals to separate the runners. The elite runners, as always, were situated in the front of the pack on Main Street. Qualifying runners were stationed on Hayden Rowe, which lies perpendicular to Main Street. Then on Grove Street, parallel to Hayden Rowe,

were the runners who had won a number in the lottery (about 5,000) or obtained one through charities, companies, running groups, or foreign tour groups (about 6,000). And finally in the rear the despised Bandit Brigade had gathered (about 5,000). Here Rad, Richie, and I stood, anxious and ready. Jack Radley was somewhere up ahead with the lottery runners. The adrenaline was flowing and helicopters were roaring overhead to the music from the bandstand. It all reminded me of the beach-assault scene in *Apocalypse Now*.

2002 At the conclusion of the National Anthem, a quartet of F-15 fighter jets performed a flyover in Hopkinton and then followed the race route into Boston. It took them four minutes to complete the race.

Lurking in the shadows, we waited and wondered. Between the bandits and the numbered runners was a makeshift barricade of bike racks, minded by ten of the biggest National Guardsmen that the state could

49

muster. Over a loudspeaker system set up in the streets, a disc jockey told jokes, called out runners' names, coached the crowd through "the wave," and played music from the Steve Miller Band ("I want to fly like an eagle to the sea/Fly like an eagle let my spirit carry me"). All this in an effort to keep the crowd settled and occupied. When the clock reached twelve, the adrenaline levels would climb to plateaus never before imagined.

1937 The original bandit runner, Peter "Old Peter" Foley, a diamond cutter from Massachusetts, was ordered to start five minutes behind the qualified runners. Mr. Foley was ruled ineligible because of his advanced age—eighty. He finished the race.

From the moment that I decided to run the Boston Marathon, I was in complete denial. Running nonstop for over twenty-six miles is unhealthy, if not asinine. Sure I've always had wild and exciting ideas, but acting on them was a different matter altogether. As the months of the calendar flipped toward spring, I buried the fear of failure deep in my subconscious. In reality, I had no right to be standing on the starting line. But there I stood with no parachute while the starter cocked the gun. All avenues of escape were closed, and the fear of failure was starting to flow from the subconscious to the conscious. I was starting to realize that I had swum out too far and was now caught in a Nantucket riptide. Who was I kidding? Maybe Marty Liquori was right—Maybe I should have stayed home. Perhaps dreams and reality occupy different states of consciousness for a reason. Maybe, just maybe, I had bitten off more than I could chew. But the tide was taking me, and I let it.

One by one the racers fall into place as they await the sound of the gun, with stern faces and elbows extended. Anxious runners in the middle of the pack are starting to gulp for air, while the elite runners in the front seem frozen in time.

The starter's arm is raised…

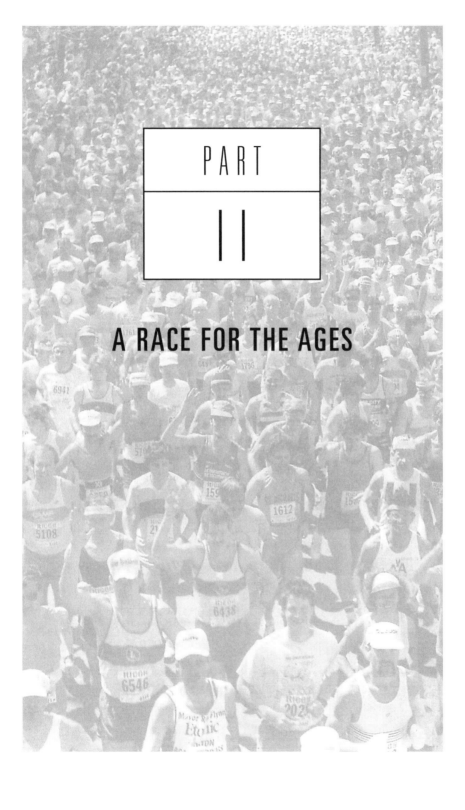

PART

II

A RACE FOR THE AGES

RUNNERS SET THEIR WATCHES AND PREPARE TO TAKE THEIR FIRST STEPS TOWARD BOSTON IN 1994. PHOTO COURTESY OF VICTAH SAILER.

MILE 1

John "Younger" Kelley described the first half of the race like this: "It's a setup. It is so easy to be suckered in by this attractive course."

— — — —

In 1897, race official Tom Burke simply organized the runners behind a line that he drew with his heel, raised his hand at 12:19 P.M., and shouted, "GO!" A decade later, the Brown family accepted the honor of baptizing the race and has held that post ever since. George Victory Brown, the family patriarch and a cattle fancier, was renowned for his ownership of the marathon. He would often be heard bellowing at the anxious runners lined up on the Ashland bridge, "Don't crowd here, you've got twenty-six miles ahead of you! Now kneel down and get ready."

For months and months the competitors have prepared for this one moment. Sometimes the anticipation is too much to take. Occasionally runners have attempted to expedite the process, causing mishap and controversy. Back in 1900, Canadian runner John Barnard jumped the gun, causing officials to order the only restart in Boston's history. Many blamed his lack of patience on the fact that the race was heavily wagered on by Canadian gamblers, and speculated that he stood to gain a share.

Eighty-five years later, many believed there was another false start that wasn't accounted for, this time in the wheel-

chair competition. Several competitors claimed that George Murray, the eventual winner, took off on the count of three, not on the shot of the starter's gun. Murray denied this accusation, as well as charges that he was guilty of drafting off the press bus later in the race. Frustrated competitors later obtained notarized letters from a motorcycle policeman and from media members on the bus confirming that Murray was told to pass the bus, but he preferred to stay behind— perhaps in an effort to avoid the blustery headwinds of the day.

Swept away by the magnitude of the race, some runners feel compelled to gain any advantage possible. In 1953 a runner showed up in Hopkinton with sprinters' starting blocks. Officials were able to convince him that the blocks wouldn't make much of a difference in the outcome.

For almost a century, a member of the Brown clan has fired an anti-quated colonial pistol into the air to christen the race and send the runners down Route 135 toward Boston. Most competitors hear a prerecorded howitzer blast triggered by the pistol; the pistol also electronically starts all the clocks along the route.

Back in the shadows of Hopkinton, we shadowy runners could barely hear the blast of the gun. A better indication that the race had started came when a tsunami of screams and exultations swept all the way from the starting line to the back of the pack. Though, mind you, the official start only produced a tempered rush of adrenaline. In the rear, the sound of the gun only meant more waiting. It was estimated that it would take over an hour for the back of the pack runners to reach the starting line— bringing more anxiety to the anxious.

The wait was bad news for Rad, Richie, and me, especially considering that we stood transfixed in the front row, flattened against the bike racks—the equivalent of being pinned against the stage during a Rolling Stones concert. We waited with teeth clenched for about fifteen minutes, until thankfully there seemed to be some movement on Grove Street, which descended onto Main Street. It was then that the National Guardsmen picked up their assigned bike racks and allowed the bandits to enter the race. The B.A.A. should be commended for their decision for two reasons: First, they continued the tradition of an "open" race, and second they averted a potential riot by 5,000 committed athletes.

The joy of joining the celebration of the 100th Boston Marathon brought a euphoric reaction from us merry bandits. As we broke into a slow jog there were hugs, high-fives, and shouts of ecstasy. We showered the trees above with sweatshirts, pants, and gloves as we worked our way toward the Promised Land.

Together we ran while sharing a special bond with the other runners. Like friendships formed during war, these momentary acquaintances come about because your fellow runners share the same fears, hopes, and feelings. We appreciate the commitment the other participants have made in order to stand in Hopkinton on this day. Only another runner can understand the draw of the race and the need to answer its call. Driven by some common intangible, every runner rejoices in this communal spirit. So as we waited to enter the arena, we all felt vulnerable, but we were strengthened by our neighbors' similar emotions. In that moment that you exchange a word or a smile, a friendship is shaped.

At the bottom of the hill, the runners bang a right turn onto Main Street, where we finally realize what the marathon is all about. The fans stand on porches and roofs and cars, they hang from trees and out windows, all of them screaming and hollering as if we were heroes coming home from war. It is like a personal surprise party for each and every runner.

Almost jogging in place, we slowly crested the Main Street hill before approaching the starting line. Little by little, my emotions rose as I realized that my dream was about to become a reality. Another forty choppy steps and I had entered an uncharted world.

As I crossed the starting line, I noticed the TV cameras rolling as they attempted to capture the ecstasy of the moment. Most runners opted to deplete some of their reserves by jumping over the line in the hopes of standing out on television from the other 40,000-plus participants. Up on the starter's podium stood Senator John Kerry and his wife Theresa Heinz, heir to the Heinz ketchup empire. As she waved to the proletariat passing below, I contemplated yelling up to her, "Bet you a million dollars that I finish!" (Might as well be bold at the start, since there won't be any boasting after the coming miles.)

Together with my brothers and sisters, I entered the first stage of the world's greatest race, joining all those who have run before me. This leap over the threshold of Boston put me in the same arena conquered by the greats, such as Clarence DeMar, Johnny "Elder" Kelley, Bill Rodgers, and Joan Benoit. Stepping out of the ranks of the spectators and into the Boston Marathon was like jumping out of black-and-white and into the Technicolor of the Land of Oz: Our lives brightened with the prospect of fulfilling a dream. Down the hill I passed the forsythia bush where Roberta Gibb, the first woman ever to run Boston, hid in 1966 as she listened for the gun before slipping into the pack. (Women were not officially allowed to run the marathon until 1972.) Further down the road, I observed the telephone pole where Mrs. Fish concealed herself in 1968 as she waited for her husband, the Reverend Howard Fish, to run by so she could join him. The minister from Cambridge and his wife were, unofficially, the first couple ever to run the Boston Marathon; Mrs. Fish beat her husband to the finish line. Living in the moment and absorbing all that we were now a part of, we were embarked toward the pinnacle of the running world and we intended to honor the race with our greatest effort.

As you glare down Route 135 in the direction of Boston, you don't see any skyscrapers but instead a sharp decline and a blind turn at the bottom of the first hill. Pumped up and ready to go, competitors must make an effort here to move smartly and safely. The start is very narrow: just under fifty feet, fitting only twenty-one bodies across. A disorderly start could result in injury or even death. Greg Meyer, winner of the 1983 race, feared the start with a passion: "With the course starting on a narrow street and moving downhill, all of your training could be for naught with one trip over someone's feet. I wish I could fall asleep, and wake up somewhere in Natick."

No one would agree with Meyer more than Rob de Castella, the winner in 1986. One year after winning the laurel wreath, the defending champ from New Zealand stood ready for the gun. Strangely, when the clock struck noon, the rope holding back the runners was still tied to a tree. Up on the podium, the starter fired the gun in the customary way, and the crowd surged forward, causing de Castella to trip over the restraining rope. Thinking quickly, a race official cut the rope with a pocketknife, avoiding further disaster, but not before the fallen champion had donated some of the skin from his knees and elbows to the streets of Hopkinton. Jumping to his feet instinctively, de Castella regained his form and went on to a sixth-pace finish. Later he recalled that he, "either had to get up or be trampled by ten thousand runners." The starting process has since been modified to avoid accidents like this.

1977 Winner Jerome Drayton of Canada voiced his displeasure with the start of the race at the post-race press conference. He ridiculed the idea of starting the race on some suburban street, complained that there was no countdown before the gun, and recalled that when the gun was fired, he was kicked, grabbed, and almost pulled down. He claimed that he actually feared for his life. (If he thinks that's bad, he should check out Filene's Basement, in Boston, when the doors open for the annual wedding gown sale.)

Down the hill, the road turns sharply left, then back to the right, and then right again, where the racers meet their first incline at about the half-mile point. The attractive opening descent can also be treacherous to the athletes' game plans, especially in the wheelchair competition. As in bike racing, drafting is an important factor in wheelchair racing: A group of wheelchair racers working together to break the wind can move faster, with the same effort, than a single racer alone. An elite wheelchair competitor who loses contact with the lead pack on the first incline will be unable to draft off the front group, and thus faces long odds to catch up later. It has been estimated that separation from the pack here can add as much as ten minutes to a competitive racer's overall time. In other words, if you don't crest this first hill in the lead pack your day is probably over, so it is essential to push the envelope here. Five-time wheelchair champion Jim Knaub puts it this way: "If you make it to the top side of the first hill before everyone else, you have a great chance of winning.

It's like God picked you up and dropped you in the lead, and said it's your day."

So it is no surprise that the charge down the first hill is reckless: Competitors reach speeds of forty miles per hour in ever-advancing racing chairs. Of course, hell-bent racing of this kind is not without risks. This was never more obvious than in 1987, when the roads were slick from a steady rain that had fallen throughout the morning. Racing for the base of the Mile 1 hill in tuck position, Jim Knaub hit a rut in the street and crashed just one hundred yards from the starting line. This miscue caused a chain-reaction crash that left six competitors on the side of the road with various injuries and damaged racing chairs. (The scene horrified the crowd, who did not consider that wheelchair athletes also face challenges and dangers—all athletes accept risks when they push themselves beyond their limitations.) Jim Knaub was able to make adjustments to his chair and finish the race. Jim Baughan, another racer, had a badly bruised forehead but also finished the race, refusing medical help until he reached his goal. Two competitors were unable to continue because of damage done to their chairs.

Some, like Fred Lebow, the late director of the New York City Marathon (who was never a big supporter of the wheelchair competition), took advantage of the accident to warn the people of Boston that they were "flirting with disaster." Boston bowed to the warnings and instituted a pace car in 1988 to hold the wheelchair athletes to a speed of twenty miles per hour for the length of the first descent. This controlled start takes ten seconds off the average competitor's time; the ten-second differential is factored in when calculating whether a finishing time has broken a course record.

For the elite runners, the first mile is not only strategically important but can also be a nuisance. Bill Rodgers, a four-time winner, doesn't particularly like the start. "The descent at the outset gives runners who aren't necessarily world class the opportunity to stay with the leaders long enough to be bothersome." On a level course the world-class runners would leave these imposters in their royal dust. Invariably, running up front each year with the elite runners is a camera hound, more interested in getting his picture taken than in finishing the race. This type of

LIKE ALL ATHLETES, WHEELCHAIR COMPETITORS FACE CHALLENGES AND OBSTACLES IN THEIR EFFORT TO REACH THEIR GOAL, AS PICTURED HERE IN THE 1985 BOSTON MARATHON. PHOTO COURTESY OF THE *BOSTON HERALD*.

showmanship is hardly new: the eccentric runner Johnny "Cigar" Connors used to drive Race Director Jock Semple around the bend in the 1930s by running in crazy outfits while smoking cigars. In 1935, he drew Semple's ire when he ran the opening miles while toking on two cigars at the same time. In the 1932 race, he took a break on the running board of a car, rejoined the runners at the twenty-five-mile mark, and finished the race. In 1937 Connors crossed the finish line wearing pink panties and a yellow beret, and sucking on his stogie.

While the elite runners fend off the pretenders in the front, the "meat of the pack" runners jockey for position by jumping up on sidewalks and around parked cars in an effort to pass slow starters. At the back of the pack, runners are moving like rush-hour traffic on the Expressway in Boston—barely.

Up the hill and to the left, in the last quarter of the first mile, the runners move by a nursery. Just beyond the nursery sits a barn from old Tebeau's Farm. From the 1920s to the 1940s, runners used to gather at this spot to change clothes and receive their pre-race physicals. Mary Tebeau, an Ashland schoolteacher, eventually sold the land to the Mezitt family. The Mezitts, the largest landowners in Hopkinton with over 900 acres, still work the land under the name of Weston Nurseries. Here they grow everything from Christmas trees to a special rhododendron that blooms for the race. Brothers Wayne and Roger Mezitt remember when the race started on their farm at a ledge called "Lucky Rock," so dubbed because of a streak of quartz that ran through the middle. And although they have fond memories of this day, their business suffers badly throughout the holiday because of the tight traffic control maintained around the race.

The running traffic for this day continues past their property and up to the top of the hill, where competitors can look over Mahar's Meadow to their left. Here the runners have completed the first chapter of this twenty-six-mile journey. Hopefully the harriers at the back are approaching the starting line. In all, the runners have descended 130 feet in the first mile, the greatest drop of any mile on the course. The starting line is the highest point on the route, approximately 490 feet above sea level. In the first four miles, the course falls over 300 feet.

The fact that the race drops nearly 500 feet, bottoming out almost at sea level in Kenmore Square at the twenty-five-mile mark, has been the source of great controversy. The descent creates the illusion, both among non-runners and within the Technical Committee of the Athletic Congress (TAC), that the race runs directly downhill and therefore is inappropriately regarded as a world-class race. The TAC ruled in 1990 that the Boston Marathon, for all its history, could not be a source of world or national records. Consequently, the TAC reversed all world records set in Boston, placing the ever-dreaded "Roger Maris Asterisk" next to the times and accomplishments of runners like Joan Benoit and Rob de Castella.

Guy Morse, the 1996 race director, feels that this decision is best handled by ignoring it. "Since the ruling, the best runners of the world have run Boston, and have been unable to break the world record, which in itself is a testament to the toughness and validity of the Boston course." The disagreement continues between the TAC and the B.A.A., but the fact remains that the beginning of the course is steep and alluring. All

JUST MINUTES BEFORE THE 1906 START, RUNNERS POSE FOR A PICTURE AT THE STARTING LINE ON THE HIGH STREET RAILROAD BRIDGE IN ASHLAND. PHOTO COURTESY OF THE BOSTON ATHLETIC ASSOCIATION.

competitors—and especially newcomers—must not forget that the easy first half of the race prepares a treacherous second half. The runners must keep close to their game plans, no matter how good they feel early in the race.

– – – –

It took just twenty-eight minutes for the 37,000 numbered runners to cross the starting line. We rolled across the line about thirty-five minutes after the gun and moved downhill past numerous parties (one of which had a stereo perpetually playing the theme from *Rocky*) and woods filled with runners relieving themselves from their fluid binging prior to the race. Pat Williams, head of the Orlando Magic and a frequent marathoner, surmises that this section of trees must be the most fertilized stretch of greenery in Massachusetts.

As we passed this area, the running was slow and circuitous as runners took time to sort themselves out and find their paces. This would continue throughout the race. Rad, Richie, and I passed the one-mile mark

RUNNERS FROM THE MIDDLE AND BACK OF THE PACK ARE JUST STARTING TO BREAK INTO A JOG AFTER CROSSING THE STARTING LINE IN 1991. PHOTO COURTESY OF THE *BOSTON HERALD*.

in thirteen minutes. The lead runners ran the first mile in 4:33 and went on to cover every mile in less than five minutes until the eleventh mile, which was run in 5:03. We weren't in any rush but we were quickly realizing that each sidetracked step added to the twenty-six miles and 385 yards.

MILE 2

Craig Virgin, the second-place finisher in 1981: "Don't do anything crazy in the first ten miles."

— — — —

Early in the race, the athletes move as a solid mass of humanity. Spectators waiting for the runners to come around the corner can hear and feel the oncoming stampede. First in sight are the wheelchair competitors and the elite runners, moving by swiftly like queen bees. Then come the followers in a thickening herd, in rows of hats and bounding hair. It's impossible for the fans to identify individual runners. Instead, the group moves like a monstrous chain gang, or like buoys bouncing up and down on a rough sea. Most of the runners have been unable to open up to a comfortable pace. Each step must be carefully placed to avoid another runner's foot—and a collision that would put you out of your misery early. Most of the spectators in the first miles live nearby; the streets of Hopkinton have been closed to normal traffic since 6:30 A.M.

> **The neighborhoods around Hopkinton are mostly rural and partially agricultural. The town is inhabited by 13,346 people spread over 28.2 square miles, with an average per-family income of $78,709. In 2001, the median house price in the town was $359,900 on an average lot size of one acre. Property taxes on these mostly colonial homes are $15.66 per $1,000.**

The town was incorporated in 1715 and named after Edward Hopkins, the governor of Connecticut. Hopkins donated money to Harvard University, which was invested in land, then inhabited by the Quansigomog Indians. The townspeople bought the plot from Harvard for $10,000.

Over the last century, the town's identity has been shaped by its association with the race. At times, the race has been a source of great argument, but in general the town has welcomed the runners with open arms, and open bathrooms.

As you leave Mile 1 and pass the Weston Nurseries on your left, the course takes a mild dip and shuffles left for about a quarter of a mile. Here the runners are delightfully entertained by the second band of the day—the Vermont Fiddlers—compliments of Art Fairbanks, the owner of Art's Auto Body, which sits on the right side of the course about 1.2 miles from the start.

In the early days, the entire field of runners could race by Art's garage in five minutes. As they passed, Art would take a break from realigning cars, bounced around by the winter's potholes, to enjoy the festivities and admire the men and women quickly moving by his shop. But as the marathon grew and eclipsed the business day, Art figured, "If you can't beat 'em, join 'em." Starting fifteen years ago, Art shuts down the shop for the day and gives the Vermont Fiddlers a stage for their biggest concert of the year. The runners make a great audience as they dance and jig, suddenly uncertain whether they're in Hopkinton, Massachusetts, or Galway, Ireland. If you get up early enough, Art and his wife, Anne, throw a nice breakfast for about fifty of their closest friends. I'm sure they wouldn't mind if you dropped by.

Mile 2 continues with a series of quick-hitting ups and downs and an occasional house among the woods and fields that line the road. Halfway through the mile, the runners pass Clinton Street and its admiring residents.

1990 Runner David Cantone had pushed himself in his training to prepare for the marathon. To make it all worthwhile,

GEOFF SMITH (LEFT) AND FRIEND PLAY THE ROLE OF QUEEN BEES WHILE BEING CLOSELY FOL-
LOWED BY INTERESTED SUITORS. PHOTO COURTESY OF JEFF JOHNSON.

**David needed to cross the finish line in Boston. Along with
the thousands of other runners, David made his way through
the first mile of the race and began his assault on the second.
The mob of runners was starting to spread out just enough**

that you could no longer tell if the runner next to you had garlic bread with his pasta the night before. Suddenly David noticed something askew: He did a double take and rushed to the aid of a runner on the side of the road. The man had blood pouring out of his mouth, and his eyes were rolled back into his head. The marathon was now a distant second on Cantone's list of priorities.

Cantone immediately summoned the help of Red Cross volunteers and teamed up with them to get the patient, who was suffering a grand mal seizure, to the nearest hospital. The stricken runner was attended to and released later that afternoon. David Cantone, who sat with his new friend throughout the day, hailed a cab so that the two of them could get back to Boston.

Sometimes things don't work out exactly as planned. David Cantone set out to run a marathon and instead he will be remembered as a Good Samaritan. As the cab rambled over the finish line, twenty-four miles later, the world was just a little better.

Right before the two-mile mark sits the Ashland-Hopkinton border, where the baton is handed from one town to the next. Standing guard over the border is a friendly local tavern called TJ's. All year long, owner John Tomasz looks forward to this weekend, which usually doesn't disappoint. From Friday through Monday, the place is hopping. On Sunday night, they offer your basic pasta dinner for runners who have found lodging out near the starting line. For five dollars, it's all you can eat. And for Monday, TJ's applies for and receives—over the police chief's protests—a permit to party-hardy outside. With a disc jockey spinning and a cook flipping burgers on the barbecue, it's a good time for all.

After TJ's, the road leading you to Mile 3 is flat and residential. By now, your breathing becomes more settled after the initial excitement of the start. As we approached the mile mark, the sidelines were still crowded and festive. Families from Hopkinton lined the streets on both sides. Parents bring their kids out to the course to expose them to a

An aerial view of the early stages of the 1935 race. Photo courtesy of the Boston Public Library Print Department.

positive and traditional pastime—a baptism in the waters of the Boston Marathon. When you live in these parts, the Boston Marathon is a part of life. Pat Williams is amazed each year to see the same faces in the same spots. He wonders, Could these families lay claim to a piece of the roadside as a function of squatter's rights?

The three of us hugged the sides of the road to high-five the fans who were extending their hands. Richie, by far the most gregarious of the three of us, rejoiced in the crowd's requests for high-fives, seemingly slapping hands with every spectator in the town. I, on the other hand, being more conservative and less certain of my ability to conquer the course, ran closer to the middle of the street, saving every ounce of energy for the later miles.

As I watched Richie's celebrations, I couldn't help but think of another sporting event, and then I couldn't help but share the analogy with Richie when we came to a gap in the row of enthusiastic fans. I was reminded of the 1995 National Championship college football game between the Miami Hurricanes and the Nebraska Cornhuskers. During the first half of that game, University of Miami defensive star Warren Sapp dominated the contest, controlling the entire Nebraska offense. After

each tackle, Sapp would dance and taunt, despite the heat of the Miami night. Later in the game, Sapp ran out of the energy and Nebraska ran the football right at him, staging a late comeback and stealing the game and championship 24-17.

Richie understood the concept and attempted to limit his celebrations to singing and arm-waving. Following the marathon, he agreed with the moral of the story: Save everything. Halfway through the second mile, a sign on the left side of the road summed up the coming journey: "Dead Men Walking."

MILE 3

Gordon Bakoulis Bloch, in *How to Train and Run Your Best Marathon*—"Hold yourself back. You should have a conscious feeling that in the first half you could be running a lot faster."

— — — —

Mile 3 starts off level as it runs through a residential neighborhood for the first two tenths of the mile. In the third tenth, the road begins to ascend without turning. Early in the third mile the runners move past a water stop at a local nursery named Prosperous Gardens. The owner, Dick Preservagi, looks forward to this day as a spectator but dreads it as a business owner. I asked him for his impression of the race, the runners, and the event in general. He was silent for ten seconds, as if he was searching for a thesaurus, and finally said, "I don't know what it is, but when the mass of humanity passes by, I… I… I just love it!"

The course moves up an incline and to the right, before turning back down to your left. Halfway through the mile, the runners pass the local Knights of Columbus and the Ashland State Park. From there, the course moves downhill for the last half of the mile.

At about 2.7 miles, the runners go by Steven's Corner, where the race was started from 1899 to 1924. This is just down the road from the spot where Holton and Graham got off their bikes and declared the original starting point of the race. In 1924 the start was moved back to Hopkinton.

The course levels off at the three-mile mark, which falls just past the entrance to Ashland High School, on your left.

1938 Since the beginning of the race, traffic and spectators along the route have posed a threat to the runners. Halfway through the third mile in the 1938 race, Leo Girard of Brockton, Massachusetts, was run over by a motorcycle. After receiving medical care for his badly cut knees, elbows, and shoulder, he jumped back in the race and climbed into ninth position, before falling back and finishing fifteenth.

— — — —

Ashland was never truly recognized for its contribution to the Boston Marathon until recent years. The town of Ashland was better known for manufacturing clocks and watches to the designs of a local inventor by the name of Henry Warren. Warren created the first self-winding clock during the Depression. People moved to Ashland to find work in the prospering clock factory. In later years, the town and Mr. Warren thrived when General Electric joined Warren as a 49% partner. Time and clocks are integral to the town of Ashland. The high school sports teams go by the nickname of the Clock-Towners, and a clock tower stands in Ashland's epicenter, down the road in Mile 4.

While researching this book or training for the marathon in Ashland, I always appreciated the relevance of time to runners. During these training runs in the months prior to the race, I would always load my Walkman with a popular album from the band Hootie and the Blowfish called *Cracked Rear View*. There was one song, called "Time," that I would play over and over again as I pushed myself forward. Here are just a slice of the lyrics I would sing out loud during my runs, causing bystanders to cross the street:

Time, why you punish me?
Like a wave bashing into the shore
You wash away my dreams...

Can you teach me about tomorrow
And all the pain and sorrow
Running free?
Cause tomorrow's just another day
And I don't believe in time

By the third mile, we were getting used to the rhythm and the pace of the race. After a couple of miles, we realized that one of the keys to this day would be patience. By this point, our pace had quickened to nine-minute miles, but that was accomplished by continual navigation among walkers and slower runners. We also figured out that attempting to get water at one of the first five tables at the water stops could be hazardous to our health. So instead, we zeroed in on the end tables, where we could move in and out of the pit stop safely and quickly.

MILE 4

Uta Pippig—"In the first five miles, it's important to run your race. The early downhills make it essential to slow yourself and stay at your pace. At the same time, on a nice spring day, I like to take the opportunity to appreciate the new green leaves on the many trees in Hopkinton and Ashland."

— — — —

At this juncture of the race, the surrounding area begins to become more commercial. The road continues on a downward grade, moving left before straightening and going right. At the 3.1-mile mark, there is a small shopping plaza on the left, occupied by your standard video store and insurance agency. You can smell the grease burning at the Honey Dew Donut Shop on your right, and see kids licking ice creams from Tasty Treat next door. Down the middle of the road lies a dangerous cement island better known to the athletes and fans of the race as "Three Mile Island." This cement protrusion stretches for about twenty yards. Wheelchair competitors need to be especially careful rolling around the bend, as they may be traveling in excess of twenty-five miles per hour coming down the long hill approaching the island impediment. Although the island is well marked with cones and police tape, it can jump on you in hurry—especially if you're drafting or following another competitor too closely. This is one of the spots in the race where being unfamiliar with the course can be a real disadvantage.

Wheelchair competitors carefully navigate the treacherous Three Mile Island in Ashland during the 100ᵀᴴ running of the Boston Marathon. Photo courtesy of FayFoto.

1997 Already feeling the pressure of running as a pre-race favorite, German Silva of Mexico was also carrying the burden of running for his impoverished village of Tecomate. After winning the New York City Marathon in 1994, he used his prize money to help his village obtain electricity. On this day, Silva was running both for the laurel wreath and for the luxury of running water for his people.

As Silva ran with the lead pack he was introduced to the Three Mile Island impediment. As members of a Kenyan group running in front of him left a water stop, they failed to negotiate the island, sending Charles Tangus to the ground. Silva, who was trailing the Kenyans, attempted to hurdle over the tangle but was tripped up. With damaged legs, he picked himself up to finish a sad fourth.

After the island, you continue past a drug store and a pizza shop. At this point, the course heads uphill and to the right. More spectators lined the sidewalks here, among them my sisters Maureen and Cathy, who were waiting for me with a sign and guarded optimism. (I had warned my family before the race that no matter how bad I looked, they must lie and tell me that I was doing great. I knew that my margin for error was slim, and there was no room for doubt.) As they waved and yelled their well-wishes, I was surprised at how excited I was to see them—and how disappointed I was to leave them. From here on in, I started to appreciate that there is a significant emotional dimension to running a marathon. Each time I came upon a family member or a friend, I remembered that I was loved and that I was not alone on the course, but pushed along and followed by their hopes and thoughts. By contrast, a quarter of a mile up the road we had planned on seeing a distant acquaintance. I couldn't believe how hurt we felt when he wasn't there. You would have thought we'd been left at the altar.

The mile turns flat and straight as the course moves briefly through a residential neighborhood before creeping past an old burial ground and then a school on the left. At the next set of lights, marking the Main Street intersection, the runners pass the spot where the old Central House and the Columbia House were located. In the early 1900s, runners received their pre-race dinner and physical here.

With nine tenths of the mile finished, the runners pass the Ashland Clock Tower on the left. This large timepiece is mounted on a commercial building called the Ashland Technology Building. At the top of the structure's face sits a giant clock facing catty-corner toward the race. In the old days, Clarence DeMar used the clock to check his

74

pace early in the race. As the runners pass the clock, they hardly glance up at the old dinosaur; they all have digital watches and numerous clocks along the route to remind them that they should have trained harder.

Happy to be known as a humble print shop worker, Clarence DeMar is probably the most unknown star in Boston sports history. Winning his first Boston Marathon in 1911 and his seventh in 1930, a staggering nineteen years later, DeMar was truly one of the greatest American athletes of all time.

DeMar might have won ten or more marathons but for a local doctor who told him that he had an irregular heartbeat that could be fatal. He warned DeMar that even stair climbing should be avoided, never mind marathoning. So DeMar dutifully skipped ten of the next eleven years.

DeMar eventually got tired of running back and forth to work as his main source of exercise, so he entered the race in 1922 and claimed the first of five victories in that decade. The seven-time champion was once asked the name of the doctor who diagnosed his cardiac condition. He answered, "I won't tell you his name, but he recently died of a heart attack. He must have been listening to his own heart."

Clarence resided in Melrose, Massachusetts, where he taught Sunday School and was a Boy Scout leader. The World War I veteran grew up in poverty and earned an associate's degree in art at Harvard in 1915 and a master's degree from Boston University.

Although DeMar was quiet and reserved off the course, he was a fierce competitor once the gun was fired. DeMar felt that the Boston Marathon belonged to him and acted that way. Two fans could attest to his intensity after suffering right crosses from the runner. One had asked for an autograph in the middle of the race; the other had poured ice water on the back of his legs.

DeMar's life was running. He once said, "I would be happy if I died while running." DeMar got his wish. Hospitalized

THE INCOMPARABLE CLARENCE DEMAR RUNS TOWARD ONE OF HIS SEVEN CHAMPIONSHIPS.

with intestinal cancer, DeMar horrified his doctor by jogging in place in his hospital room. The doctor pleaded with the great runner to rest, but DeMar continued on. Hours later DeMar died a fulfilled man. Clarence certainly was DeMar(velous).

— — — —

1976 Because there were no clocks along the course to provide split times, Jack Fultz used his placement in the race as a timer. He knew that if he was running in the top ten, then his splits were consistent with what he needed to run a good race. He won the race.

Diagonally across from the clock on the right is the annual marathon flea market put on by the local chamber of the Lion's Club in an empty lot before the intersection. The event is their best fund-raiser of the year, sending people home with smiles and junk they don't really need. (You

VICTOR MACAULEY, CLARENCE DEMAR AND CHUCK MELLOR (L TO R) RUN STRIDE FOR STRIDE IN 1925. PHOTOS COURTESY OF THE *BOSTON HERALD*.

wonder if some of that stuff is as old as the race.) Marathon-related yard sales like this have gone on since 1923, when the Red Cross held a Red Tag sale in Ashland before the race. Proceeds were used to purchase first aid kits for the local schools.

Continuing down the road, the runners enviously sneak a peak at the Dairy Queen ice cream stand on the right side of the road. This is one of those spots where you see a complete nutritional polarization between the runners and the spectators, many of them apparently season ticket-holders at the ice cream establishment. Although on hot days, Dairy Queen has been known to see the occasional marathoner at its run-thru window.

As the end of mile approaches, you are sandwiched between two businesses. On the right is a Chinese food restaurant by the name of the Cherry Blossom. Each year the restaurant sets up tables of water out in front to provide the runners with some refreshment (no substitutes). The restaurant doesn't do anything else during the day—and actually loses money—but they hope their hospitality creates some goodwill.

1989 The area in front of the Cherry Blossom was the site of a near tragedy. As a pack of runners was passing by the gathered spectators, a deranged runner reached into the crowd and grabbed a little girl. As he dragged her down the street, spectators followed in pursuit. The crazed wanna-be kidnapper released the girl and jumped into a nearby pond to evade the mob and the police. He was quickly reeled in from his impromptu biathlon screaming, "I'm Jesus Christ!" which made it seem unnecessary to test him for narcotics.

Across from the Cherry Blossom sits Tom's Autobody, which is perfectly situated above the course on the left side. Because of this ideal setting, the owner Tom McClements has often been approached by real estate agencies, television crews, and marathon revelers seeking to take advantage of his vantage point.

The structure that houses Tom's Autobody holds great historical significance in the town of Ashland. In the late 1800s, the Perini family, who are known in these parts for owning the Boston Braves and Perini Construction, owned an estate on this site. The estate was the envy of the town. The mansion had a fishpond in the shape of a fish, cathedral windows, and Old Man Perini's favorite toy—a baby grand piano. On spring and summer days, Perini used to enjoy sitting up on the hill with the windows open, treating the town to a piano concerto.

Along with its many other amenities, the Perini estate was the first house in the town to have electricity. This blessing proved to be a curse when a northeasterly storm blew into town. The blizzard, accompanied by blustery winds, ignited a fire at the Perini mansion that burned the estate to the ground. As the old man reviewed the damage, he was overjoyed to find that his pride and joy, the baby grand piano, had survived to play another day.

The town of Ashland was itself named after a rich country estate. A town incorporator who admired Senator Henry Clay adopted the name "Ashland" from one of Clay's three properties in Kentucky. Previously known as Unionville, Ashland was incorporated in 1846 after acquiring land from the three surrounding towns, including Hopkinton.

Ashland is a fast-developing area of Massachusetts, as are most towns in close proximity to Route 495. The town covers almost thirteen square miles with an estimated 2001 population of 14,674 and an average per-family income of $72,021. In 2001, the median house price in the town was $293,500, with most houses set on half-acre lots. Property taxes for the same year were $16.07 per $1,000.

More than halfway through Ashland Pat Williams keeps urging himself "Just make it to Framingham."

MILE 5

The Boston Globe reported in 1968 that race official Jock Semple was in charge of keeping "babes" off the course. He was later quoted as saying, "They will run over my dead body!"

— — — —

As they finish the fourth mile, the runners are greeted by the refreshing sight of Bracketts Pond on the left side of the course. In the middle of the road, another set of cement islands demands the runners' attention. The road then moves uphill and forks left, before passing a garden shop and nursery, on the left, by the name of Beckongreen Ltd. The shopkeepers post the names of friends and associates running the race on a display board outside that is normally used to advertise flower sales. Many sweatshirts and tops are thrown into the parking lot here by runners who are beginning to overheat.

1976 With thermometers topping the 100-degree mark in Hopkinton, getting enough water and staying cool were matters of necessity. As Jack Fultz ran toward the Framingham border, he noticed a makeshift shower on the side of the road: Someone had connected a hose to the top of a stepladder and ran the water throughout the race. Fultz decided to deviate off the course and enjoy this oasislike respite from the baking sun. Fultz stood under the shower

JOCK SEMPLE FEELS THE WRATH OF KATHY SWITZER'S RUNNING COMPANION, TOM MILLER, IN THE 1967 BOSTON MARATHON AS SEMPLE ATTEMPTS TO RIP KATHY'S NUMBER FROM HER JERSEY. WOMEN WERE NOT ALLOWED TO "OFFICIALLY" RUN THE BOSTON MARATHON UNTIL 1972. PHOTO COURTESY OF THE BOSTON PUBLIC LIBRARY.

for over five seconds, convinced that he was making an "investment in time." Fultz went on to win the race.

The course continues to snake uphill, left and right, until reaching the barbecue at the DRC Auto Service garage and the Sri Lakshmi Temple at the Framingham-Ashland border.

The Sri Lakshmi Temple draws Hindus from all over the Northeast. With a mailing list of over 8,000, worshipers come from as far away as New Jersey to shed their shoes and pay homage. On the temple's magnificent tower, which rises fifty feet into the sky, is a statue of Lakshmi, the goddess of Wealth. On her sides are the dwarapalika—the female gatekeepers.

Mile 5 is a mixture of residential, commercial, and undeveloped land. Many runners feel indifferent during this stretch and must bear down in order to stay focused. That was not the case in 1967, when the race changed forever at Mile 5.

With the entire country seemingly involved in some form of change or protest that spring, the Boston Marathon was not exempt from the challenges of the oppressed. Kathy Switzer was not primarily a rebel or a troublemaker or a feminist—she was, in her words, an athlete "in pursuit of a goal." In 1967 the college runner entered the historically all-male event as K.V. Switzer and came to Hopkinton to challenge herself athletically. In the process she became the first numbered woman ever to run the Boston Marathon, thus putting the marathon and the entire sporting world on an irreversible course toward equality.

With her head covered by the hood of her gray sweatshirt, prominently displaying the number 261, Switzer took her spot with the other runners at the start. Walking among the competitors to confirm that they were registered was Race Director Will Cloney. When he reached Switzer, he placed his hand on her shoulder, checked the number on her sweatshirt, and pushed her back behind the snow fence with the other runners. In all the chaos Cloney didn't realize that he had just sent through the first numbered woman ever to run the race. Five miles down the road, Cloney and fellow race official Jock Semple would attempt to extract Switzer from the race.

The gun was fired and the numbered men and woman trotted through Hopkinton and into Ashland. With each step Switzer took toward Boston, the word spread further that there was a *woman* running with a number. The rumblings soon reached Jock Semple and Will Cloney, who immediately sped off in the press bus to stop the renegade.

Five miles into the race, Switzer's main concern was one of vanity: "I couldn't wait to take off my old gray sweat suit and show off the beautiful running suit that I had on underneath. I wanted to prove that a woman athlete didn't need to be masculine or a tomboy, but could be feminine and an athlete." As Switzer worried about her garb, she was overtaken by a flatbed truck carrying the photographers and the bus carrying the print media and the two infuriated race officials. The bus pulled over ahead, and Cloney and Semple disembarked determined to remove the official number that hung mockingly on the front of the genderless sweatshirt.

Little did these dynamic defenders of male separatism know that, before they could remove the irritant, they would have to get by Switzer's muscle-bound boyfriend, Tom Miller, a collegiate hammer thrower who was running side-by-side with his girlfriend. Semple got to her first ("Cloney tried to catch her first—he was too bloody slow," he later recalled) and yelled for the alien marathoner to "get out of my race." Unaware of Miller's presence, he reached for Switzer and began to pull off the number 261. Instinctively, Miller knocked Semple to the ground, introducing the race official to the hammer throw event, allowing Switzer to escape, and proving that chivalry is not dead. (Semple later claimed that he never hit the ground.)

After the press had finished snapping their historic pictures, and Semple and Cloney had sped off in the bus, Switzer was left to contemplate the events. "I was embarrassed and mortified. I was treated like a common criminal when I was only hoping to run a race. The next miles were sad and eerie. Everyone was silent. The only sounds you heard were the quarter-sized snowflakes hitting the leaves of the trees and the runners' feet pounding the pavement." Switzer finished the marathon, changing the complexion of the race forever.

In fact, a woman had already completed the Boston Marathon: In the previous year's race, Roberta Louise Gibb of Winchester, Massachusetts, finished 124th out of 416 runners. Because Gibb ran without a number, Semple chose to ignore her—although his blood pressure reportedly sky-rocketed when the post-race media coverage focused more on the woman runner than on the actual winner, Kenji Kemihara of Japan.

The 1967 race was different. Cloney and Semple were rabid at the post-race press conference. "I am surprised that an American girl would do something like this, and go someplace where she wasn't invited," Semple fumed. Still, Semple's attempt to save "his race" had been captured for all to see, and the snowball had started rolling. Katherine Switzer was eventually banned from the Amateur Athletics Union (A.A.U.) on the following four counts:

- **Running without a chaperone**
- **Fraudulent application (Switzer applied for her number using her first initials; 267 out of 700 applicants did the same that year)**
- **The A.A.U. did not permit women to race distances over one and a half miles**
- **She ran in an all-male race (although that was not stated on the application)**

Switzer's unintentionally defiant run cost her her A.A.U. status but gave women a irreversible foothold in American sports. No other athletic conquest has had a greater impact on women's sports.

1967 When Roberta Gibb repeated her trek of 1966, the spectators and runners were well aware of her presence. One runner in the 1967 race was an Assistant Professor of Classics at Yale University by the name of Erich Segal. After finishing the race, he was asked by *The Boston Globe* what he thought of Ms. Gibb's run. "For ten miles I saw nothing but those beautiful legs—I should have asked her to dinner." Erich Segal went on to write the hit novel *Love Story*.

IN AN EFFORT TO LOOK BOTH ATHLETIC AND FEMININE, KATHY SWITZER RUNS THE FIRST FOUR MILES IN 1972 IN A LOVELY BLACK-AND-WHITE ENSEMBLE. PHOTO COURTESY OF THE BOSTON PUBLIC LIBRARY PRINT DEPTARTMENT.

1970 An unofficial woman runner, commenting on the idea that women shouldn't run long distances: "Women are human beings—not baby mills. Maybe some of these men don't have confidence in their own virility."

The B.A.A. finally swallowed its pride in 1972 and allowed women the opportunity to participate in "their" marathon. Nina Kuscsik was the first official female winner, with a time of 3:10:26, which placed her 410th out of the field of 1,081 runners. To date the queens of the Boston Marathon, with three wins each, are Rosa Mota of Portugal, Uta Pippig, a medical student from Germany, and Fatuma Roba of Ethiopia.

After the landmark years of 1966, 1967, and 1972, women's marathoning evolved gradually until 1984, when two-time Boston Marathon champion Joan Benoit captured the hearts of women and men alike with her dramatic gold medal victory in the first-ever women's Olympic Marathon in Los Angeles. During that period, women made up 10.5% of all marathoners. Twenty years later that number has grown to 38% and is climbing.

While Switzer and Gibb had blazed a trail to Boston, I was more concerned with making it out of Ashland. At about the five-mile mark, I admitted to myself that I was exceeding my limits by attempting to run with my friends. I had to let them go: It was a sad necessity. I would have loved to share the entire experience with Rad and Richie, but it was more important for all of us to stay within ourselves. There would be plenty of time after the race to share our stories.

So quietly I stayed behind with the runners who ran nine-minute miles. My new friends included an Englishman dressed as a Court Jester, a man with a shirt from Scituate, Massachusetts (where I used to summer as a child), two runners named Whit and Paul who had their names emblazoned on their shirts, and a runner dressed as a cow who caused the crowds everywhere to moo. Later in the race, as my grip on sanity slipped, I found myself becoming jealous when fans would yell for the other runners after yelling for me. "How dare they? I thought that I was their favorite!"

1983 At the five-mile point, Ethiopian runner Abraha Ge-brehiwet Aregha was the early leader. Along with his run-ning form, his musical taste was highly critiqued by the analysts and the other runners: Abraha was wearing a Sony Walkman as he rolled down Route 135. Marty Liquori, the well-known television analyst, told his audience to ignore the leader because, in his eyes, anyone who would wear a musical device while running in a world-class race shouldn't be taken seriously.

Abraha eventually fell from the lead after seven miles and finished without his Walkman. It was later learned that the music lover was actually doing a live commercial for Sony. He finished 110th with a time of 2:21:57. In later years, fellow marathoners grew to respect Aregha as a for-midable runner: He has a sub-2:12 marathon on his resume.

MILE 6

Past winners Geoff Smith and Jim Knaub will tell you there is no such thing as a game plan. Both runners have a common strategy: attack every inch of the course the same. Knaub says: "Go for broke from the beginning to the end. If it's not your day then it's not your day." Smith say: "Line up and let's see who's best—whoever wins was the best that day."

— — — —

After the five-mile mark, the runners' brains are busy with calculations as they divide five into their time and then multiply by twenty-six and a bit. The route has been fairly easy to this point, with the pace quickened by adrenaline for the first thirty to forty-five minutes. Passing this point, the runners should be ahead of their per-mile target pace because of the downhills and the excitement. Runners who are new to the Boston Marathon can easily fool themselves into thinking that they can maintain this pace for twenty-one more miles. This will be proven false not far down the road.

At this juncture, the runners begin the first of many tugs-of-war between the mind and the body. Here they rejoice that they have passed the first real benchmark of the race, but at the same time they realize that they haven't even completed a fifth of the course. The devil, on the runner's left shoulder, is starting to tell the angel on the right shoulder that this might not be the day. With more than twenty-one miles to go, and the easiest part of the course left behind, it takes a calm mind and

a well-trained body to take the next step and convince oneself that the ten-mile mark is just around the corner.

Luckily, the crowds start to increase here: By this point the runners are starting to need and crave every "looking good" or "you can do it" they can get. At the beginning of the sixth mile, the course moves uphill and to the right before leveling off through a wooded, residential neighborhood. Halfway through the mile, the course inclines again and swings right. On the left, diners may step out of the Italian restaurant LaCantina's between bites of their chicken cacciatore to wish the runners well.

1972 Wherever Kathy Switzer traveled, her femininity and her running ability always seemed to be intertwined. In 1966, the year before the Switzer-Semple encounter, *The*

***Boston Globe* ran a story, which was sent over the wire by the American Press, about a woman runner who was competing in the half-mile for the men's track team at Lynchburg College in Virginia. This woman was Kathy Switzer. The story stated that the runner had some unusual statistics (34-25-37) and that she was going to play the accordion in the talent portion of the Miss Lynchburg beauty contest later that week. Other interests were listed as tennis, karate, and fencing.**

Six years later, Kathy continued in her effort to prove both her running prowess and her womanliness. In the inaugural women's race of the Boston Marathon, Kathy Switzer appeared at the starting line decked out in a beautiful white tennis dress over a black leotard, despite the humid conditions. After passing the infamous spot where Jock Semple had tried to rid her of her number five years before, Switzer began to overheat. Desperate, she ran off the course into a gas station and, catching the station attendant by surprise, she grabbed the women's restroom key and one of the steak knives that customers used to receive when they bought a full tank of gas. In the bathroom—with no light—Switzer began to cut and mend. Some minutes later she emerged with the tennis outfit pinned up, no legs to her leotard, and no socks and ran off to an eventual third-place finish.

After bending right, the runners get a brief respite with a short descent past a commercial area, before another right-hand bend and a slight uphill at 5.8 miles. Through this section, trees provide some temporary protection from either sun or rain and offer the runners a moment to gather themselves. Up ahead, the increasing noise signals a tumultuous welcome around the corner.

In the last two tenths of the mile, the runners come upon the intersection of Route 135 and Winthrop Street, an ideal viewing area where fans stand five- or six-deep, drawing in the runners like a magnet. Here, the athletes are treated like guests of honor, but they must pay attention because the big right turn a half mile back is reversed here with a huge left turn that stretches for a tenth of a mile through the intersection. This curve in the road appears to have been molded for the sole purpose of straightening out the marathon course: For the next four miles, it will be straight and relatively level.

In 1660, the deputy governor of the local colony, Thomas Danforth, Esquire, was compensated for services rendered to the Crown with a grant of 250 acres of land in the western section of the colony. Over the years, he added 15,000 additional acres, which he combined to create Danforth Farms. In 1700, the area was incorporated as the town of Framingham in honor of Danforth's hometown in England, called Framlingham (the l was dropped).

In the nineteenth century, Framingham became an important railroad hub because of its location halfway between the cities of Boston and Worcester. In the early- to mid-1800s, train tracks were laid through South Framingham from Boston because the people on the main stagecoach road (now Route 9) didn't want the dirty, noisy trains in their area. Later the railroad was the catalyst for the development of this previously wooded area.

Today, Route 135 in Framingham is primarily a commercial area with a scattering of modest homes. In 2001 the average home in town cost $285,000, while businesses pay $10 to $15 per square foot for space. The town of Framingham stretches over 26.4 square miles and has a population of 66,910 with a median family income of $78,709. Property taxes are $16.55 per $1,000.

MILE 7

Jim Knaub's advice on how to approach the train tracks in Mile 7: "Just hit them and hope for the best. It's either your day or it isn't."

— — — —

The first substantial stretch of level and straightforward running begins in the seventh mile. This flat section provides the leaders with the opportunity to feel out their opponents and begin their cat-and-mouse games. A front-runner may initiate a surge here to weed out the pack, while upstarts running in the pack may gain confidence from the fact that they are still running with the leaders.

At the 6.1-mile mark, Mark Noe, the owner of Mugs Away Pub, is hosting his own form of marathoning. By the time the wheelchair leaders pass at approximately 12:15 P.M., the sports bar (formerly a biker bar) will have had the beer taps flowing for four hours. They will continue to work them for another twelve.

Mark Noe, who prays for rain on Marathon Day to keep his patrons belly up and not on the sidewalk, has been a lifelong admirer and spectator of the event. He grew up on the race route and was excited to purchase the pub in the early 1990s because of its location. With cold beers, steamed dogs, and public bathrooms, this location is popular with his neighbors and the occasional runner who needs a quick pit stop.

Just past the Mugs Away Pub, the course reaches the ten-kilometer mark. Many runners can be seen checking their watches at this point to assess their pace. When I passed this juncture, my time was just over fifty-three minutes (adjusting for the slow start). For me this was more than acceptable. The last time I had run ten kilometers in a race was in the autumn edition of the Falmouth Road Race, five months before. In that race, I went out too fast and then struggled through the first three miles. As I waited for a second wind, I couldn't help but be disheartened by the number of runners passing me. To be successful in my mission going forward, I realized that it would be necessary to adjust my competitive instincts. In the future my focus needed to be on the course and not the other athletes around me. It was imperative that I concentrate on making my challenge singular while ignoring my surroundings.

To accomplish this task I drew on the advice my father once gave me: "Don't concern yourself with being the fastest. Your only goal in life should always be to maximize your God-given talents and never settle for anything less."

I survived the race (barely), finishing with a time of one hour and seven minutes. I crossed the finish line tired and wiser, but also excited about reaching another benchmark in my journey. Now I was the proud owner of a 10K finish; one month before I couldn't have accomplished such a feat. Still, it wasn't lost on me that I had just struggled to complete a race that was twenty miles shorter than what I would attempt in the coming April. I learned two valuable lessons that day: to run within myself and to focus on finishing the course, not on the other runners.

Just past the 6.2-mile mark, the course moves past the car dealerships of R.H. Long, which surround the route on both sides. The Long family has been a commercial leader in South Framingham since the turn of the century. Originally a shoe manufacturer, R.H. Long converted his trade to a product he thought might be the wave of the future—motorcars. Long manufactured the first Bay State Sedan in the area and sold it for $2,300. In addition to his interest in shoes and cars, Long ran for governor of Massachusetts but lost to Calvin Coolidge. R.H. Long's son, Charles, was born around the turn of the century and is the present owner of R.H. Long Auto Sales.

Charles Long and the Boston Marathon are chronological brothers: Over the last ten decades, each has grown and prospered. During that time, the car dealership has taken advantage of Marathon Day to throw one of the most entertaining parties on the whole course. The Melchonian Dixieland Hoboes set up their ensemble on the roof of one dealership, playing upbeat Bourbon Street music for the runners and spectators. Across the street, at Long's other facility, another band performs more modern music (recently the Generators played). Thus all markets are targeted as the two bands engage in a musical duel, in stereo, over the passing runners. Inside the dealership, youngsters can get balloons and autographs from some of their favorite race car drivers, who bring along their race cars for all to see. Radio stations also take advantage of this location to bring live updates to their listeners in between songs.

Because of the entertainment and the wide-open viewing area, the crowds are very large in this location, bringing the noise to a level not yet experienced. Over the last mile, the crowds more than anything personify the wonderful spirit of the Boston Marathon. From Hopkinton to Ashland and into Framingham, the competitors seem to be the entertained rather than the entertainers. Running through Framingham, I found the crowds of thousands in a festive and celebrating mood. Together they were singing and dancing and hopping and hollering. Sitting on lawn chairs and standing on curbs, boys and girls, moms and dads, girlfriends and boyfriends, and grandmothers and grandfathers were all joined together in a generation-busting version of "Hot, Hot, Hot (Ole, Ole, Ole, Ole, Ole)" as I ran by. The singing and clapping brought a great smile to my face and raised goose bumps on my arms as I and the other runners threw our hands in the air and joined in with the clapping and singing.

This type of treatment, usually bestowed upon rock stars and celebrity athletes, was now raining down on us ten-minute milers. It was an amazing feeling, bringing with it a tangible energy boost that runners feed on—but also need to harness. Such rushes of adrenaline can sometimes deplete athletes' reserves and hurt them in the long run. This juncture of the course is famous for inspiring the runners and accelerating their strides. Jack Fultz experienced just such a spike in adrenaline and pace at this spot on the course during his wicked-hot championship run in 1978. While running comfortably in the second of two lead packs, Fultz experienced a strange phenomenon. "The crowd in the Framingham area was really getting into the race as we moved together in a pack. At one point, the crowd noise rose to such a frenzy that the strength of their enthusiasm caused the pack to surge." It has been estimated that a sudden rush of adrenaline can cause a runner's heart rate to increase by as much as 5%, potentially causing problems down the road.

Now the route runs straight ahead, allowing the runners to pound the pavement while appreciating the carnival atmosphere. As they come up on the 6.4-mile mark, it is important for the competitors to pay attention to the old railroad tracks that cross the road. Runners, and especially wheelchair competitors, need to maneuver either to the left or to the right as they pass over the tracks because of the pronounced rise in the middle of the road. Most veterans of the race are aware of the rise and act accordingly, while some hit the tracks aggressively anyway. In 1988 Andre Viger, two-time winner of the men's wheelchair division and pre-race favorite, suffered the penalty for choosing the hell-bent over the parochial. While rolling with the lead, Andre attacked the protruding tracks at full speed and suffered a flat tire. By the time he could mend the damage, he had lost contact with the lead pack. His lead disintegrated into an eventual sixth-place finish, costing him money, glory, and a tire. Some wheelchair competitors have suggested that a truck with spare wheels and parts should be on hand to spare future racers from the fate of Andre Viger.

1907 The ten-man lead pack made their way across the tracks in Framingham just barely beating a scheduled freight train that moved across Route 135. On the other side of the train were 114 challengers, including the two pre-race favorites. Frustrated and stiff, the runners waited for the train to pass while Tom Longboat, a member of the lead pack, took advantage of their bizarre good fortune and ran through the day's snow to the finish line and the laurel wreath.

Some witnesses reported that Longboat actually jumped through an open door into a freight car and out the other side to get by the train. In 1973, Harry

Augusto, who had witnessed the event, recalled the race: "I was 14 at the time and the fact that I saw Tom do this has always stayed with me. I was amazed he took the chance he did."

Two years later, the train would again sever the lead pack from the rest of the field. One of the pre-race favorites, Robert Fowler, claimed that he was twice robbed of a potential championship by a badly timed freight train.

At the 6.5-mile mark, on the left side, sits the old Framingham train station designed by H.H. Richardson, the same architect who created the Boston landmark Trinity Church, which stands just yards from the race's finish line. The station building, where the passengers used to wait, for years housed a famous restaurant and bar called Ebeneezer's (recently re-christened as Grand Central Station). Like TJ's in Ashland, the bar hosts a loud and festive marathon party that spills out into the street. Giant balloons in the shape of beer bottles and cans, kindly provided by the distributors, bounce in the wind above the tavern. Running past the aroma of the barbecue and the tunes spun by an outdoor DJ, the racers start to ask themselves in earnest why they're punishing their bodies when they could be throwing back a cold one and gnawing on some barbecued ribs.

Six train routes used to run through this bustling station, moving west to Worcester and east to Boston; in 1885, the station handled over 100 trains a day. These days, the tracks mostly carry commuters who prefer to sit and read the paper on the way to Boston instead of fighting the traffic.

Every other Sunday in February and March, Rad, Richie, Jack Radley, and I would ride out to Ebeneezer's to train on the course in order to familiarize ourselves with the route and gradually build up a tolerance to the marathon distance. Prior to our runs, we would use the facilities one last time and stand inside the foyer of the restaurant, stretching our tight muscles. As we extended our quads and attempted to touch our toes, curious patrons moseyed in and out of the breakfast buffet. The eggs and bacon inside looked a lot more attractive than the fifteen- to eighteen-mile run in slush and car traffic that lay ahead.

LUTZ PHILIP, THE TEMPORARY LEADER OF THE 1973 RACE, RUNS PAST THE FRAMINGHAM TRAIN STATION. PHOTO COURTESY OF RICK LEVY.

Nonetheless, despite the arduous and sometimes tedious nature of the training, these long runs ultimately were a wonderful part of the overall marathon experience. From the moment you decide to run the race, the journey commences; the race doesn't start when the clock strikes twelve in Hopkinton, but as soon as the commitment is made. The fact that Richie, Rad, Jackie, and I all went through the hard training together deepened the marathon experience for all of us, and brought us closer together.

We would follow the same routine for each workout. During the early stages of the run, we ran single file through Framingham and into Natick, catching up on each other's families and related interests. Eventually, Jackie would pull ahead while Rad would turn up the volume on his Walkman and get lost in his music. Richie would be kind enough to slow his pace and keep me company. Our conversations followed every tangent possible to distract us from the run. From work, to the Red Sox, to family, we babbled and breathed heavy as we made our way down the road. Needless to say, by the time the run was finished, the world's problems would almost be solved (except for the problems of the Red Sox). In retrospect, these moments of friendship were in a lot of ways as important as the race itself.

Across from Grand Central Station is a family-run business named John and Sons' Bakery, established in 1955. John doesn't do much business on Patriot's Day except for coffee when the weather is cold. John lets spectators and media people park in his driveway, while volunteers hand out water to the runners in front of the store. The one-day inconvenience is not a problem for John and his son because it brings a little life to the town.

1957 Past winner Veikko Karvonen of Finland was running with the lead pack past the Framingham train station when he was surprised by a woman who approached him with flowers. Karvonen graciously accepted the flowers, smelled them, and continued on with his bouquet in hand. He finished second.

Until the checkpoints were moved to more conventional intervals, the 6.5-mile mark was a traditional monitoring point for the Boston Marathon. Checkpoints provide race officials with well-known, central locations to track the competitors for time and placing. The 6.5-mile checkpoint was originally chosen because of the train station. Officials would take the train from Boston out to Framingham to monitor the runners; after the hundreds of runners had passed, officials could jump back on the train and arrive in Boston fifty-five minutes later for the

GERARD COTE (LEFT) AND TARZAN BROWN BATTLE FOR THE LEAD AS THEY PASS THE FRAM-
INGHAM TRAIN STATION IN 1939. PHOTO COURTESY OF BOSTON PUBLIC LIBRARY PRINT DEPT.

finish and the first bowls of beef stew. Other checkpoints along the race
were also picked for their proximity to train stations or watering holes
for horses.

Runners came to disdain the odd placement of checkpoints because
it made it difficult for them to calculate split times and keep track of their
pace. The B.A.A. and race traditionalists defended these checkpoints for
their historical significance to the race. Eventually, in 1983, the runners
won the battle between common sense and tradition, and the checkpoints were moved to fall at each mile mark and at five-kilometer intervals.

1959 While monitoring the proceedings at the 6.5-mile checkpoint, Jock Semple almost landed in the local jail. While checking off the numbers of the passing competitors, Semple was infuriated to see a spectator wearing a mask and clown shoes run out of the crowd and start drawing laughs from both the masses and the runners. Enraged that his temple of running was been mocked, Semple leaped at the individual, grabbing the mask but missing the comedian. Semple rolled into the gutter with the mask in hand, while the clown ran down Route 135, clomping his clown shoes to the delight of many. A policeman approached the red-faced race director on the ground with the intention of arresting him for assault, but was persuaded against it.

John "Jock" Semple did more to give color and identity to the Boston Marathon than any other individual in the hundred-plus-year history of the race. Born in Glasgow, Scotland, Jock traveled across the sea and took up residence in Philadelphia, Pennsylvania. In 1929, Semple hitchhiked to Boston for the opportunity to run the famous marathon. He ran that year and eighteen more times, finishing in the top ten six times (his personal record was 2:44:29). Semple eventually made Boston his home and joined the B.A.A. The marriage between Semple and the Boston Marathon became a successful and passionate union. With his Scottish brogue and hot temper, he soon became known as the Cardinal of the Boston Marathon, with the unusual ability to make grown men act like first-graders being scolded by a nun. When asked for an application, Semple was known to loudly demand: "Are you sure you can run twenty-six miles?" Ken Parker of Canada felt that being the recipient of Semple's wrath was a solemn part of the Boston Marathon experience: "It was an honor to be yelled at by Mr. Semple." Jock passionately administered to the race from 1947 to 1982.

Jock Semple will always be remembered for his extrication attempt on Kathy Switzer, but without him the race

wouldn't be the premiere event it is today. Jock died in 1988 at the age of eighty-four, but many will swear that you can still hear his brogue echoing over the hustle and bustle of the pre-race activities.

The rest of the seventh mile carries on along the same plateau. The route is almost completely commercial here. At the 6.8-mile mark, the runners again have to cross train tracks. Of the three sets of tracks, these are by far the most treacherous. Even cars move to the right as they proceed over this obstacle.

On the left side of the course, over the tracks, are the remains of the brick factory of E.W. Dennison. In 1897, Dennison moved his gum label and box factory from Roxbury to South Framingham. The factory, which employed over 2,000 workers, was world famous for baggage labels. The skeletons of the old factories make this section somewhat haunting, but the runners appreciate this stretch for the level topography and the helpful tailwind that traditionally blows here. In particular, a tailwind here allows the wheelchair racers to sit up from their aerodynamic crouches and enjoy the ambience of the course and the support of the spectators.

2000 **A teenager standing outside Colonial Floors waited for the leaders to come into sight. When they approached where he was standing he ran out in front of them with a camera, snapping pictures of himself leading the race.**

With Framingham coming to an end, Pat Williams always says to himself, "Just make it to Natick."

MILE 8

Ricky Hoyt from the team Hoyt and Hoyt: "When I'm running, I feel like I've never been handicapped."

— — — —

At the start of Mile 8 the road remains level and straight. The Boston-Framingham train tracks run parallel with the race route on the left. In the old days, spectators could watch practically the entire race by boarding the local train to Boston and peering out the window, their view broken only by the occasional horse-drawn carriage parked on the side of the road. These days, so many trains clog the tracks from Framingham to Boston that a train probably couldn't keep up with the runners.

1950 South Korean runner Yun Chi Choi was brought to a halt when a red chow dog attacked him early in the eighth mile. After nipping at the runner's sneakers, the dog seemed satisfied and moved on. Choi continued on to finish third in an all-Korean sweep: His countrymen Kee Yong Ham and Ki Yoon Song finished first and second, respectively.

The eighth mile is mostly wooded, with an occasional house, vacant lot, or business. After the first third of the mile, the runners leave Framingham behind and move into the town of Natick, now on West Central Street.

The town of Natick is just over 16 square miles in area and peopled with more than 32,000 Natickians with a median

THE FATHER AND SON TEAM OF DICK AND RICK HOYT INSPIRE ALL WHO WITNESS THEIR QUEST TO MEET THE CHALLENGE. PHOTO COURTESY OF THE *BOSTON HERALD*.

family income of $70,855. The average home costs $282,000.

"Natick" is an Indian word meaning "place of hills." Native Americans settled in this area in 1651 with the help of

Puritan missionary John Eliot, who was known as the "Apostle to the Indians." Over the following years, the Indians built a prospering town here while being preached to by Eliot. In 1675, after violent incidents, the English settlers laid claim to this attractive area and shipped the unusual "Praying Indians" to Deer Island in Boston Harbor out of fear of retaliation. Many died from illness and starvation on this barren and exposed island.

Mile 8 is generally level until the 7.7-mile mark, where the route rises for a tenth of a mile. Greg Meyer, the 1983 winner, points to this hill as a spot in the race where runners can assess their condition: "You'll have a good idea at this point if it is your day or not. This incline certainly makes an impression on the runners." Some know this slight rise as "Heartburn Hill."

Greg Meyer's view is shared by Dick Hoyt, one half of the crowd's favorite team of Hoyt and Hoyt. Dick Hoyt points to this hill as the first of many that will test his calves and quads as his pushes his son Ricky up the hill.

Hoyt and Hoyt is not a law firm but simply a father-and-son team that has become one of the most inspiring stories in the history of the Boston Marathon. Rick Hoyt, the son, was stricken with cerebral palsy as a child. An avid Boston Bruins fan and a Boston University graduate (class of 1993), Rick loved athletics but his disabling disease restricted his participation. That was until his father Dick decided to take up running and included Rick in his new passion.

Dick started out running around the block while pushing Rick in an old wheelchair; eventually they graduated to road races, marathons, triathlons, and Iron Man competitions. (During the swimming segment of triathlons, Dick pulls his son in a small rowboat with a rope held in his mouth.) Through these endeavors, Dick and Rick entered a whole new world and formed a new bond. They now share their

pain and triumphs together as a team. As Dick pushed his son through the streets of Hopkinton and all the way into Boston, another bond formed—between Team Hoyt and the Boston Marathon fans. With this new passion, Rick's sense of humor also blossomed—after each race he takes the opportunity to remind his father that he beat him by a second.

1935 **Two Natick policemen working crowd control on motorcycles were hit by a car, which then sped off. Officers Ray Tanner and John Flynn were brought to Leonard Morse Hospital; Tanner had a fractured pelvis, while Flynn was released with minor cuts and abrasions. The culprit was never apprehended.**

After this limited but trying hill, the road works its way down. At the bottom of the descent sit rows of residential condominiums, whose inhabitants gather to cheer the runners along this quiet stretch. The West Natick train station is located at the end of this mile.

As I approached the bottom of the hill, I couldn't help but smile at the sight of volunteers happily giving their time to pass out water and assist the runners with whatever needs they might have. In this sometimes cynical and unfriendly world, people seem more likely to keep their heads down, as they hurry by, than to offer a hello and a smile to a passing neighbor. This is not the case with the Boston Marathon—which is one reason that the event is so special. If only for one day, the runners give each other assuring smiles, the fans genuinely wish the competitors well and inspire them to go faster and farther, and the volunteers freely give immeasurable support to the athletes.

Across from the Natick condos, a volunteer was handing out dabs of Vaseline near the mile mark. As a runner came upon the table, he reached out and grabbed a gob. As he moved on, he yelled in thanks, "I love you!" The volunteer shouted back, "I love you too!"

MILE 9

Local marathoner Mark Coogan: "Boston is the only marathon where you can't walk off the course. The fans are going to push you right back out there."

— — — —

For the wheelchair competitors, drafting becomes a game of cat-and-mouse through the flats from Mile 6 to Mile 11. It has been estimated that a wheelchair racer who is drafting off a competitor needs to exert only about 70% of the effort that would be required to maintain the same pace alone. Eight-time winner Jean Driscoll takes advantage of this stage of the race to soften up her competitors. When it's her turn to lead, she picks up the pace aggressively, forcing other members of the lead pack to push their limits to stay in contact—which may cost them dearly on the infamous hills ten miles down the road.

For the past three miles, the runners have been treated to a pancake-flat course, allowing them to settle into a consistent pace with limited downshifting and upshifting. Mile 9 on the other hand hits the runner like a sneaky uppercut, with inclines at the beginning and again toward the end of the mile. Here the route passes by a combination of commercial enterprises and wooded lots. Just past the halfway mark in the mile, the runners reach Natick Auto, where owner Charles Ribicoff treats his employees and their families to barbecued hamburgers, hot dogs, and sausages and an opportunity to cheer on the competitors.

Moving past the dealership and up to the Speen Street intersection (named after John Speen, a Native American who first built on this land

in the early 1700s), the runners are greeted by the beginning of Fiske Pond on their right and Lake Cochituate on their left. These waterways stretch for the next half mile on both sides of the route into Mile 10.

It was here in 1938, with the temperature approaching 80 degrees, that past winner Tarzan Brown surrendered his lead in order to take a swim in the refreshing waters of Lake Cochituate. After finishing his dip, Brown returned to the race and finished in fifty-first place. Later asked about his decision to sacrifice a shot at the first place trophy, he retorted, "Sooner or later, they [trophies] get black and you have to throw them out." One year later, Brown returned to Hopkinton and proceeded to set a Boston Marathon course record of 2:28:51 on the way to his second laurel wreath.

Ellison Meyers "Tarzan" Brown was the pride of the Narraganset Indian tribe of Rhode Island. Known as Deerfoot to his fellow Native Americans, Tarzan was one of the true characters of the race. He first came to the attention of the marathoning world in 1935 when he finished the Boston Marathon in thirteenth place while running barefoot. One year later, he won the first of his two championships, despite his traditional pre-race meal of hot dogs and orange soda pop. In all he would race Boston nine times.

Running in these days of racial intolerance, Brown was not treated well by the press. Following Brown's first victory, *The Boston Globe* reported: "Brown ran the panting palefaces into the ground with a modern day tomahawk of a killer pace." They continued, "Many Indians cheered on their blood brother. They must have been notified by smoke telegraph." In 1939 Brown again showed them by winning his second marathon, although it didn't curb the poison of the Boston scribe who wrote: "The indomitable Narraganset brave whooped more powerfully than his warlike ancestors."

Over the years the coverage of the Boston Marathon has evolved and matured along with the rest of society. Still, it is hard to believe that language like that above, or headlines such as "Atomic Boy" (in reference to 1951 winner Shigeki Tanaka, who was from Hiroshima), or "Jap wins" (referring to Keizo Yamada in 1953), could ever have been considered acceptable.

Twice in Tarzan's career he won consecutive marathon events in the same day. In 1936 he represented the United States in the Berlin Olympics. Ellison led the Olympic Marathon for thirteen miles only to be disqualified after a German fan placed his hand on him as the runner attempted to work out a cramp. In 1974, Tarzan was elected into the Indian Hall of Fame in Albuquerque, New Mexico.

As I neared the end of Mile 9, the crowd was sparse and the scenery was limited to the pavement in front of me. Here for the first time, a feeling of insecurity stole into my mind. Would I have the physical and mental strength to finish the race? The questions and doubts began to crowd out the blondes, beers, and barbeque grills that had so far occupied my attention.

As I ran toward Mile 10, I could increasingly feel the effects of an injury I suffered to my iliotibial band during a run back in early March. The IT band is a tissue that runs from the hip to the outside of the knee; the result of my injury was intense pain in the outer left knee. Recovery had been slow and never quite complete, although not for lack of effort. At the time of the injury, I was four months into my training and had already undergone heart surgery in order to line up in Hopkinton. I was not going to let some knee soreness ruin my dream of running Boston.

From early March until the gun went off, I dedicated myself to remedying the ailment. I attended physical therapy sessions where therapists Sandra and Jennifer pushed, massaged, shocked, and manipulated the leg back into shape—despite the fact that my quad muscles were, in their words, as tight as piano strings. After each session, I downed ibuprofens, iced my knee with bags of frozen vegetables, and devoured books and articles that dealt with strategies for coping with pain. One of my readings offered a method called "imagery." This theory called for the injured to concentrate on the pain and imagine that the area of discomfort is a square of butter sitting in a heated pan; remaining completely focused on the pat of butter, you are supposed to envision the pain melting away, as the butter does in your imaginary pan. It all seemed pretty hokey to me, as did the article that recommended that you run tall and strong, not allowing the mind to acquiesce to the pain.

Gradually, my combined efforts allowed the knee to heal somewhat. After multiple therapy sessions, I was finally cleared to test out the knee on the treadmill at the local YMCA. After tentatively mounting the machine, I cautiously ran my ten-minute miles relatively pain free. On the next treadmill, my old friend Jack Linso was busy covering his miles at a 6:30 pace. When I finished my workout, I dismounted and said goodbye. He returned the wish as he continued his sprint. While I worked my way behind his treadmill, still gasping from my exertions, I accidentally kicked out the cord to Jackie's treadmill, causing his machine to screech to a halt. Fortunately, Jackie wasn't catapulted across the room like a cartoon character. Feeling two inches tall, I quietly slunk out of the gym.

One week later, I stepped out onto my front porch with three miles on my mind. I did all the pre-run stretching as instructed, and then loped down the street for two blocks before folding up my tent and limping home. The pain was still holed up in the knee, meaning I now had to take the next and most drastic step. I had endured heart surgery and then flat-lined on the recovery table. I had trained for almost six months now. I had no choice but to take the next leap: I placed a call to Dr. Diane English, orthopedic surgeon extraordinaire, and asked for a cortisone shot.

Much to my chagrin, she agreed and told me to come into the office. Sitting in the waiting room, the last two words I wanted to hear were Michael Connelly. When my name was called, my face went pale and my palms turned sweaty. The thought of a needle puncturing my skin and injecting burning cortisone into my body was not what I had in mind back in October. I walked forward with clenched fist and grinding teeth. The doctor rubbed the spot with an alcohol swab, inserted the needle, and it was over. I didn't cry, but I didn't get a lollipop either. It wasn't as bad as anticipated, and the results were promising. With just weeks to go, I needed to be patient while the cortisone did its job.

Five days later, I stretched out on the infamous porch and held my breath, wondering what the coming steps would hold. Slowly I ran down my street and hardly exhaled. A hundred yards became a half mile and then two miles and then one more. Every time my left foot landed, I wondered if it would be my last step toward Hopkinton. About two blocks from home, I felt the twinge I had been dreading—the same place, the same pain. I cringed and tried to convince myself to keep running. I summoned up the imagery exercises that I had mocked earlier. To stop now would have extinguished any hope. There was no way I could stop running. "Stand tall! Be strong! Melting butter! Melting butter!"

After attempting the mental exercises, I realized that the whole imaging thing was a bunch of nonsense, except that it had diverted my attention for the last block and my house was in sight. I just had to push through the pain. Fifty yards, forty, thirty, ten, five, one—I made it! I collapsed on my porch as if I had found a life raft floating in the middle of the Atlantic Ocean. I knew that I would live to run again.

I picked myself up and proceeded to increase my workouts to ten miles. In my mind, I felt healthy enough to stand in Hopkinton and give it a shot. My last runs before the race were relatively pain free, allowing me to cloak my physical weakness with a false sense of bravado. But no matter how much I tried to fool myself, there was no denying that I would enter the race grossly unprepared. I had never run more than eighteen miles in my entire life; the race on Patriot's Day would exceed that distance by 30%.

I tried to keep in mind that injuries, colds, and other restricting ailments were just part of the game. In the months before a marathon, all runners push their bodies close to the point of breaking (or beyond it) as they build up the endurance to run twenty-six miles. Inevitably, the immune system weakens and the chances of sickness and injury climb. Toeing the line in Hopkinton at less than 100% is the norm. Many other runners were also doubting their fitness or engaging in denial that morning. I had to focus on one thing: survival. Suck it up and grind it out. No one wanted to hear about why I didn't or couldn't run. I either had to do it, or not do it.

Now I was nine miles into the race, and my leg was beginning to talk to me. Starting back around Mile 6 the injury had flared up, resulting in very limited extension of the knee. My left leg had to stay straight, leaving my right leg with a lot of responsibility. The course was conspiring with my wavering confidence to open a space of doubt in my mind—an unhealthy incubator for rambling thoughts. I didn't need an abacus to figure out that I had almost seventeen miles left as I finished Mile 9 in front of the VFW Post 1274.

MILE 10

Rob De Castella: "If you feel bad at Mile 10 you're in trouble. If you feel bad at Mile 20 you're normal. If you don't feel bad at Mile 26 you're abnormal."

— — — —

Mile 10 begins with a winding right bend at Horseshoe Curve. The road hugs Fiske Pond on the right and the train tracks and Lake Cochituate on the left for three tenths of the mile. This stretch of the route is best known for the Henry Wilson Historical District, which it traverses.

Henry Wilson was the vice president of the United States from 1873 to 1875 under Ulysses Grant. As a young man with only ten months of education under his belt, Wilson came to Natick from New Hampshire. He found employment in a local shoe factory, educated himself by reading over a thousand books in his spare time, and then turned his attention to politics. Given the nickname "Cobbler" by his adversaries, Wilson became a U.S. senator before moving on to the White House. Known as a friend of the soldier and common man, Wilson gave away most of his money to the needy and died in office leaving a humble personal estate.

Even though Wilson has a whole district named after him, he's actually the second most popular citizen of Natick, next to Heisman Trophy winner Doug Flutie. Flutie was a football star at Natick High School before moving onto Boston College, where he will forever be remembered for throwing the "Hail Mary Pass" against

TEN MILES INTO THE RACE, RUNNERS CAN BE TEMPTED BY THE REFRESHING SIGHT OF FISKE POND. PHOTO COURTESY OF THE BOSTON ATHLETIC ASSOCIATION.

the University of Miami, beating the defending national champions as time expired on the clock. After college, Doug moved on to the pros where he became the most prolific player in Canadian Football history and an All Pro in the NFL.

Here on the right side of the road, just past the two bodies of water, I encountered a rock-and-roll band by the name of Free Lunch jamming away in a front yard on the right. How many garage bands can claim they played for 40,000 people?

After leaving an open area at the end of the lake, where the runners are exposed to the random weather of April, the course works its way up a slight incline toward the protection of West Central Street. Uta Pippig enjoys this part of the route: "For some reason, I look forward to this small hill. I don't know why. Maybe it's the way it twists back and forth. But I know it's up ahead, and I am excited to get there."

At the top of the hill, West Central Street (still Route 135) straightens and begins to move through the residential portion of the Henry Wilson District. Here magnificent trees line the road on both sides, providing the athletes with a protective tunnel as they parade toward Natick Center. Over the years nature has ravaged the trees with ice storms and disease, but still they rise dramatically toward the sun, their tops meeting over the road like a marine honor guard crossing swords at a wedding. In 1909, Lucy Child, a resident of Framingham, described the site as "a row of stately trees which fling their arms across W. Central Street forming a green roof in the summer and a brown arch in winter." In the late 1800s and early 1900s, this segment of West Central Street was used for buggy rides on spring and summer afternoons; in the winter, the street was scraped, rolled, and roped off so that the affluent could race their horse-pulled sleighs here each afternoon.

While the runners pull their own sleighs through the Henry Wilson district, they cross a neighborhood of great historical significance. At the intersection with Taylor Street, just past the half-mile point, runners in a far more urgent race used to pause from their journey to rest. The Edward Wolcott estate, on the left side of the road, sheltered runaway slaves in the 1800s. With twenty-one rooms, the mansion was the most impressive property in the town, but its real stature is due to the tunnels that ran from the rear of the estate to the Boston-Albany train tracks one hundred feet away. Fugitive slaves who jumped from passing trains and made their way underground to the estate would receive food and shelter here before continuing on to Canada.

Proceeding forward the runners pass the Forest Street intersection where another house related to a dark chapter in American history sits. Major Daniel Henry Longfellow Gleason lived at 71 West Central Street, on the left of the road, after serving in Washington, D.C., during the

Civil War. Gleason is famous in town because of his intimate connection with the assassination of Abraham Lincoln. When Gleason was working in Washington, an associate of his attended secret meetings where a plot to kidnap President Lincoln was discussed; one of the individuals present at those meetings was John Wilkes Booth. When he learned of the plot, Gleason warned officials but to no avail. After the assassination, authorities turned to Gleason for help hunting down the culprits. With his assistance they tracked down Booth, but the others escaped. Gleason died in Natick in 1917.

With the Mile 10 demarcation visible in the distance, the lead pack drives on at a blistering pace. Within the pack, the elite runners are busy assessing their opponents and calculating strategies. Bill Rodgers used to look forward to this stage of the race to throw a surge at the pack and shake off his rivals. By contrast, some runners like to glide along in the pack and bide their time—the front-runners shield them from the wind and relieve them of the psychological burden of leading the world's greatest race. Amby Burfoot, the 1968 winner, compared the security of the pack to "a comfortable, cozy nest." As for Uta Pippig, she doesn't care whether she runs in a pack or by herself. "I am confident in my abilities and what I can do—although, if in a pack, I respect everyone in that group. I feel solidarity with the other runners. I appreciate the physical and emotional investment that they have made in order to run in this race. Although I might not know some of the runners in my pack, I must respect them because at that moment they are the same distance from the finish line as I am."

While the lead pack is sometimes an amicable group, the 2000 contest between Ethiopian runner Gezahegne Abera and multiple Kenyan runners proved to be a battle. The usual pack-running tactics, in which the leaders work together to conserve their energy, degenerated into a shoulder-knocking, arm-pushing tussle that sent the Ethiopian tumbling to the ground halfway through the tenth mile. As he picked himself up, blood poured from his elbow and leg. Sixteen miles later, Abera was literally nosed out at the finish line by Kenyan Elijah Lagat, with both runners recording a time of 2:09:47 in the closest finish in the race's history. Following the race Abera complained that the Kenyan runners (especially

Lagat and Moses Tanui, who finished third) had "ganged up" on him, pushing and shoving him throughout the race, and then working together to beat him at the end.

In the last two decades, African runners have left their mark on the race. From 1988 to 2002, thirteen of the fifteen men's races have been won by African runners, with Kenyans claiming the prize twelve of those times. African women have won six straight races from 1997 to 2002.

In the early decades of the race, Canadian and American runners dominated. In the 1940s, the 1950s, and into the 1960s, the laurel wreath was most often claimed by Japanese (eight wins), South Korean (two), and Finnish runners (seven). In 1963 the Boston Marathon community was treated to a glimpse of the greatness that lay ahead for African runners when Ethiopian heroes Abebe Bikila and Mamo Wolde came to Boston and almost grabbed the laurel wreath before falling off their record pace at Mile 20. Since the late 1980s, Cosmas Ndeti of Kenya, Ibrahim Hussein of Kenya, and Fatuma Roba of Ethiopia have all claimed three championships each. In 1996 the first eight finishers were from Africa, and seven of them were from Kenya.

Boston Marathon guru Tommy Leonard shared his theory on why the African runners were controlling recent races: "They're hungrier. They train harder. They are like the Taiwanese Little League team in baseball." Dr. David Martin, a physiologist at Georgia State University, offered this explanation: "The African runners live together, eat together, and train together. Each is pushed to become their country's national hero."

While the lead pack rolls on toward Boston, the crowds in Natick are the deepest yet seen on the course. Police have their hands full holding the crowds back and plucking rollerbladers and bikers off the course. Aggressive crowds and unwelcome travelers present a significant hazard to the competitors. This was demonstrated clearly in the early 1990s when a biker ran over a runner near the Natick Common, sending her to the hospital. After spending an entire year training for this day, she finished the marathon in a Framingham hospital with ice bags on her legs and an unfinished dream in her heart.

As they spend the day pleading with the crowds to respect the runners' quest, police and firemen must also remain vigilant for any emergency that might arise. With thousands of competitors and fans converging in such tight surroundings, civil servants and B.A.A. officials are ever mindful that the potential for a calamity exists and have thus spent months coordinating with the towns to create what Race Director Dave McGillivray likes to call "Plan B."

2002 In response to the terrorist acts of 9/11, six hundred policeman ran the race; in addition, this race saw such other security devices as radiation detectors and bomb-sniffing dogs.

The plan is designed as a response to a major emergency along the course, such as a broken water pipe, a sinkhole, or even the threat of a terrorist bomb. Natick's Plan B includes rerouting the marathon to either Route 9 or Route 30, both of which run adjacent to the marathon course and would allow the competitors to rejoin the original course in either Wellesley or Newton. (I'm sure the Technical Committee of the Athletic Congress [TAC] would have a field day with measuring that route). In addition to planning course deviations, officials have to be sure that the town has adequate police and fire coverage. Because the runners present a human wall from approximately 12:30 to 3:00 P.M., fire trucks and other emergency vehicles have to be placed carefully on both sides of the route in critical sections—although the Natick fire chief has said that if an emergency arose that required additional units, the race would be stopped to let them cross. Luckily, such events have yet to arise. A more typical emergency is a marathoner stopping in at the local station with dehydration or blisters.

Although the marathon brings overtime pay for most of the affected civil servants, the blasting sirens, screaming kids and overexcited fans make for a long day. By the end of the race, and after months of planning and late-night meetings, their job is finally done—until they have to start planning next year's race.

– – – –

With sixteen miles to go, I was revitalized by the sight of the Mile 10 sign. Another benchmark, on the long list of benchmarks, is conquered. My exhilaration was tempered by the fact that the race wasn't even half-finished. Still, it was an opportunity to take satisfaction from my efforts, while remembering the challenges that loom ahead.

Many recreational runners call it a day here. A good number of the early participants, mostly bandits, enjoy the pageantry of the start, get in some exercise, and then drop out after ten miles for a beer and some chicken wings instead of a PowerBar. I couldn't help but chuckle at a sign next to the Mile 10 sign that read "Shortcut to Boston" with an arrow pointing toward the kegs of beer in the yard on the right. The thought crossed my mind.

MILE 11

Bill Rodgers on Mile 11: "There are two things that excite runners. They are people and clocks—you've got both here."

— — — —

The runners move through Natick Center at the beginning of Mile 11 and cross the Route 27 intersection. At the 10.2-mile mark, they pass what was the second checkpoint of the race prior to the standard conversion. It's also here that West Central Street becomes East Central Street. The route here is level and provides an ideal viewing point for townspeople and fans.

Like Hopkinton, Natick Center has a villagelike atmosphere. From a mile away you can spot the town center by its church steeples—one for Protestants and one for Catholics. The First Congregational Church, which was built in the 1850s, sits on the left side of the intersection, with a large clock at the top of its steeple. Opposite the Congregational Church is the Natick Common, created in 1856. In 1868 the Soldier's Monument was built to honor the eighty-nine Natick soldiers who died in the Civil War. This area is usually busy with a concert on the bandstand or teenagers playing Hacky Sack.

1919 As he neared Natick Center, a lead runner, William Davis, stopped and stuffed newspaper into his shoe in an attempt to stop the bleeding caused by a nail that had punctured the sole.

The variety of faces and interesting outfits add a distinct flair and color to the 1996 race. Here, "cowman" passes through Framingham. Photo courtesy of David Morey.

Like the start of the race in Hopkinton and Grand Central Station (Ebenezer's) in Framingham, the Natick Common is a prime spot for spectators. The fans' affection is always heartfelt—with a drink in one hand and a pretzel in the other, they shout out encouragement, searching the shirts of the runners for names or phrases they can use to personalize the cheers. Throughout the history of the race, spectators have enjoyed cheering on certain runners because of the cause or affiliation promoted on their shirts. Over the last century a wide range of causes, from Pro-Life to No Nukes, have been advertised from Hopkinton to Boston on the chests of the sweating athletes. I wonder if anyone running in the early 1900s would have worn a shirt asserting "Horse manure smells better than gas fumes"?

1965 John Marchant of the North Medford Track Club wrote "Pass" on the back of his left shoulder and "Don't Pass" on the back of his right.

1983 After being married on Saturday, Fred and Paula Palka ran the Boston Marathon wearing shirts that read "Just Married."

Prior to our own run, my friends and I debated what to inscribe on the front of our shirts. Richie suggested that we have shirts made up in some attention-grabbing color with the letters BOB written in bold, black letters; underneath the shirt would read "Boston's Official Bandit" with the number 37,501 (the field of numbered runners was 37,500 when the shirts went to press). Rad, Jackie, and I agreed only because we weren't creative enough to come up with something better.

On the eve of the race, Richie reached into his bag and produced four shirts in an orange-yellow mustard color—the ugliest color imaginable. After harassing him for his temporary bout of color blindness, we accepted the shirts knowing that we would soon have bigger problems. Little did we know Richie had hit a home run. The crowds loved the bold print and the crazy color, allowing us to stand out from the masses. Throughout the race, people would scream "Go Bob! Go Bob! Go Bob!" as we ran by, or yell out "What about Bob?" (a reference to the Bill Murray movie). BOB was a stroke of genius. For four and a half hours, I was the happiest Michael ever to be called Bob.

All the same, our outlandish shirts were tame compared to some of the getups worn on the course. Jock Semple, as you might guess, was dead-set against any running outfit that might give the impression that the sacred event was a circus. Nevertheless, runners have always used the forum of the Boston Marathon to add their personal piece of color to the race's history. Crowd-pleasing characters that have run by over the years include the Viking, Superman, Groucho Marx, the Blues Brothers, Kermit the Frog, a rhinoceros, an astronaut, and—of course—the obligatory runner with the beer-can hat, in which the beer dangles forever four inches in front of the runner, thus giving him something to run for.

1985 As John "Elder" Kelley ran through Natick Center during one of his sixty-one marathons, a vendor ran up to him and patted him on his back. The vendor was selling buttons displaying Kelley's face. Kelley later said, "Would you believe it? I'm hurting and this son of a bitch is trying to make money off me!"

After passing the town green, the runners continue on a level path past the beautiful new municipal buildings on the left side of the road just before St. Patrick's church. Working their way toward the end of the mile, the runners approach Nick's, the popular Natick ice cream and hot dog stand. Nick's is best known for its Saturday night gatherings of classic 1950s automobiles and Corvettes. For years the Boston Marathon marked opening day for the ice cream establishment; now it's a year-round operation, but they still look forward to the marathon as a sign of spring. Outside, they like to dress the place up for the big race with balloons and American flags. If you are in need of an ice cream some Saturday night by all means drop by, but don't pull in with your minivan—there's a dress code.

Continuing on toward Mile 11, the runners pass the courthouse and, at the 10.6-mile mark, the Natick Battalion Armory, which was built to honor the veterans of the Spanish-American War. The route continues past some stores, the Central Street Grill, Glidden Autos, and then through a residential neighborhood to the end of the mile. At this point Pat Williams keeps saying to himself, "Just get me to Wellesley."

RUNNERS IN THE 1996 MARATHON PASS THROUGH NATICK CENTER. PHOTO COURTESY OF STEVE ROSSI.

MILE 12

Pioneering runner Kathy Switzer: "For most, running Boston is an amazing opportunity to compete in the same arena with the best athletes in the world, no matter your talent level."

— — — —

The route continues through Natick passing through a mostly residential neighborhood with the occasional business. House parties are popular and the fans are polite. This is a mile that can lull the runner into a mode of indifference—although eight miles later, as they trudge up Heartbreak Hill, the same runners would give a piece of their souls just to be back on the flats of Natick. As Jim Knaub once noted, "There is no such thing as an unimportant mile."

During the quiet moments on the course, when the ranks of lawn-chaired grandfathers thin and the screams of beer-slugging college kids temporarily subside, your mind sometimes drifts away from the sightseeing and the running. At these times, the race seems more like a daydream than a concentrated effort.

One of the wonderful aspects of running is that it strengthens you both physically and mentally. Until I started my journey to Hopkinton six months prior to the race, I didn't realize that training runs almost always included movement in the spirit as well as the body. The simple act of separating myself from the distractions of my daily grind gave me the opportunity to release whatever needed to be released. With sneakers double-knotted and water in hand, I welcomed the chance that each run offered. Out on the road, I found a respite from the day as I ran in my solitary world.

Off the porch and down the street, it would take a mile to get the blood flowing to the muscles and the breathing settled. But once I had found my rhythm, I would begin to reflect on my life and all that it included. Each step seemed to correspond with my contemplation. Whether the subject was my past, present, or future, I would always come to realize a little more about myself. Running can be lonely and at the same time cathartic, cleansing, and thought-provoking. Questions that stymied me before a run—as an employee, a father, or a husband—always seemed clearer from the perspective I gained on the road.

Throughout my runs, both in training and during the marathon, I invariably came to recognize my limitations, both as a runner and as a person. So, as I tried to resolve my concerns, I found myself drawing upon my friends and family who have prematurely left this world for a better existence. Friends such as Tom, Nana Connelly, Billy, David, Henry, Tommy, Tony, Mrs. L, Judy, Dr. Phil, Mr. Y, Joe B, Mike, Michael, and Betty all provided me with guidance and inspiration in my efforts to achieve my dreams and solve life's riddles. These friends motivate me because of the fullness of their lives. In a chronological sense, their lives were limited. But during their existence, they learned how to appreciate life at a level that most eighty-year-olds don't. They appreciated the beauty of every snowflake, raindrop, sunrise, and breath. They stared longingly at life and loved it and hungered for what it offered. Whenever my quads would tighten and my breath would shorten, warm reflections of my earthly-departed friends would help me push forward toward my goals in the running and non-running worlds.

Ultimately, running showed me that to move forward, I am best served by bringing my spiritual being to the effort. Each run was an opportunity to become reacquainted with my blessings. During difficult stretches, when answers were scarce and the running was tough, I would routinely find myself reciting verses of my favorite poem, "Forgive Me When I Whine," in order to maintain proper perspective. A few follow:

Today upon a bus I saw a lovely maiden with golden hair;
I envied her, she seemed so happy and, Oh, I wished I were
so fair
When, suddenly, she rose to leave, I saw her hobble down
the aisle;
She had one foot and wore a crutch, but as she passed
a smile.

Oh, God forgive me when I whine;
I have two feet, the world is mine...

With feet to take me where I'd go,
With eyes to see the sunset's glow,
With ears to hear what I should know,
I'm blessed indeed, the world is mine
Oh, God, forgive me when I whine!

Alone with my thoughts for a half hour, an hour, or sometimes two, I had ample time to mull over my life and its direction. Often, as I stretched or iced down after a run, I would suddenly realize that issues that had troubled me before the run had been resolved. Work, family, and finances are all placed in better order if you have time to converse with yourself.

— — — —

2001 In the months after his father, Lee Hae Ku, died from cancer, the South Korean runner Lee Bong-Ju struggled to accept the loss. To escape from his pain, he ran and denied. Before toeing the line in Hopkinton, he dedicated his marathon effort to his father's memory. Twenty-six miles later, he brought great honor to his father's life by winning the Boston Marathon.

Now the runners hear the first, faint echoes of a faraway din. Veterans of the race know that they are a mile away from the rallying cries of the women of Wellesley College. John Kelley, the patriarch of the Boston Marathon and local hero, always warned of the need to stay focused at this juncture of the race. With the impending excitement in the next mile, he believes it is essential to stay within your game plan and not push yourself too early. He knows this from personal experiences that may have cost him two championships: "Running past the girls at Wellesley College, your mind tells you one thing, but your legs do something different. I was always impatient both in life and in running, and it cost me dearly later in the course."

John "Elder" Kelley, who is best known for running the Boston Marathon over sixty times, won the race in 1935 and 1945. He finished second seven times and third once. He dropped out of his first race in Wellesley with blisters.

Kelly was once told by a reporter that if he had run during today's era of professionalism and prize money, he would have won more than $500,000 for his eighteen top-ten finishes. To which Kelley responded: "Different times, different values. I ran for the love of it. My good friend Ted Williams, baseball's greatest hitter, was asked the same question. He responded that he once begged Red Sox owner Tom Yawkey to cut his $70,000 contract because he had a sub-par year. We both had a passion!" In the absence of prize money, Kelley worked several jobs, including painting houses and toiling for Boston Edison. Loved and admired throughout the running community, John is a member of the Track and Field Hall of Fame and was recently named the most Prolific Runner of the Twentieth Century (he has competed in more than 1,500 races from Boston to Japan). The five-foot three-inch, 145-pound runner will forever be linked with the Boston Marathon because of his accomplishments and his love of the race.

THREE-TIME CHAMPION LES PAWSON (LEFT) AND TWO-TIME WINNER JOHNNY KELLEY WERE BOTH FAN FAVORITES IN THE 1938 RACE BECAUSE OF THEIR RUNNING SKILLS AND THE FACT THAT THEY BOTH HAILED FROM NEW ENGLAND. PHOTO COURTESY OF THE BOSTON PUBLIC LIBRARY PRINT DEPT.

Leaving Natick, the runners are guided east by the same train tracks that escorted the founders of the race, a century ago. At the 11.7-mile mark, you bid Natick a fond adieu and enter the beautiful town of Wellesley.

The Wellesley Historical Society retains several accounts of the town's history. In one version the following was observed about the town in the 1800s: "Wellesley was getting a reputation as a town that gets what it wants. Might was right. There was no problem too big [that it couldn't] be solved with money." The town was named after Isabella Pratt Wells, wife of the town's largest benefactor, Horatio Hollis Hunnewell. Along with his wife's maiden name, Hunnewell also gave Wellesley much land and financial support.

These days, the average home in Wellesley is a three- to four-bedroom colonial on a lot of 10,000 to 15,000 square feet with a price tag of almost $750,000. The town is spread out over 10.5 square miles and is home to more than 26,000 citizens with an average household income in excess of $128,500. Shop owners in the town can pay as much as $40 a square foot in order to peddle their product and trade. The tax rate in 1886 was $9.50; in 2000 it was $8.85 for every $1,000 of assessed property.

The executive secretary of Wellesley, Arnold Wakelin, appreciates the marathon and is grateful that his town can contribute to the event. "It's a privilege for the town to host the race and the halfway point," he says. "The marathon acts as a precursor to spring and good weather. With the contribution from the B.A.A., we are fully capable of living with any inconveniences. On a personal note, it is amazing to see the runners still coming by, one and two hours after the winners have finished."

As we finished Mile 12, a fan yelled out that Uta Pippig had just won her third Boston Marathon. Spontaneously, many of the male runners started to chant "Uta, Uta, Uta, Uta!" I wondered if they admired her running ability or her blond hair, pleasant face, and wonderful disposition. Little did they know at the time how she had struggled to overcome adversity throughout the race to wear the laurel wreath.

Earlier we had heard that Cosmas Ndeti of Kenya had lost to his countryman, Moses Tanui. It was sort of a letdown to us runners: The people of Boston had adopted Cosmas as a brother and Cosmas had adopted Boston in return, naming his child after the city. But Ndeti had had his time. Now there is another hero in Kenya.

With more than fourteen miles to go, it was best not to focus on the fact that some fellow competitors were relaxing with medals around their necks while you still had over two hours of work in front of you. As an athlete who had worked hard to prepare for the event, I found it difficult to comprehend that there are athletes who can run so fast for so long. I didn't know whether to respect or envy their superhuman ability. Either way, it was never more apparent than at this point in the race that the light of the Lord's gracious hand shined on the 2:10 marathoners, while a cloud hovered over the sweaty non-endorsed plodder somewhere back in Wellesley.

While the winners are busy claiming their winnings, the runners finishing Mile 12 are excited to enter the next one, where the decibel-defying divas of the local college sit in waiting right up the hill from the mile mark. So put in your earplugs and stay within yourself, because here they come.

As the course moves into Wellesley, the road widens to four lanes and the speed limit goes up to forty-five miles per hour. The road drops for two tenths of a mile until the mile mark. Here Pat Williams keeps telling himself, "Just make it to the college… they'll help me."

MILE 13

In his landmark book, *The Complete Book of Running*, Jim Fixx writes, "The modern world's most appreciative marathon fans [are] the girls of Wellesley College."

— — — —

The beauty of the Boston Marathon is the way the route takes on a life of its own. Mile 13 is a story within the story, and a big part of the identity, history, and uniqueness of the Mecca of all marathons. And a big part of Mile 13 is Wellesley College. The school is renowned as an educational institution, boasting such graduates as former First Lady and now Senator Hillary Rodham Clinton, journalist Diane Sawyer, former Secretary of State Madeline Albright, and Katherine Lee Bates (class of 1880), author of "America the Beautiful."

Founded in 1870, this all-women's school enrolls about 3,000 students, each costing $34,944 a year to live and learn. (A century ago 704 students paid less than $250 per person to be similarly accommodated.) In the late 1800s, there was a four-story factory situated near the Wellesley College campus. Horatio Hunnewell did not feel that industry was good for the image of the town. So he simply bought the factory and donated the land to Wellesley College for dormitories. Currently the college is the town's largest employer with over 1,200 workers. Despite its educational mission, Wellesley College is best known to marathoners as the high-water mark on the course in terms of shrieks and screams.

Since the first race in 1897, the women of Wellesley College have hurried through lunch in order to stand on the old stone wall outside Cazenove,

LES PAWSON TRIES TO FOCUS ON THE DUTY AT HAND AS HE RUNS PAST THE WOMEN OF WELLESLEY COLLEGE IN 1940. PHOTO COURTESY OF BOSTON PUBLIC LIBRARY PRINT DEPT.

Pemeroy, and Munger Halls in time to encourage, inspire and deafen the athletes who are attempting to meet the marathon challenge. Runners need to stay disciplined in this stretch, known as the "screech tunnel."

Like Johnny Kelley, Uta Pippig warns of the need to stay within yourself as you run past the campus. "I appreciate the support we receive as we pass the college. I don't let it excite me to the point of running faster than my capabilities. I use it more as a boost to my energy level, which I can then utilize somewhere later in the race." Uta has truly experienced the pinnacle of sound as she cruised past the women of Wellesley: Although the Wellesley students cheer on all the runners, they reserve the highest pitches for the female competitors. And no runner in the history of the race received a more riotous greeting than an athlete in white shorts and a black top in 1966. That runner, Roberta Gibb, was the first woman ever to compete in the marathon. As she passed the students of Wellesley College, she heard them cry, "It's a woman! It's a woman!" Thinking back on the passionate response Gibb would later say, "It was like I was setting them free."

Three decades later Gibb returned to Wellesley as the guest of honor at a rally held at the school prior to the 100th running of the race. A number of current world-class runners waited in line to obtain her autograph. Over the years, Gibb has felt somewhat slighted by the massive attention given to Kathy Switzer for her run in 1967. There is no question that Gibb—running in a black bathing-suit top, her brother's white Bermuda shorts, and a pair of boys' size-six Adidas sneakers—was the original trailblazing woman of the Boston Marathon a year earlier.

Over the years, elite women runners from marathons past and present have participated in the John Hancock Financial Services "Women on the Move" rally, first held in 1985. These rallies at Wellesley have been a wonderful opportunity for top women runners to be recognized for their contributions to the marathon, while at the same time thanking the students for theirs. The rally features clinics and speeches from elite runners. Past speakers include three-time Boston Marathon champion Uta Pippig, Olympic champion Valentina Yegrova of Russia, and New York City Marathon champion Tegla Loroupe of Kenya. But no one has spoken more eloquently about the rewards in life that come out of meeting challenges than Wellesley Athletic Director Louise O'Neil, who talked about the mission of the college: "There is no limit to what a woman can accomplish if she has confidence in herself and a determination to make her visions and goals a reality. Every day women from Wellesley College work a little harder and come a little closer to achieving these goals. Members of the college community encourage students to take chances to break down barriers, which stand in our way, and to embrace success."

GEOFF SMITH TRAVELS PAST THE CROWD OF WELLESLEY COLLEGE WELL-WISHERS. PHOTO COURTESY OF JEFF JOHNSON.

– – – –

Male runners react in different ways to this high-volume siren song. Some are disturbed by the earsplitting experience, which makes it almost impossible to concentrate on the task at hand. Halfway through his run to glory, Greg Meyer struggled to focus on the course and not the wailing women as he ran the gauntlet: "In the old days, the girls were on the street and were literally yelling in your ear. They were so loud that you had no idea what your legs were doing. It was impossible to concentrate. I never thought I would say that running through hundreds of college girls would be a challenging experience."

Other men love soaking up the atmosphere as they move past the campus. Tommy Leonard, of Eliot Lounge fame, always enjoyed the run past Wellesley. In the book *The Boston Marathon*, he was quoted thus: "These girls, I love them when they come out. They're all good-looking chicks. I try to make dates. See you at the Eliot Lounge, but none of them show up—I'm 0 for 21."

1988 Runner Michael Goldstein was so thrilled by the Wellesley students that he decided to turn around and run the stretch again.

The famous Wellesley College stretch has always received extensive coverage from *The Boston Globe*. Below is a sampling of stories going back to the very beginning:

1897 "As the runners passed Wellesley College, several young girls received them."

1898 "The girls cheered for Grant of Harvard."

1899 "A bevy of beautiful girls are gowned in fashionable varicolored gowns sitting on a stone wall."

1902 "Pretty college girls flaunted their handkerchiefs."

1904 "Coterie of pretty girls were sitting by the roadside."

1907 "Wellesley college students gave the runners a great cheer. . . . Thomas Longboat caught sight of the girls waving to him. He grinned broadly and nodded his head."

1916 "On the hill leading up to Wellesley College, the fair collegians stood along the road within the grounds. They smiled at runners but only a few took notice of the men following in the motorcars who tried to get a flirtatious twinkle."

1928 "The girls gave a cheer. Runner Joie Ray came along and smiled and laughed at the students. He was seen to wink once or twice, but he kept going as the girls smiled back. He ended up collapsing at the finish."

1934 "Leaders passed the Gothic Building of Wellesley College where the fair undergraduates turned out by the hundreds to applaud the laboring runners."

1943 No girls—Easter Vacation

1970 "Wellesley College students were following more serious pursuits. There was scarcely a girl in front of the college."

1977 Vin Fleming, a dishwasher at the Eliot Lounge, thought it was a bigger thrill to pass the girls at Wellesley College than to finish fifth.

1995 The majority of the Wellesley College students wore special edition Wellesley College T-shirts as part of a promotion by Nike. Students also displayed shirts with their own personal endorsements. One shirt read, "Wellesley College girls have been on top for 120 years," and another proclaimed, "Wellesley College is not a girl's school without men but a women's school without boys."

1996 "The cheering began at 12:25 when the first wheelchair contestants began to roll by. It reached a crescendo shortly after 1:00 when the first pack of a dozen male runners approached, and it remained constant for more than three hours."

2000 "Signs outside the college read, KISS ME, YOU'RE HALFWAY THERE and RUN LIKE A FAUCET."

2002 "The festivities included a nonstop music broadcast by the college's radio station and scores of signs on both sides of Route 135 including, ALMOST THERE BABY and AN ENERGY BOOST! WELLESLEY'S WOMEN!"

By the time you reach the thirteen-mile mark, the anticipated struggle is slowly becoming a reality. The route is increasingly hilly, and the tough half of the course still lies ahead. So as your head begins to droop just a notch, you gladly come upon this oasis of sound.

I arrived at the gates of Wellesley College more than two hours after the wheelchair competitors had passed. I didn't expect much at that time of the day, but I still looked forward to passing the area that veteran runners had talked so much about. As I came upon the campus, I was amazed to find the place still packed with enthusiastic college students. The cheering was unbelievable—it made me wonder if Wellesley applicants had to send in recordings of themselves screaming along with their transcripts and SAT scores. To maintain such a level of volume for so long must be at least as challenging as running the race. This great outpouring of passion truly lifted my spirits. I felt I owed it to these women to keep working hard. To stop now would be to betray their trust and let them down; the only way I could repay them was to dig in and concentrate on putting one foot in front of the other.

Throughout the mile, the runners are sandwiched between the train tracks on their left and the Wellesley campus on their right. Until the 12.6-mile point, the route moves consistently uphill. At 12.7 miles, the road dips before climbing into Wellesley Center and then flattens out toward the end of Mile 13.

MILE 14

Uta Pippig: "As you move past the halfway mark, the road narrows. It's not a concern, but I am aware of it."

— — — —

Mile 14 begins at the end of the upper town center. At two tenths of a mile, you hit a slight decline and a subtle twist left. This takes you past an intersection at Grove Street. On the left corner is a commercial building, on the right is a group of upscale shops.

For the last five or six minutes, the women of Wellesley College have drowned out the voice in your head that keeps asking, "Why are you doing this to yourself?" Now, as you move deeper into Wellesley Center, you reach another psychological landmark: the halfway point.

The 13.1-mile mark falls in the middle of Wellesley Center where the runners are squeezed between architecturally pleasing brick and stucco-faced buildings, a sharp contrast to the abandoned factories and boarded-up buildings that lined the course just a few miles before.

1982 **In probably the greatest Boston Marathon of all time, Alberto Salazar and Dick Beardsley battled each other from Hopkinton to Boston while simultaneously fighting off every obstacle the course could throw at them.**

Just after the halfway mark in Wellesley, an intoxicated fan took a swing at the runners. His fist barely missed Beardsley and struck Salazar in the stomach, knocking the wind out of him. Salazar regained his breath, and the runners

THE LEAD GROUP OF RUNNERS WORKS ITS WAY THROUGH WELLESLEY CENTER AND PAST THE HALFWAY POINT IN 1994. PHOTO COURTESY OF VICTAH SAILER.

continued stride for stride into Kenmore Square. Here another drunken fan grabbed at Beardsley's shirt, impeding his stride. Beardsley shook the fan off just in time to be sideswiped by the press bus, which the runner pounded with his fist in frustration.

Continuing down Commonwealth Avenue with barely a mile to go, Beardsley stepped in a pothole so deep that his foot seemed to land in Chinese territory. (This was a blessing in disguise as it shook out a cramp that Beardsley had been hobbled with for some miles.) Escaping the pothole, he

moved onto Hereford Street in pursuit of the leader Salazar. Between the two runners rode about ten motorcycle policemen. From Hereford to the finish, Beardsley was twice blocked by a motorcycle and was actually hit by one, forcing him to push away the motorcycle and its officer. Salazar went on to win the race by two seconds in a time of 2:08:52.

On days when the Boston Marathon is not being run, people can gallivant around the town and shop for cheese at the Cheese Shop, leather goods at London Harness, a cup of hazelnut java at the bagel shop, or antiques at Swan and Stuart, where race day is not good for business. ("We usually get gum-chewing, ice cream-dripping kids who need to use the bathroom.") But today the runners are the consumers, and they're only interested in water, oranges, and taking another yard off the course.

As I ran through Wellesley Center, my stomach was starting to clamor for replenishment. By this point in the day, the oranges offered by well-meaning fans were starting to warm. During training runs, I had tried orange slices but swore off them because of the acid's effect on my stomach. Prior to the race, I had reminded myself to limit food and fluid consumption to items that were acceptable to my system.

But here, almost fourteen miles from Hopkinton, I was starting to get desperate. Strangely my mind began to pull up random files that I had tucked away deep in my subconscious, as it would throughout the second half of the race. Spying the volunteers' table up ahead with the oranges, my brain selected the file titled "Bataan Death March." This was the horrific incident that took place in the Philippines during World War II when 70,000 American POWs were forced by the Japanese to march seventy miles in 100-degree temperatures with almost no food or water. During this sadistic parade, the prisoners were told that if they attempted to obtain water they would be executed. Nonetheless, many risked the consequences and tried to quench their thirst. Approaching the oranges, I suppose my subconscious felt itself to be in a dilemma like that faced by the POWs—although of infinitely less importance, of course. I stuck out my hand.

Needless to say, the warm oranges didn't cure my ills. To the contrary, they made my stomach turn and triggered bouts of queasiness that would be intensified over the next thirteen miles by every roadside cookout.

With a churning stomach, I turned my attention to search for a college friend who told me he would be waiting in Wellesley. Although the odds of finding him were slim, I needed to see him: The cheers from Wellesley College were wearing off.

— — — —

Up ahead the course continues past the town hall and a small duck pond on the left. On the right, at the half-mile mark, is the end of Route 135. The course follows the green sign that reads ROUTE 16 EAST—CAMBRIDGE/BOSTON. Following a left fork, the runners move past St. Paul's church on the right and a stone monument across the road that commemorates the first-ever high school football game. Wellesley beat Needham 4-0 on November 30, 1882.

Starting here and continuing for the next mile, wheelchair competitors have noticed an unusual bumpiness to the road surface that seems to hurt performance. Women's wheelchair champion Jean Driscoll observed, "For some reason, you can't stroke as fluidly at this section, so you have to bear down more than you should through a level stretch."

Jean Driscoll, the only eight-time champion in the race's history, began her reign at Boston in 1990. She won seven straight championships, tying the great Clarence DeMar. It would take her three exhausting and memorable duels with friendly rival Louise Sauvage to finally capture her eighth laurel wreath and make history. She holds the Boston Marathon course record, 1:34:22, which she set in 1994.

Jean sees Boston as the ultimate event—"bigger than the Olympics!"

Every year she began her training regimen at the University of Illinois (a trailblazing institution in the study and training of disabled athletes), where Jean would push herself

141

WOMEN'S WHEELCHAIR CHAMPION JEAN DRISCOLL MOVES TOWARD HER SEVENTH CHAMPIONSHIP IN THE 1996 BOSTON MARATHON. ONLY THE GREAT CLARENCE DEMAR HAS AS MANY. PHOTO COURTESY OF FAYFOTO.

to the limits to improve the ever-important strength-to-weight ratio. While preparing for the 1996 marathon, the 112-pound champion bench-pressed 200 pounds. This strength gave her the physical and mental ability to attack the hills instead of fearing them. Two weeks before the race, Jean would travel to the south shore of Massachusetts to train on the area's hills.

After claiming one of her eight championships, Jean was invited to run with President Clinton. During the run, the president from Arkansas remarked, "You have the best-looking arms in America."

Like many segments of the course, Mile 14 was the site of historic and dramatic confrontations. In 1901, a local man on a bike became a hero when he raced up alongside a riled horse and grabbed him by the bridle seconds before he trampled the oncoming runners. In 1922, the spectators turned from heroes to adversaries. As Clarence DeMar ran toward his first of seven championships, a car turned onto the marathon route, just missing the runner. DeMar was so infuriated that he took a swing at the driver, missing the man behind the steering wheel but striking a passenger in the stomach. DeMar spent the next mile watching over his shoulder for retaliation.

As the mile continues, the road proceeds along a slight rise into a commercial neighborhood before it levels off at the end of the mile.

MILE 15

Halfway through Mile 15, Denise Scwabb and Ed Walters stopped to exchange wedding vows at the Wellesley Hills Congregational Church. Said the Reverend Craig Adams, "To run this far was an effort, but the contest you face beyond the finish line is going to be even greater." The happy couple kissed and returned to the course to finish the 1996 race.

— — — —

Mile 15 is the calm before the storm, the last "placid" mile in which you can work out a cramp or adjust your game plan. After this mile ends, the runners discover that the first fifteen miles were nothing but a dress rehearsal. From this point forward the ring announcer is yelling, "Let's get ready to rumble!"

At the beginning of the mile, Hunnewell Park runs along the right-hand side of the course. (The park is named after the town's generous benefactor—it's the least the town could do.) On the opposite side, the railroad tracks continue to shadow the course up to the half-mile point, where the Wellesley Hills train station and the local post office are located. After the depot, there are a variety of innocuous commercial buildings and businesses leading up to the Unitarian Universalist Societal Church and the sixty-five-foot Wellesley Hills Clock Tower, built with the famous Wellesley fieldstone. In years past, the bells of the tower used to be rung to greet the runners. Modern editions of the marathon are so large that it would be impractical to keep ringing the bells.

144

As the runners pass the town clock in Wellesley in the 1994 race, they quickly approach the topographic nightmares of the Boston Marathon. Photo courtesy of Victah Sailer.

As this mostly level mile ends, the runners approach a multi-street intersection with stores on all sides. One of these, on the left, is appropriately called Marathon West. Here the entrepreneurs take advantage of their namesake event to hand out PowerBars and fit sneakers on individuals who have suddenly pledged to run the next year's race.

Up ahead, the runners fork left and continue east on Route 16, heading over Route 9 via a bridge. At the beginning of the bridge there is a substantial bump, which forces the runners to pick up their feet and the wheelchair competitors to cross carefully. Across the bridge, the Wellesley Hills Congregational Church stands on the left, facing some small shops across the road. The course is residential and shaded for the last level section.

Here four-time winner Bill Rodgers used to assess the situation again and adjust his strategy. With the steepest downhill of the race approaching in the next mile, good downhill runners like him prepare to attack.

If Johnny Kelley is the Patriarch of the Boston Marathon, then Bill Rodgers must be the Archangel of the world's greatest race. While individuals such as Brown, Semple, DeMar, and Switzer brought the running world to the universe, Bill Rodgers is almost single-handedly responsible for bringing the universe to the running world. From 1975 to 1980, Rodgers won four Boston Marathons, four New York City Marathons (in a row), and the Fukuoka Marathon. During one six-month stretch in 1977–1978, Rodgers won all three of those races, achieving the Triple Crown of marathoning in what was one of the great athletic feats of all time. In all, he won twenty marathons. Twice during his reign over the running world, Bill graced the cover of *Sports Illustrated*, further introducing the sport to the masses.

A talented runner at Wesleyan University, Rodgers roomed with 1968 Boston Marathon champion, Amby Burfoot. Toward the end of his college days and after graduating in 1969, Rodgers took an indifferent approach to his gift—in his senior year, he actually gave it up. Smoking a half a pack of cigarettes a day and drifting between jobs, Rodgers was forced back into running when his motorcycle was stolen. With no other way to make his way back and forth to his job, Rodgers transported himself with his feet. Running to work and anywhere else he wanted to venture, Bill regained his passion for the sport and eventually won his first of four Boston Marathons in 1975.

In the year following Rodgers's first Boston championship, an estimated 25,000 Americans finished marathons. Since then, the number has grown exponentially to over 450,000 in 2000. The running boom that he helped ignite eventually provided a comfortable living for Rodgers. He

currently owns the Bill Rodgers Running Center in Boston's Fanueil Hall with his brother Charlie and appears throughout the world at running clinics and expos.

Famous for his swinging left arm and gloved hands, the five-foot nine-inch, 128-pound Rodgers broke onto the scene in the mid-1970s and ended up athletic royalty, sharing a spot with a very short list of names like Larry Bird, Ted Williams, and Bobby Orr.

Training on the marathon route, as I did, has its good and bad points. A runner who is unfamiliar with the route probably enjoys Mile 15 as a level, forgiving mile. But for those of us who are acquainted with the course, this stretch only produces fear and apprehension. At the end of the mile, there are no breaks, no fun, no high-fiving fans, no dancing to the music from house parties—just outright pain.

As I ran toward Mile 16, I couldn't help but be filled with trepidation: I was heading into, not away from, the hurricane that awaited me in the miles ahead. Knowing this, I could feel my mind shifting out of attack mode and into an attitude of reluctance I used to fall into during training when my body really didn't want to run—a state I called "apathetic rationalization." Once in this mind-set, I could amaze myself with my ability to validate the most absurd reasons *not* to run. Sometimes it was too hot, sometimes it was too cold. Sometimes I needed quality time with my son, sometimes I needed private time at the house. Or I needed to rest my weary legs, or save my fresh legs, or let my blisters die down, or avoid new blisters. Too early, too late, too wet, too dry, too many carbohydrates, too few, full moon, half moon, can't run on days that end with the letter *y*—you name it, I used it. Whatever the excuse, it was all too easy to persuade myself to grab the clicker and a spot on the couch instead of my Walkman and sneakers.

As I approached the end of Mile 15, I continued to put one foot in front of the other in a twisted suicide mission into the eye of the Boston Marathon. But how could I not? The answers lay ahead. Somewhere in the coming miles fulfillment waited. How could I pass up the opportunity to search the undiscovered depths of my soul? Six months ago, I had

FOUR-TIME WINNER BILL RODGERS (RIGHT) RUNS STRIDE FOR STRIDE WITH THE NOTORIOUS JEROME DRAYTON IN 1975. PHOTO BY JEFF JOHNSON.

flat-lined. There had to be a reason why I was prompted to run Boston. I needed to go forward to find it. So I ran.

Still, I was desperate for someone to pull me forward. I needed outside support to validate this bout of insanity. With just a half mile left in the town of Wellesley, I still hadn't found my college friend. I longed to see a familiar face, and so I kept looking.

MILE 16

Paul Fetscher—"Five minutes of disclipine—that's all it takes when you get up in the morning. Hit the head. Pull on your stuff and get out the door. Everything else just falls into place."

— — — —

As Mile 15 turns into Mile 16, the race begins to resemble a visit to the dentist: You feel a little pain at the moment, but you know that very soon you're going to experience some real agony. Up to this point, the elite runners have been like boxers feeling each other out in the early rounds. Now it's show time.

When I think of the beginning of Mile 16, I'm reminded of the time when, somewhat younger, I sat at the peak of a roller coaster with my friend Steve Alperin. As we anxiously waited to plummet back down through the clouds, Steve closed his eyes and made peace with his maker. I punched him in the arm and yelled at him to throw his arms up in the air.

Starting in Wellesley, the route descends sharply for almost half a mile into Newton Lower Falls. This drop brings the runners to fifty-five feet above sea level—a descent of 100 feet in all. The downhill moves past the Warren School and its field on the right and some small businesses on the left. Although this downhill is less publicized than other sections of the course, it is of great strategic importance. Until now, race tactics have probably been limited to occasional surges on the flats of Framingham and Natick. Good downhill runners take advantage of this stretch to roll: A well-timed surge may separate them from the other leaders before getting to the hills in the coming miles. Bill Rodgers liked to attack here. As did Uta Pippig, who when asked about her strategy for the downhill, "How I approach this section of the course is my own little secret."

For wheelchair competitors, this downhill is both strategically important and potentially dangerous. Some push the envelope and attack this section of the course at speeds approaching forty miles per hour. Depending on the weather, crowd control, and the condition of the street, a hell-bent style can be hazardous.

Even if the runners proceed down the hill with caution, most are unaware of the internal side effects of a 100-foot drop over a half mile. Having completed fifteen highly taxing, adrenaline-filled miles, a steep descent can cause real problems for the legs and arms of competitors. The effect can be similar to body shots in a boxing match.

1897 J.J. McDermott of New York made his move on the downhill leading into Newton Lower Falls. After taking the lead on the descent, he never looked back en route to winning the first Boston Marathon.

1898 As Louis Liebgold ran down into Newton Lower Falls in tenth place, he caught his heel on the train track running down the middle of the street. Bloodied, he crawled over to the side of the road where he was eventually picked up and taken to Boston.

1969 Scandinavian champion Pentti Rummakko of Finland was running on the heels of the lead pack as it passed through Newton Lower Falls. As he focused on each step, a fan by the name of Paul Cahill from Wellesley came out of the crowd and knocked the Finnish runner to his knees. Off-duty Newton policeman Richard Gunn arrested Cahill, while Rummakko picked himself up and finished tenth. The reason for the attack is still a mystery.

— — — —

Trying to regain their equilibrium after their leap from Wellesley, the runners approach the last quarter of the mile. The street widens to five lanes, allowing the runners to spread out and the spectators to get a good look at the athletes.

Grete Waitz, who won the New York City Marathon nine times between 1978 and 1988, pointed to the downhills in Boston as the most challenging aspect of the course. Struggling after the quad-crushing descents, she dropped out of the 1987 Boston Marathon with the lead, just a few miles away from the winner's circle. The experience gave her great respect for the course in Boston: "I never train downhill. No one I know trains downhill—we only train uphill. It can be hard to run downhill. Next year, I'll be ready." She never came back.

Many other elite marathoners, including Alberto Salazar, Dick Beardsley, Greg Meyer, Rob de Castella, and Craig Virgin, echoed Waitz's observation about the course. After pushing themselves in Boston, they were never the same.

The beating these runners were subjected to on the descents is not uncommon. Dr. David Martin of Georgia State University has studied the impact of downhill running on both elite and back-of-the-pack marathoners. In his findings he discovered that downhill running takes so much out of a runner because the dual need for running and braking forces the runner to use more muscles. Even the recovery is affected: "It takes many more weeks to recover from Boston because of the delayed muscle soreness caused by chronic eccentric downhill loading."

B.A.A. Race Director Dave McGillivray (who has conquered Boston multiple times) feels that how well a runner withstands the downhills of Boston all depends on his or her individual style: "If you land like a helicopter, the course can beat the heck out of your quads, knee joints, and feet."

When the TAC disqualified the Boston Marathon as a course where new world or American records could be set, they mostly argued that the dramatic drop in elevation from Hopkinton to Boston gave runners an unfair time advantage. This reasoning raised the eyebrows of many veterans of the race. They respond that it is precisely the downhill running of the Boston Marathon, followed by the daunting hills in Newton, that makes the course uniquely punishing among top marathons. In their view, most runners are unaccustomed to the tricky combination of braking and forward running demanded by the hills, and so the Boston course is actually much harder than the pancake courses where world records are normally set. Maybe the TAC should ask Frank Shorter, gold medal winner in the 1972 Olympic Marathon and past critic of the Boston course. Shorter, who once mocked the course's descents, ran Boston in 1978. The course reaped its revenge on the condescending marathoner, sending him home with a twenty-third-place finish.

— — — —

Eventually the runners reenter the atmosphere and arrive in Newton Lower Falls. After experiencing such a fall, the runners probably should wave their hands above their heads like the Acapulco cliff divers do as they surface to let the spectators know that they're all right. At the bottom of the hill, the runners reach the end of the mile and cross the Charles River by way of a small bridge. (The Charles River also begins in Hopkinton and ends in Boston, but it takes a meandering route of eighty miles.) Pat Williams—who would have spent the last mile pleading with himself to "Just make it to Newton"—will now be able to scratch another town off his list and start pleading for the next landmark. Here the runners have a moment to catch their breath before they will be introduced to the first hill of Newton, and what some consider the ugly sister of the Newton Hills.

As for me, I wasn't looking forward to the prospect of climbing after I just finished falling. The injury to the outside of my left knee was severely tested on the downhills, making me wonder if anyone at the TAC had ever run the course. My inability to roll the knee normally made the 100-foot drop a painful undertaking. I had to extend my left leg straight out, like a peg leg, while my right leg did the rolling. By this point in the race, I had stopped checking my splits at the mile marks. Time was no longer a factor. From here on, it was just a matter of survival.

When I reached the valley at Newton Lower Falls, I spotted a young girl with oranges on the right side of the course. I was desperate for some

nourishment but I didn't want to waste the steps it would take to reach the side of the road. So I yelled to her to throw an orange. She misjudged the distance and the orange sailed behind me. In dire need of that orange, I threw my left hand behind me and made a behind-the-back catch that would have impressed Nomar Garciaparra.

Just then, with the Route 128 hill rising up ahead in the foreground, a fan ran onto the course. It was my college friend Jim Delaney. He had a beer bottle in one hand and a glow on his face, which made me jealous. Twelve years earlier I had leaned on Jimmy's shoulder when I fell unconscious in the college baseball game; now, over a decade later, I leaned on him for support again. He ran with me for a hundred yards and asked me how I was doing. I answered, "I feel like shit, but I'll do it." As he turned off he yelled, "You're the man! Go get 'em!"

Although I was psyched to see him, I was equally disappointed when we parted company. The pain and misery I was experiencing was made more difficult by the solitude of marathoning. It was a lonely pain: The struggle of a marathon is personal. Throughout the run, I wondered if the thousands of other competitors were feeling similar discomfort or if the course held some kind of grudge against me and was saving its best shots for my run. Nevertheless, Jimmy had pumped me up enough. His well-wishes were enough to get me over the hill to the Newton-Wellesley Hospital, where my parents would be waiting.

MILE 17

Two-time winner Geoff Smith observed: "This extended uphill [over Route 128], coming off a downhill, is an example of the reverse muscle usage which beats the hell out of the runner's legs."

— — — —

In the first half of Mile 17, the runners' quadriceps—which were just put through the spin cycle on the last downhill—are put to the test. At first the course is relatively flat and wide open. At the start of the mile, the athletes move past the historical Baury House. Built in 1755 by shipbuilders, the house was situated on the old Natick Road almost as if they knew that some day the world's greatest race would pass this way. In recent years, the landmark was remodeled into a professional building and turned to face a road perpendicular to the race course. The architect was obviously not a running fan.

At the base of the hill, on the right, sits Gregorian Rugs. Like most successful businesspeople, the folks at Gregorian Rugs recognize a marketing opportunity when they see one, so they take advantage of the Boston Marathon to sell rugs while they cheer on the runners. Each year during race week, Gregorian puts on a special sale on carpet "runners" for hallways and stairways, and hangs a sign out front depicting a marathoner in order to remind potential customers of the ongoing sale. During the day, thousands of living and breathing reminders will pass the store.

Two tenths into the mile, just past Gregorian Rugs, the five lanes become four and are divided by cement islands. A sign on the right welcomes

JON ANDERSON (LEFT) AND TOM FLEMING (RIGHT) ARE ESCORTED BY THE POLICE AND BIKERS
DURING THE 1973 BOSTON MARATHON AS THEY WORK THEIR WAY UP THE OVERPASS WHICH
CROSSES OVER ROUTE 128. PHOTO BY RICK LEVY.

runners to NEWTON, THE GARDEN CITY. The course moves past the old
restaurant the Pillar House, which was built prior to the Civil War, before proceeding over a bridge spanning Route 128 and Interstate 95. If
the runners took a right onto Route 128 here, they could wind up in
Florida—fitness permitting. A left turn points you toward Maine.

156

Although the three hills ahead on Commonwealth Avenue get most of the attention, many runners feel that the Route 128 overpass is the most difficult challenge on the entire course. Like climbers on Mt. Everest, who must ascend to base camp before attacking the peak itself, the runners must climb for almost three quarters of a mile over the highway before being in a position to scale the hills up ahead. This gradual but continuous climb often fools runners into using more energy than they planned when surveying the route from a tour bus the day before. Wheelchair competitors in particular must pay attention to their pace and plan of attack, as wind can be a factor during the exposed run over the bridge.

1967 As Kathy Switzer approached the intersection before Newton-Wellesley Hospital, she spotted a policeman who was suspiciously eyeing her. She turned to her coach Arnie Briggs, who was running alongside, and told him, "If this cop tries to arrest me, I'm going to resist arrest. I haven't come this far for nothing." Running with a rebel's gait, Switzer proceeded up to where the officer was directing traffic. As she passed him, he turned toward her with a stern expression and said, "Your hands look cold. Take my gloves." Switzer went on to finish the race and make history.

As I ran up the hill over Route 128 (the image of the condensation dripping down Jimmy's beer bottle still fresh in my mind), I started to get excited about the prospect of seeing my parents a half mile ahead. Here again I felt a profound vulnerability that I never would have imagined in a road race. The thought of briefly reuniting with my mother and father provoked powerful emotions within me. I felt juvenile for getting so sentimental over a road race, but at the same time I was deeply moved as I thought of the sacrifices they had made and the countless gifts they had bestowed upon me. Over thirty-some years they firmly steered me through my childhood, tolerated me through the teenage years, and subtly guided me in my adult years, when I was too old to have my parents tell me what to do.

WITH WHITE RUNNING GLOVES TUCKED NEATLY INTO MY WAISTBAND, I APPROACH THE SPOT WHERE MY PARENTS ARE STANDING. I HAD TO FIGURE OUT WHETHER TO KEEP RUNNING OR TO STOP AND ASSURE MYSELF A RIDE HOME. PHOTO BY JOHN CONNELLY JR.

Six months earlier my father had sat in the hallway with my wife and prayed for my recovery while my mother relied on the power of her rosary beads to find solace and strength. Half a year after my heart decided that it preferred to restart rather than call it quits, I was granted the wonderful gift of sharing yet another significant moment of my life with them. I broke into tears, knowing that my new lease on life would be celebrated with the very two people who gave me my life.

After reaching the crest of the hill, which is a fifty-five-foot rise in elevation over a half mile, the runners work their way up to another cement island at a set of traffic lights. On the right is Newton-Wellesley Hospital, which is busy caring for wayward runners as a primary source of care, while at the same time testing their catastrophe plan.

By law, all hospitals across the country are required to have a disaster plan in place in the event of a catastrophic occurrence. The disaster plan must be rehearsed twice a year. For Newton-Wellesley Hospital, the chaos of the Boston Marathon approximates closely enough the chaos that would follow an earthquake, a flood, or a nuclear attack, so the marathon is used as one of the hospital's two annual disaster drills. With runners streaming by outside, doctors, local police, firefighters, nurses, and hospital social workers are busy running their own synchronized race. After September 11th such an exercise has taken on a new relevance.

1909 Runners Lewis Fine and Louis Tewanima, pride of the Hopi tribe of Arizona and school friends of Jim Thorpe, pushed themselves beyond their limits in 90-degree weather. Their inevitable collapse gained them beds at Newton-Wellesley Hospital.

1911 A Boston Globe reporter covering the marathon drove by the Newton-Wellesley Hospital and wrote this the following day: "It's a pathetic sight to see invalids and convalescents waving to these sturdy athletes."

— — — —

Founded in 1881 as one of the country's first "cottage hospitals" (so named because patients with common infectious diseases occupied designated cottages), Newton-Wellesley Hospital not only serves as a medical center for runners, but also served as the birthplace of one of the race's most famous journalists, Henry Nason.

From the moment Nason was born, it seemed he was destined to contribute to the world's greatest race in some fashion. Just five days after his birth, he saw his first Boston Marathon when a maternity ward nurse held him on her shoulder while she peered out the window to catch a glimpse of her boyfriend, who was running the race. Some

**years later, as a boy, Henry became a volunteer lemon car-
rier for the race and later a sports writer for *The Boston
Globe*. Nason covered the race for over a half a century,
making his own contribution to the marathon's folklore.
Journalists like Nason and Lawrence Sweeney and Joe Concannon, who also covered the race for decades, provide a
historical bond, linking runners in the modern marathon to
past participants all the way back to 1897.**

The runners move on a declining grade past the hospital. On the left
sits the Woodland Country Club, which was built in 1897 to offer recreational activities for vacationers at the posh resort known as the Woodland Park Hotel a mile down the road. Its beautiful clubhouse, which
burned down in both 1970 and 1983, is situated down the driveway
about a five iron from the road. The famous golf course architect Donald Ross designed the course.

The current club manager says that Woodland doesn't do anything
special for the day. "In reality," he confessed, "the race is a nuisance. We
can't book any events for the day and the streets are shut down from the
early morning to late afternoon. Some members play golf in the morning, have lunch, and then take in the race from the club grounds. But in
general, the day is more an inconvenience than anything."

Back in 1960, my parents had their wedding reception at the Woodland Country Club. Now, six kids later, they stood across the street from
where they celebrated their union and anxiously awaited my arrival.

As I finished the first of the four hills, I could see my parents a hundred yards down the road. My mother had a look of maternal concern on
her face, while my father stepped out onto the course to take some pictures, just like in the old days during birthdays, first communions, and
graduations. As I passed, they asked how I was doing and stretched out a
bottle of Gatorade. I told them I was all right and waved off the drink.

While I ran past, I smiled and stood tall in the hope of disguising my
discomfort: I was afraid that they would see through my guise and demand that I end this foolishness. Fortunately, they understood the meaning of this endeavor. They knew I had to prove something on this day. So

WOODLAND PARK HOTEL,

WASHINGTON STREET, CORNER WOODLAND ROAD,

AUBURNDALE.

JOSEPH LEE, Proprietor.

This New and Elegant Hotel is now open for the reception of Guests at all Seasons of the year. Steam Heating during the Winter Months.

BOWLING ALLEYS, BILLIARD AND POOL ROOMS

OPEN TO THE PUBLIC.

JOSEPH LEE, Caterer.

ICE CREAM, FANCY CAKE, AND DELICACIES MADE TO ORDER.

Mr. Lee will attend to the Catering for Parties, Weddings, Etc., in Newton or Boston; has unrivalled facilities for giving Dinner Parties, Class Suppers, Etc., at his Hotel. Ice Cream delivered in any part of Newton.

An 1896 advertisement promoting the Woodland Hotel bragged about its ability to deliver ice cream anywhere in Newton. Illustration courtesy of the *1896 Newton Registry.*

my father gave me the thumbs up, my mother waved, and once again I was all alone. After I passed my parents, a strange thought came to my mind. I suddenly realized that I might have missed out on an opportunity to get a ride home. The last thing I wanted was to end up passed out on someone's front lawn and have some B.A.A. official walk by shaking his head and saying "Bandit."

Although Woodland Country Club would rather the race didn't happen, many Newton residents claim that the race should be called the

Newton Marathon. By their calculations, Newton hosts a larger portion of the race (six miles) than any of the other seven towns. Within those six miles lie a hospital, two colleges, two country clubs, a town hall, and four hills. Arguably, more races have been won and lost in Newton than in any other town along the route.

Once a part of Cambridge, Newton was known as New Towne in the late 1600s. Upon being separated from Cambridge, it joined the words and dropped the e.

The town of Newton boasts a population of over 83,000 people spread over 18.2 square miles with a median household income in excess of $91,000. Residents live in homes with an average price of $579,000. In addition to its role in the Boston Marathon, Newton is probably best known as the home of the Fig Newton, the third most popular cookie in the country, which was created in 1891 by baker James Henry Mitchell.

The former mayor of Newton, Theodore Mann, was always concerned with the cost of sponsoring such a large event as the marathon. At the same time, he felt the town of Newton had a historical obligation to make it happen.

Newton Mayor Thomas Concannon echoed these thoughts when he described the race as a cultural event that provides a carnival atmosphere and a kind of reunion for the people of his town. "The Boston Marathon serves as a coming-out party for the people of this town. After a long winter, the race provides them an opportunity to reacquaint themselves with their neighbors. The event is culturally enriching, allowing the town to benefit in many ways which far outweigh the monetary costs."

— — — —

1961 As the lead runners ran from Wellesley into Newton, a black Labrador shadowed the lead pack, matching them

stride for stride. After passing the border of the Garden City, the dog darted into the road, as if possessed. Eino Oksanen of Finland leaped over the dog, but John "Younger" Kelley was knocked to the ground. English runner Fred Norris stopped and helped Kelley to his feet, while Oksanen never looked back on his way to victory. At the press conference after the race, Oksanen laughingly said, "The dog should have been shot." John Kelley reflected on the irony of the Englishman jeopardizing his dream in order to aid an Irishman. "What a wonderful representative of his country."

An eighth of a mile past the golf course on the opposite side, the local Green Line train (part of the Boston subway system) drops off passengers at the Woodland stop. Many spectators take the train from the city to watch the race here, making this a congested and supportive area. If you're thinking about throwing in the towel, the train from this stop to Kenmore Square (one mile from the finish) covers the distance in twenty-six minutes.

The end of the mile turns residential and flat for one last breather before the road turns the corner at Mile 18. Pat Williams keeps saying to himself, "Get me to the fire station."

MILE 18

In 1909, *The Boston Globe* wrote, "The long, hard, smooth hills in the distance have proved to be the undoing of many ambitious lads."

— — — —

The route is level for the first two tenths of the mile as the runners approach the turn from Route 30 onto Route 16 East. On their left before the corner, the runners proceed pass the footprint of the famous Woodland Hotel.

Back in the late 1800s and early 1900s, the Woodland Hotel was frequented by well-to-do Bostonians who made the trip from the city by horse and carriage. Along with the blue bloods from Boston, President Taft once graced the hotel as did the Yale Bulldog football team, which made the hotel its headquarters each year on the weekend of the big game with the Crimson of Harvard. At one time the hotel was owned by a Newton socialite named Joseph Lee who was also the son of slaves in Charleston, South Carolina. As a young man Lee witnessed the bombing of Fort Sumter, which signaled the beginning of the Civil War. Along with the hotel, Lee ran a very successful catering business and owned a patent for a bread-crumbing machine.

In 1917, the Woodland Hotel was bought by Lasell College, although there was a delay before the college could put its new property to use: In the first year after the purchase, the Newton-Wellesley Hospital commandeered the property during an influenza epidemic. In 1952, the property was sold to a contractor who built twenty-seven houses on the site. This location used to be the fourth checkpoint of the race before they were switched to even intervals in 1983.

1925 Frank Wendling from Buffalo, New York, pulled out of the lead pack to enjoy a hot tea at the Woodland Hotel. After finishing his tea, he rejoined the snowy race and finished tenth.

1948 Bill Lanigan stopped his run to admire two girls playing tennis at Lasell College. He proceeded to grab a racket and join the girls in a volley before continuing his run, which he eventually finished.

At the intersection of Route 16 and Commonwealth Avenue (Route 30), the course takes a ninety-degree turn at the Newton Fire Station. Many runners look to this spot as another landmark on their long list. Knowing that the hills lie just ahead, you round this corner like a boater drifting helplessly toward a waterfall.

The Newton Fire Station, located on the right corner of the intersection, is conveniently situated for viewing the race. Firefighters can watch the last level stretch of Route 16 and then cross the room to the Route 30 side to see the start of the first hill. Depending on the weather, the firehouse may serve as an impromptu first aid station for runners who have pushed too hard. When the marathon has fallen on warm days, the firehouse has seen long lines of distressed runners in need of assistance.

Along with providing care for participants and spectators throughout the day, fire personnel are also still responsible for protecting the ordinary citizens of Newton. As in Natick, they place firefighting equipment on both sides of the race route. Inevitably the fire engines that sit on the carriage road across the street turn into a carnival ride for bored kids.

— — — —

By this point, I later learned, Richie and Rad had gained almost twenty minutes on me. While I ran, I would occasionally overhear a spectator say, "There goes another BOB shirt." It gave me comfort to know that they were still alive and kicking. It was like finding a strand from one of their shirts stuck to a branch somewhere deep in the jungle. Coming into the race, I suspected that they were better prepared than I was. If I had spotted one of them on the side of the road, I would have been deeply demoralized: If they couldn't do it, then I was a goner.

During my long training runs on the race course, I used this turn at the fire station as a benchmark to assess my physical condition. Before making the turn, I took the opportunity to take inventory. In past runs I approached this spot in a variety of physical states. Invariably, how I felt here was a good indicator of whether the run would end in success or failure. If I was struggling at the fire station, it would be an early exit.

On this day, all in all—and despite my whining throughout this book—other than my knee and the nausea, I was feeling pretty decent. My wind was strong, and I had the blessing of having my wife, son, and friends two miles up ahead. I was still pessimistic about the outcome, but I felt good enough to put my blinker on and take the right turn.

1907 Canadian Charlie Petch was running stride for stride with Thomas Longboat at the turn onto Commonwealth Avenue. As he took the corner, he allowed the excitement of the crowd to get the best of him and danced his way around the turn. Longboat kept his head down and moved on to the championship. Petch finished sixth.

1979 Toshihiko Seko's coach, Kiyoshi Nakamura, informed the press that his runner would stay on Bill Rodgers's shoulder until the fire station, where he would then destroy Rodgers on the hills. Rodgers proved to be the destroyer, beating the second-place finisher Seko by forty-five seconds.

— — — —

Two-time New York City Marathon champion German Silva respects the hills on the Boston course, but is more concerned with the five

sharp turns that occur on the race route: at the fire station in Newton, at the top of Cleveland Circle, at the bottom of Cleveland Circle, heading onto Hereford Street, and heading onto Boylston Street. "Everybody talks about Heartbreak Hill, but I'm more interested in the corners. You can take advantage of the corners. If you are prepared, you are prepared for everything."

Runners make the turn onto Commonwealth Avenue with caution and a wide circle, compliments of tiring legs. Wheelchair competitors approach the corner at speeds of twenty-five miles per hour. Soon, their downhill muscles will be taking a break, and their uphill muscles and rotator cuffs will confirm whether or not they spent enough time in the weight room. Wheelchair competitors who are on the heavy side must wait for the downhills to make their move. For lighter wheelchair competitors, who have a high strength to weight ratio, it's time to attack.

Just after the turn onto Commonwealth Avenue, hill number one rises ahead for approximately a half mile with a roundabout swing to the left. Here on the right side of the road, Uta Pippig always looks for information on the race leaders: "After turning at the fire station, I look forward to seeing the sign on the side of the road that lists the leaders. Every year I look for it. I train with some Kenyan men, so I am interested in how they are doing up ahead." On the left, the runners are boxed in by a grass island that protects a carriage road. This island will continue into Mile 22. On the right, at the start of the hill, sits Brae Burn Country Club.

The manager of the club informed me that their members, like the members at the Woodland Country Club, show up early to play a round of golf and grab lunch before working their way out to the street to watch the competitors. Brae Burn attempts to coexist with the race by allowing some parking and the use of bathroom facilities. The day is long and arduous for the club's security staff. Many years ago, Brae Burn's golf course used to cross over Commonwealth Avenue. So beware of some elderly golfer who lives off interest income and thinks FDR should run for another term. He might just hit a low seven wood over the race route.

Sometime back, Brae Burn sold land to developers who built beautiful Georgian estates. These $700,000 to $1,000,000 abodes dot the course on both sides for the next three to four miles.

The first of the three Commonwealth Avenue hills is like the first punch to the face of the runner: If you're still standing, you may proceed to the next hill. Greg Meyer, the 1983 winner, feels that this hill is the most difficult of the Commonwealth Avenue hills. "It's steeper and longer than the other two. Heartbreak Hill is a gradual rise which levels off, whereas the first hill at the turn is a real test to your physical condition at this juncture of the race."

As I climbed the first of the three peaks, I couldn't help but feel like I was back at the YMCA working out on the stairmaster machine (which is like attempting to go up a down escalator). The steepness of the slope made me exaggerate my stride, pulling my knees higher while I carefully landed on the balls of my feet to compensate for the added pressure on my calves.

As I scaled the hill, I could feel my physical condition deteriorating. The aroma of cookouts was starting to sicken me, while my left leg continued to bother me, almost giving way at one point. The simple act of lifting and dropping my feet was starting to become an adventure. Halfway up the hill, I decided it was too discouraging to look up toward the top; the reward seemed scant for all the effort I was exerting. I dropped my head and forged on, as I would on all the future hills.

Three quarters of the way up, I became aware of my heart for the first time during the race. As I struggled toward the top, I was conscious of the fact that my engine was working harder than it ever had before in thirty-two years of service. I could literally feel my chest being pushed and pulled with each pump of blood. Somewhere in the shadows of my mind I wondered, What if the surgery hadn't been successful? I knew then that if I survived this test, I could survive anything.

When I finally did reach the top of that first hill, my energy was pretty much zapped, and I still had two of the three Commonwealth Avenue hills to go. For the first time in the race, my self-evaluation was turning negative. I was starting to make concessions. I had now been on the course for over three hours—an accomplishment, considering that my longest training run had been 17.5 miles, covered in 2:48. The voice inside my head was whispering negative nothings: "You've already surpassed your best efforts. There's no disgrace in stopping. Look how many competitors are walking, or are sitting on the side of the road! There is no way they can feel worse than you do."

This type of thinking is very dangerous. Like a prisoner of war succumbing to torture, my mind was starting to betray the mission. My months of mental conditioning were being severely tested, and so my physical effort teetered on the cusp of failure.

But my heart held strong and rebuked the overtures: "Who cares how far or how long you've run, if it isn't 26.2 miles?" So I continued on.

At the top of the first hill, the course swings left, giving the runners a brief respite on a slight decline that extends to the eighteen-mile mark. Now Pat Williams is pleading to himself, "Just make it to the second hill."

MILE 19

Ibrahim Hussein: "I will sacrifice myself on the hills."

— — — —

It is impossible to do justice to the stature of the three Commonwealth Avenue hills with verbose prose. The truth of the hills is better described by the beholders:

Four-time winner Bill Rodgers: "This is the most significant stretch of course in the road-racing world. The Fukuoka route [in Japan] has its spots, and other races have nice scenery, but there is no section that identifies the challenge and beauty of marathoning more than this section of the Boston Marathon."

John "Elder" Kelley, who conquered this course sixty times: "Those hills have special meaning to me. I have great respect for them. They've caused me a lot of problems."

In 1907, the media and fans predicted that runner Tom Longboat would "fag out" in the hills of Newton—he didn't, and went on to win the race. *The Boston Globe* has described this section in various ways over the years: as the "teasing Newton Hills" in 1933; as a "topographical booby trap" in 1952; and as "topographically terrorizing" in 1965.

Other experts on the hills:

- **Writer Jerry Nason: "These hills separate the men from the boys."**

- **Geoff Smith:** "The hills are mountains by the time you hit them."

- **Jean Driscoll:** "The marathon is won and lost on the hills. Those who fear the hills will falter, while those who attack the hills can win."

- **Canadian runner Ken Parker:** "It's like meeting the queen."

- **Robert Dill of Glenrock, New Jersey:** "It was tough, those hills. That's where I got my ass kicked."

- **Sara Mae Berman:** "It's at this point that your physical effort becomes more of a mental effort. You have to want to keep going."

- **Uta Pippig:** "The first time that a runner participates in the Boston Marathon, they can get confused with how many hills there are on Commonwealth Avenue. But after you run the race once, you'll always remember that there are three hills."

At this point, the runners continue to assess their bodies and adjust their estimated times of arrival at the finish line. The fibs that runners told themselves back on the flats of Framingham are meeting the truth on the hills of Newton.

Uta Pippig says, "I always reserve some extra energy for the hills. I know back in Framingham and Wellesley that they are up ahead, so I plan accordingly. While running them, I stay within my game plan unless I'm running with someone that I am unfamiliar with. Then I will try to push myself and test my competitor. If they are fast, then they can go ahead. If I'm faster then I'll go ahead."

In 1895, the Newton Boulevard Syndicate built Commonwealth Avenue; the trolley was added the following year. This mode of transportation was popular among affluent Bostonians who enjoyed taking the five-cent ride out to the country. During the same year, the twins Freelan and Francis Stanley introduced their own form of transportation, called the Stanley Steamer, which they used to race up and down the road, defiantly exceeding any speed limits. The steam-powered motor car set a land speed record in 1906, reaching the speed of 127.6 miles per hour. The Steamer sold for $600, two times the average annual American salary at the time. Francis died in a car accident in 1918.

1909 Riding his motorcycle over the second hill, George Proctor of Waltham, Massachusetts, broke a sprocket on his bike and went crashing into a family of marathon watchers. Two children were taken to the hospital and later released with minor injuries.

1947 Yun Bok Suh of Korea was running with the lead when a fox terrier ran onto the course and tripped him to the ground. Suh was bloodied by the fall but seemed to get an adrenaline rush from the incident: He got to his feet, took off, and won the race.

— — — —

The first hill has been conquered, but there are still two to go. The course levels off and then declines, as do the runners' pulses. The mile zigzags through a residential neighborhood and then continues past a set of traffic lights at the Chestnut Street intersection and onward to the Newton Cemetery, which lies on the right halfway through the mile. Across the street from the cemetery is Wauwnet Road.

The Wauwnet Road-Commonwealth Avenue corner, a quarter mile from the town hall, marks the site of the old Wauwnet Dairy Farm. During the Great Depression five hundred Jersey cows used to stop their grazing to cheer on Clarence DeMar as he ran past.

1980 As he struggled to beat the Newton hills, runner John David Knows was knocked to his knees by a well-meaning

**fan who was spraying the overheated runners with a gar-
den hose. During the fall, Knows' contact lenses were dis-
lodged. After spending priceless minutes searching for them
on hands and knees, he finally gave up and finished the race
without them.**

After the Newton Cemetery, the runners move down a knoll to the
Newton Town Hall, which was built during the Depression. The steeple
on top of the hall has a large timepiece on its face, alerting runners to
their tardiness.

John "Younger" Kelley used to hate the clock on the town hall. During the race he made a point of ignoring his watch, fearing that the time
would demoralize him. As he ran toward the Newton Town Hall, the
clock on the steeple would inevitably sneak into his line of sight, invariably showing the big hand five minutes further along than he had hoped.

On the left at the Town Hall, there is a quaint little walkway presided
over by a statue sculpted by Rich Munroe. The monument portrays two
runners holding hands as they run up Heartbreak Hill. One of the fig-
ures is a rendering of the young John "Elder" Kelley as he crossed the finish line to win the 1935 championship; the other depicts an older version
of John "Elder" Kelley as he competed in the race in 1992.

During our training runs in February and March, Rad, Richie, Jack,
and I used to share the duty of buying drinks, pretzels, and oranges. After
meeting somewhere around Mile 22, we would drive together down the
course toward Framingham. For some reason, we always stopped along
the way at the John "Elder" Kelley statue in order to leave a jug of water
or a bottle of Gatorade. It was almost like lighting a candle at the foot of
a patron saint. I guess in a way we were.

Later, during the run, when we deviated from the workout to grab
some fluids, we would find ourselves humbled by the fact that the race's
patriarch completed this course at an age fifty years senior to ours. By
that point in the run, we were the ones who felt like the octogenarians.

As I ran by the monument to Kelley on race day, my appreciation for
the ageless wonder was greatly enhanced after tasting the first nineteen
miles of the race. As I stared at the second hill up ahead of me, just past

the Mile 19 signpost, I took strength from the man who had conquered the course for over half a century.

1987 After winning back-to-back championships in 1984 and 1985, Geoff Smith was again in the hunt for the laurel wreath. After chasing the leader Toshihiko Seko up the first hill of Newton, he finally pulled even with the runner from Japan. As they ran shoulder to shoulder, Smith looked into Seko's eyes and smiled at him. Seko ignored the salutation, turned away, and ran on to victory. Smith, the eventual third-place finisher said later, "I guess I shouldn't have smiled at him."

MILE 20

Olympic silver medalist John Treacy on the difference between the runners' demeanor before the race and at the twenty-mile mark. "There is no animosity between the competitors at the starting line because we all understand the mortality of a marathon. There is no reason to get the competitive juices flowing at that point. The twenty-mile mark is where you evaluate and assess your competition."

— — — —

In my mind, no mile on the course better exemplifies the physical and mental challenge of the Boston Marathon than Mile 20. Here the second of the three hills on Commonwealth Avenue pummels the runners with its cruel topography. Just past the Walnut Street intersection and the mile marker, the hill moves up and to the right. The uphill stretches about seven hundred yards. Twenty miles into a race, it seems a lot farther.

1999 As Fatuma Roba climbed the second hill with her reserves emptying and her legs tiring, her attempt to claim a third straight championship was in serious jeopardy. That was until several fellow Ethiopians ran out of the crowd and briefly joined her on the course, carrying their country's flag and a headband displaying the same colors. As Roba donned the headband, she seemed to ignite a reserve of adrenaline that carried her all the way to Boston and the

MILE
20

winner's podium. "I was very tired," she later recalled. "To be honest, the flags gave me a boost."

As I ran up the second hill, feeling the cumulative toll of the previous miles, I flashed back to a disaster I had experienced on this same stretch during a training run two months before in February. After starting out at the 6.5-mile mark, I was forced to stop on the second hill because of dehydration. Stranded alone somewhere between the Town Hall and Newton Center, I wandered up the hill desperate to find fluids. Fortunately for me, the Boston area had been inundated with over 100 inches of snow during the winter. Reaching deep into the two feet of snow that lined the road that day, I started to eat snow voraciously, solving the dehydration problem but not restoring my lucidity.

Distraught that my dream of running the Boston Marathon seemed to be over, I walked a mile up the road to a convenience store across from Boston College and started to feast on pretzels. I later wondered how I must have appeared to the other patrons at the store—snow plastered around the perimeter of my face, a runny nose, and the look of a serial killer.

For me, the second hill exceeds the others in difficulty. The first hill is attacked with great zest after the turn at the fire station. Running up Heartbreak Hill, the third hill, is a battle within the war. Runners are so geared to run the famous obstacle that excitement and emotion can take them over the summit. The second hill just hurts.

As I struggled up the second hill, I was shocked to see how many runners were walking. The number was so great that at one point, a volunteer yelled out, "I only see one person running—lets go!" Luckily, I was that one person.

1950 Leader Kee Yong Ham ran past the Center Street intersection and off the race route on the left side of the barricades. Police eventually directed him back to the course and on to victory.

1963 At the Centre Street intersection, Newton South High School student Jane Weinbaum jumped into the race on a bet

Coaxed on by her friends, Jane Weinbaum entered the 1963 race at the Centre Street intersection in Newton and went on the become the first woman ever to cross the finish line in Boston. Photo courtesy of the Boston Public Library Print Department.

with her friends. She ran the final six miles, making her the first woman ever to run across the finish line.

1983 Running shoulder to shoulder with Benji Durden, Greg Meyer decided to throw a false surge at his competitor to test Durden's resolve. Surprisingly Durden immediately fell back and Meyer ran on to victory.

Halfway through the mile, the second hill ends. The now-level road snakes back and forth until reaching the Centre Street intersection, where it straightens. At this point the residential neighborhood runs into a small commercial district. On the right at the intersection is the Ski & Tennis Chalet. Tom Foran, two-time third-place finisher in the men's wheelchair competition, looks for the black sign on the front of the Ski & Tennis Chalet to remind him that he has one hill to go. Store owner Lyle Shelly lives for the Boston Marathon. Taking advantage of his store's excellent location just before the twenty-mile mark, Shelly sets up a six-foot ladder outside the store and takes in the race perched high above the other spectators, who line up here six- and seven-deep for a glimpse of the runners.

Frank Shorter: "Why couldn't Pheidippides have died at 20 miles?"

One of the most dramatic moments in Boston Marathon history occurred near here in 1985. Running in Mile 20 on world record pace, leader Geoff Smith came to an abrupt halt, feeling as if he'd been shot in the leg. With severe cramping and limited mobility in his hamstrings, the English runner limped forward, looking to the skies for divine intervention. He finished the mile in 6:17. His dream of adding his name to the record book was crushed.

When Smith left Hopkinton he had every intention of setting a world record. He completed his first mile in 4:31 and the first three in under fourteen minutes. He passed the half marathon in a blistering 1:02:51. He was not out just to break the record—he was out to abuse it.

Smith acquired his passion for running as a fireman in Liverpool, England. During civil service training, the brigade was routinely asked to run in order to keep their legs in shape for ladder climbing. The privates ran through the Liverpool fog, knowing their commanders awaited them at the

RUNNING ON A WORLD RECORD PACE IN 1985, GEOFF SMITH SCREAMS IN PAIN AS HIS HAM-
STRINGS AND HIS RECORD PACE BOTH CRAMPED. PHOTO COURTESY OF VICTAH SAILER/MC-
MANUS.

finish line, which happened to be situated at a local pub. Geoff figured out that running faster than the others would net him a well-deserved pint while he waited for his slower, less thirsty comrades. This thirst to run provided Geoff purpose in his runs, and a star was born. From the soccer fields and fire poles of England to Providence College and ultimately to the streets of Boston, Smith proved himself a runner of remarkable versatility. He has run a sub-four-minute mile, a sub-1:02 half marathon, and a sub-2:10 marathon—an accomplishment matched by very few.

"I'm a dinosaur in track and field events," he says. "I used to compete in thirty, forty races a year at all different distances. These days, runners like Cosmas Ndeti run two, maybe three marathons a year and that is it. Marathoning is a career. People like myself, Alberto Salazar, and others used to run the marathon as part of the normal rotation of events. It wasn't unusual for me to run a five- or ten-kilometer race and then weeks later run the marathon. These days it's unheard of."

Smith was still on pace to break the world record when the course reared its ugly head. For a hundred years, the marathon has had a way of humbling even the great runners, and this year was no different. "I thought it was all over," he says recalling the race. "With the pain biting at my hamstrings, I didn't think I could take another step. But the cramp let up somewhat and I was able to run slowly and cautiously to the finish line."

Smith held onto his lead and claimed a ragged victory six miles later with a time of 2:14:05. Many involved with the race saw this as symbolic. The quality of the field had diminished in the recent years as world-class runners migrated to races that rewarded their efforts with prize money. Smith's painful saunter across the line allowed critics to point out that while the winner walked across the finish line, he still beat his nearest competitor (Gary Tuttle, 2:19:11) by five minutes.

In retrospect, Smith's 1985 run embodied the essence of the Boston Marathon. There was no prize money, no cars, no hidden purse—just a medal and a laurel wreath. Smith already had won the year before. He could have walked off the course in Newton and still had his name in the circle of champions. But he fought the pain and anguish because his heart told him to. As Geoff Smith walked across the finish line, his run evoked pathos but not pity. He had taken the Boston Marathon's best punch and was still standing. Somewhere high above, the late great champions William Kennedy and Clarence DeMar must have been smiling as Smith broke the tape.

On a flat stretch near the end of the mile, the runners pass the Newton Tennis and Squash Club on their right. When the manager of the club was asked if the club did anything special on race day, he answered in his most refined British voice, "Only the squash courts are available for the members at that time of the year."

1905 Fred Lorz had to jump past a horse and two bikers in the twentieth mile in order to continue on his way to the championship.

1906 *The Boston Globe* reported that the Newton police were like Yale football players, tackling interlopers.

After conquering the second hill with great difficulty, I ran toward the end of the mile and again found myself being overcome by emotion. It was in this mile that I used to stand as a young boy with my grandmother, Nana Connelly, and my two brothers and three sisters to watch the marathon. Every Patriot's Day, Nana used to squeeze the six of us into her Mustang convertible and treat us to a special day in the way only a grandparent can. As we kids were busy absorbing the race, Nana used to rejoice at the sight of her grandchildren adopting this special day as our own. Nana died in 1984 having fulfilled her responsibility as a Bostonian of passing on the Boston Marathon tradition from one generation to another.

Running past this spot provoked so many warm memories that my eyes began to swell with tears. Two hundred yards up the street, past the Centre Street intersection, the emotional roller coaster would continue, as my wife would be waiting at a house party with friends and a member of yet another generation of Connellys—my son Ryan. With the mile sign in my sights, I finally spotted my friends and family up ahead. In my mind, I made a special note to my legs to look strong. I didn't want to scare my child.

My wife came to the edge of the course to cheer me on with my son in her arms. As I approached them, I was struck by the sacrifice they both

As 1976 winner Jack Fultz gets cooled down, the author's grandmother, Catherine Connelly (in white dress), cheers him on. Photo by dick Raphael/*Sports Illustrated*.

had made. It was thanks to them that I was able to run in this extraordinary race. Many a weekend they had sat at home alone while I pursued this singular, self-absorbed goal. So I committed myself to run nobly in appreciation of their dedication. Their gift only added to my motivation: I had to be successful to honor their contributions.

When I finally came upon them, my friend Jay Parker came out and gave me a high-five while my wife had my son wave to his daddy. On the outside, I slapped Jay five and smiled at Ryan. Internally I was confused.

With Heartbreak Hill in sight, and running gloves still in place, the author tries to put on a good face as he approaches his wife, son, and friends who were patiently waiting at the 20-mile mark. Photo courtesy Noreen Connelly.

I didn't know what I wanted to do. Should I quit after completing twenty miles, running non-stop for over three hours and fifteen minutes and assuring myself a ride home? Or should I keep going? My head said stop, but the nerve impulses being sent to my legs got no response—so I just kept running.

On the sidewalk, my wife stopped to take pictures and then ran along the side of the road to wish me well. The sad thing was that she was running faster than I.

MILE 21

Rob de Castella: "The race is broken down into two halves. The first half of the race is the first twenty miles. The second half of the race is the last six miles."

— — — —

Some run, some walk, some crawl, and some surrender, but without doubt all who pass do so with respect.

During the race's infancy, *Boston Globe* writer Lawrence Sweeney described the hills in Newton as "heartbreaking hills." As the years went by, and the hills claimed more victims, the latest race correspondent, Jerry Nason, built on Sweeney's description and formally christened the last and most treacherous of the three hills (because of their cumulative effect) with the befitting name of Heartbreak Hill.

By the time I reached the base of Heartbreak Hill, my family (and ride) had been left behind. I was alone yet again. On the left side of the road, a spectator was pounding a huge base drum again and again and again. The drumming seemed to keep time with my heartbeat; I felt like a warrior being sent off to battle. I couldn't help but get pumped up as I prepared to attack the last of the three hills.

2002 Before scaling Heartbreak Hill, veteran marathoner Tom Frost stopped his run for a moment of silence. It was here where Tom's daughter used to stand and cheer for her father. On September 11, 2001, Lisa Frost perished on United Flight 175. On this day, Lisa ran beside her father.

RUNNERS ARE FORCED TO NEGOTIATE BOTH HEARTBREAK HILL AND THE UP-CLOSE-AND-PERSONAL CROWD. PHOTO COURTESY OF FAYPHOTO.

The twenty-first mile began relatively flat before quickly scaling upward. The runners get a brief fifteen-yard respite at the intersection of Grant Street before they face the concrete monster.

1975 As leader Bill Rodgers ran up the base of Heartbreak Hill, he stopped and kneeled down for more than ten seconds to tie his sneaker. This was one of five times that

AT THE BASE OF HEARTBREAK HILL, THE RUNNERS ARE INSPIRED BY THE PRIMAL BEATS OF AN ENTHUSIASTIC WELL-WISHER IN 1996. PHOTO COURTESY OF FAYPHOTO

Rodgers stopped on his way to setting a new American record for the marathon (and course record) of 2:09:55.

From mile to mile, town to town, the crowd gradually turns into a mob. On Heartbreak Hill, spectators rally five, six, and seven deep to see men and women wage their own personal battles. The fans arrive in droves here, both to support and to witness. It's not every day that you can see the human spirit emerging from the inner core of so many. One by one, the athletes dig in and push, plumbing depths of the soul not known by most. The masses clap and urge them on if only for the opportunity to share in the moment and take home with them the hope of limitless possibilities.

— — — —

While former Boston Mayor Ray Flynn stared upward to the top of Heartbreak Hill, his running partner Donald Murray

A passionate spectator congratulates a runner after cresting Heartbreak Hill during the 100th running. Photo courtesy of FayPhoto.

said to him, "This will be the closest you'll be to God all day." Flynn responded, "How can't I make it to the peak after that?"

One writer likened the marathon crowd to "the sadistic mass at the Indianapolis 500 who are more interested in human wreckage than the sporting event itself." Another writer declared, "The fans at this vantage point are sadists, flog artists, and bunion mongers."

While some spectators may take pleasure in the inevitable crashes, the majority of the fans are invaluable in providing support as the runners try to maximize their effort. With the fans at the top pulling and the fans behind them pushing, the runners scale to the peak of Heartbreak Hill. For four tenths of a mile, teeth are gritted and fists are clenched until somehow the runners arrive in the Promised Land. To the spectators, it appears that the arms and legs have done all the work, but in actuality the competitors relied mainly on one muscle—the heart.

For me, struggling up Heartbreak Hill didn't seem any harder than the steps on level ground. Every time I put my foot down was a painful experience. Each new step presented an obstacle and passed by as an accomplishment. The discomfort I was feeling was cumulative pain, deepening the farther I swam out from Hopkinton. Halfway up the hill, the pain spiked when I had to sidestep a toddler who had run out into the middle of the course when his mother lost track of him. This small deviation from my running pattern caused me extreme distress.

Somewhat irked by this parental negligence, which had almost caused six months of training to be for naught, I continued up the hill. At one point, I picked up my head to sneak a peek at the crest of the hill. While I assessed the situation, I noticed an older runner working it hard. Looking more closely I saw that the man had a prosthesis on one leg. His effort inspired me and made me proud to be part of an event where courage was just as important as athletic ability. Later that day, watching highlights of the race on the news, I caught sight of the man crossing the finish line. His success made a powerful statement about the will of someone who refused to be denied. It made me reflect upon my own physical ailment and what a metaphor this race was playing in our lives. Resilience, persistence, and a refusal to accept the limits that life attempts to place upon us—these traits serve us well not only on the road from Hopkinton to Boston, but just as well in our daily efforts to survive, and then to thrive.

Finally the SUMMIT! I had reached the peak! I had done it! I had won the famous battle within the battle. For years, I had read and witnessed tragic stories of wasted efforts and futile ascents. Now I had defeated the mountain. I rejoiced in my accomplishment: Goliath had been slain.

Up on top, the crowd welcomed me as if I had just been voted into a special fraternity. With the fans going absolutely crazy, I didn't know whether to plant my flag in the mountain's peak or collapse on the ground. Parked on the grass island to the left, Lieutenant Feeley of the Newton Police was busy proclaiming over the loudspeaker on his squad car, "Congratulations! You have just conquered Heartbreak Hill!"

The scene was a picture of elation: The crowd saluted the runners for their effort, and the runners showed their appreciation by throwing gloves and hats into the crowd in thanks. The display of adoration was so overwhelming that I moved to the side of the road to join the party and thank the crowd for their support. With my hand raised, I ran along the sidewalk slapping palms—and it was here that I realized that the crowd had probably been drinking for over four hours. One enthusiastic student almost knocked me back into Mile 15 as he reached back and crashed his hand into mine to congratulate me.

A group of Boston College students partying at the curb of the 1970 marathon were awestruck by the sight of a passing competitor by the name of Eugene Roberts. Roberts, a casualty of the Vietnam War, mesmerized the glowing students as he pushed past the campus in his hospital wheelchair. Never before had an athlete undertaken such a challenge. Now, after racing for over four hours, Eugene ran with the skyscrapers of Boston in his sights.

In preparation for the race, Roberts practiced both pushing in his wheelchair and hand jockeying to figure out which approach would be more efficient (hand jockeying is the method of using the two hands as crutches and pulling the body forward). Before the gun sounded Eugene had only completed three miles in training by hand jockeying and just one mile by wheelchair. Roberts and his brother decided on the wheelchair and stirred countless fans along the route to tears. When they arrived at Boston College, many of the students were inspired by this man's mission and honored his effort by joining him for the remaining miles.

Some five miles later, Eugene became the first wheelchair athlete ever to complete the Boston Marathon. In just over seven hours, the Baltimore native finished the race by getting down out of his chair and using his two hands to pull himself across the line.

Alongside the courageous warrior was his brother and the crowd of admirers who joined them in a chorus of "Praise the Lord" as they covered the last mile.

Halfway through the mile, at the top of the hill, the road drops to the right before rising cruelly for one last, brief moment of pain.

THE GOTHIC STEEPLES OF BOSTON COLLEGE STAND GUARD AT THE 21-MILE MARK. PHOTO COURTESY OF FAYPHOTO.

Dick O'Brien, a citizen of Newton, lives at the peak of Heartbreak Hill. Each year, he celebrates Marathon Day with a cookout for his family and friends. Dick usually misses the race because he has to man the barbecue grill, but one year he let the burgers burn so he could see his oldest son run the race.

"When my son approached, it looked as if he was near death. As he passed in front of the house, the only thing he could think about was stopping and going to bed. But the crowd wouldn't let him. Like a supernatural act, the crowd lifted him over the hill with their screams of support." The eldest O'Brien child went on to finish the race. Afterwards, he described his feat like a true Bostonian: It was, he said, like hitting a baseball over the Green Monster at Fenway Park. By the way, now that the town of Newton has placed some portable bathrooms at the top of Heartbreak Hill, the O'Briens don't need to hire a guard for their front door anymore.

The end of the mile moves right and downhill past the front gate of Boston College, which was founded by Jesuit priests in 1863. By

1897 Boston College was home to 450 male students, who paid less than $100 in annual tuition (plus a $1 library and athletic fee). Now it costs almost 15,000 young men and women $35,200 a head to live and learn at BC. Famous graduates include football star Doug Flutie, Ed McMahon of *The Tonight Show* and *Star Search* fame, and the late Speaker of the House Tip O'Neal. The most heralded faculty member is Raymond McNally (who happens to be the country's foremost expert on Count Dracula).

Past the school there is a downhill that is famous for testing spent quads and reminding elated runners that they have five more miles to go. Kathleen Beebee, who has twice finished in the top forty, and who in 1996 placed third in the age 50-59 division with a time of 3:16:47, recalled a trip down this challenging hill that she would like to forget: "I had just reached the top of Heartbreak Hill and I felt terrible. I knew that I had to finish if I had come this far. So, as I ran down the backside of Heartbreak Hill, I took a peek at the John Hancock skyscraper, which sat in the sky six miles away, and noticed that it was swaying back and forth. This was not a good sign. But being a stubborn Irishwoman from County Mayo, I worked my way into Boston to the turn onto Hereford Street. My friends there said that I looked deathly gray before I collapsed to the ground with the finish line in sight. I was taken by ambulance to the nearest hospital where I recovered physically but it took me a year to recover from the depression caused by the agony of falling so close to the finish line."

Kathleen Beebee went on to run other marathons and the Hancock has since stopped swaying. But her experience is a reminder to all runners. The best time to enjoy the conquest of Heartbreak Hill is later, when you replay the race in your mind or swap war stories with fellow marathoners. There is no time to rest on your laurels. There is more to the Boston Marathon than conquering Heartbreak Hill.

1923 In hot pursuit of Clarence DeMar, Frank Zuna was brought to a stop in Mile 21 by a traffic jam of motor cars. The time Zuna lost negotiating the congestion foiled any hope of catching the great DeMar for the victory.

JOHN "YOUNGER" KELLEY WITH THE 1959 LEAD PAST ST. IGNACIUS CHURCH, WHICH STANDS
ON THE BOSTON COLLEGE CAMPUS. PHOTO COURTESY OF FAYPHOTO.

After leaving the merry group at the top of Heartbreak Hill, I started
to descend. Outside the Boston College gates my brother Kevin was waiting with our friends Tim and Mary Kate Rose—both past survivors of the
race. Tim and Mary Kate wished me well, while Kevin joined me for the
final five miles. As we took off, I was hoping he would say, "You look terrible—you have to stop." But instead he said, "You look great. Let's do it!"

MILE 22

John Treacy, silver medalist in the 1984 Olympic Marathon, once noted, "The great mystique of Heartbreak Hill is not getting up it. It's getting down it."

— — — —

In the months leading up to the race, Rad, Richie, Jackie, and I were made aware of the struggle that lay ahead simply by training on the course. During our training runs, we beginners were brash in our speculations on how to solve the riddle of running Boston. Though, in reality, our boldness was a cloak for insecurity.

One of the many theories we concocted concerned the last five miles of the race: "Make it over Heartbreak Hill, and the rest of the race will be smooth sailing." Mind you, we were not the first to advance this (false) hypothesis, nor will we be the last. For over a century, the backside of Heartbreak Hill has made mincemeat of runners who committed the sin of disrespect. Don't forget Jim Knaub's advice, that "There is no such thing as an unimportant mile." The hills are done, but the race goes on. Runners must be careful not to let their guard down too early. There are still more than five miles to go before the athletes earn the right to wallow in their glory.

Ever since 1903, when Sammy Mellor was forced to surrender the lead and walk down the Mile 22 hill, both elite and back-of-the-pack runners have feared that they too might fall victim in the eerie mile known by some as the Graveyard

of Champions (so nicknamed by the writer Jerry Nason). Many suspect that the spirits housed in the Evergreen Cemetery down the road are to blame for wreaking their sadistic whims upon the runners. Whatever the cause, unexpected outside forces have played a significant role in this segment of the course throughout the history of the race. Menacing vehicles, illegal stimulants, and schizophrenic behavior have all conspired to turn this stretch of course into the running edition of the Bermuda Triangle. Below is a sampling of past occurrences that support the runners' dread of Mile 22:

• Festus Madden was running a close second to Clarence DeMar when a car crashed into him. DeMar ran on to one of his seven championships unopposed.
• Thirty-six years later, runner Michael Kish was sent sprawling onto the sidewalk at Boston College by a speeding car. After receiving medical care for his bleeding head and arms, he continued on to finish the race.
• 1972 Leaders Olavi Suomalainen and Jacinto Sabinal were scared clear into Mile 23 when they were almost run over by the press bus just after passing the college. In an effort to brace themselves, they held on to each other to keep from being crushed.

The runners move past Boston College in a continuous descent of almost a half mile. At this point, runners must assess their energy reserves to determine whether they can push themselves or whether they should hold on for dear life. Those in the second group now understand that their split times, which looked so good back in Natick and Framingham, are out the window. Survival is their only goal now.

As in Mile 16, runners are again forced to shift gears as they did at Newton Lower Falls: After fighting over Heartbreak Hill, they now need to mobilize leg muscles used in downhill running. This tormenting of the runners' legs prompted past champion Rob de Castella to refer to this section of the race as "an anatomical challenge."

Toward the bottom of the hill, runners are greeted by the pleasing sign of BOSTON. For rookies this border placard is a welcome sight. Little do they know that the course mockingly cuts through Boston for a moment before regurgitating the runners into Brookline in the coming mile. Former Boston Mayor and veteran marathoner Ray Flynn used to compare the sign to a punch in the stomach: "When you see the Boston sign, you feel like you're rounding third and heading for home. One mile later when the runners are welcomed into Brookline, it can be psychologically demoralizing to have Boston offered and then taken away from you."

Plodding forward, the runners can't help but notice that there are just as many victims scattered on the sidewalks of the downhill as there were on the ascent of Heartbreak Hill.

At the bottom of the hill, after Boston College, the route passes St. Ignatius Church on the right and the Boston College Green Line trolley station on the left. Here many a runner has boarded the B train after surrendering to the course, including Stylianos Kyriakides, who hitched a ride at Boston College in 1938 and pledged, "Come back again? I think not—never again." Eight years later he won the championship.

Leaving the station, the road now becomes a four-lane thruway divided down the middle by the train tracks. Runners stay to the right of the road. An eighth of a mile farther on, the course moves past the Lake Street intersection and up a slight incline with the St. John's Seminary and the cardinal's home on the left, and the poltergeist-filled Evergreen Cemetery on the right. The road inclines slightly again and the runners are now sandwiched by the student-occupied apartment buildings that line both sides of the street. Ahead at the end of the mile, the road hugs the Chestnut Hill Reservoir on the right until Chestnut Hill Street, where the runners turn and temporarily leave Commonwealth Avenue.

With the mile coming to an end, the runners' quads are almost wrung dry. If you approached the course with a plan, this is a good time to make your move. Three-time winner Cosmas Ndeti always pointed to this juncture of the course as the critical spot during the race saying, "The race doesn't begin until the thirty-five-kilometer mark." In the 1993 race, he was in sixteenth place at the base of Heartbreak Hill, in third when he crested the peak, and first at the finish line. Two years later, he again waited for this moment to dominate his competitors, claiming the lead at the thirty-five-kilometer mark and never looking back.

Mile 22 was the site of a bizarre episode in 1901. Ronald MacDonald—local hero, past champion, and Boston College student—was running with the leaders past the Chestnut Hill Reservoir when he took ill. Subsequently, the runner was handed a solution of unknown ingredients causing him to collapse, ending his dream of capturing his second laurel wreath. Some witnesses claimed that a certain Dr. Thompson had given him stimulants, which had an effect other than the one intended. Dr. Thompson disputed this account and claimed someone had intentionally handed MacDonald a sponge saturated with chloroform. "It couldn't well have been an accident," Thompson said, "when there was so much money up on the race."

MacDonald himself claimed that a soldier assigned to assist him during the race had handed him a sponge soaked with the contents of a mysterious canteen. After sucking the sponge dry, he said, he fell to the ground with his throat burning from the unknown fluid. MacDonald further claimed that Dr. Thompson gave him two strychnine pills to counteract the sponge, thus saving his life. Upon hearing this explanation, Herbert Holton of the B.A.A. called the story "an excuse of a crybaby who was trying to cover up the disgrace of letting down the number of American bettors who had put their trust in him."

A similar incident occurred in 1923, though with a different outcome. Albert Michelson apparently made a deal with the devil when he was handed a flask at the Lake Street intersection by an attendant who had ridden next to him on a bike throughout the race. The flask was reported in *The Boston Globe* to contain peppermint water and a pill of "unknown purpose." The spark he received from the remedy allowed the elite runner to capture fourth place.

1922 Leader James Henigan's legs began to tighten as he made his way down the hill at Boston College. Approaching the Lake Street intersection, his worsening legs forced him to stop. In an effort to restart his engine, Henigan grabbed a yardstick from a fan and beat it against his legs, with few results other than red welts. Henigan was forced to drop out of the race, while Clarence DeMar raced on to victory.

1936 Two-time champion John "Elder" Kelley fell victim to what he would later call the "Haunted Mile" in the year following his first victory. After chasing leader Tarzan Brown through the hills, Kelley finally drew even with the fading leader on the downhill. As he passed Brown, Kelley made the mistake of tapping the reined-in leader on the shoulder and saying, "Nice try kid. I'll take it from here."

Kelley's ill-advised bravado backfired, as Brown powered forward all the way to the winner's podium, leaving Kelley alone to feast on humble pie with his post-race beef stew.

1942 Massachusetts Governor Maurice Tobin followed his favorite runner, Fred McGlone (the "Galloping Golfer") in his car. McGlone slowed after passing St. Ignatius, causing the Honorable Governor to disembark and minister to the faltering runner with water. (Apparently the governor felt his office entitled him to affect the race's outcome.) As the governor reentered his car, the car door was accidentally slammed on his hand, bringing him to his knees.

For the first half of the mile, I attempted to converse with Kevin to distract myself from the pain. The downhill was pulverizing my injured left knee, so my sentences came out as fragments. Kevin politely helped finish my thoughts and added small talk. My head was beginning to droop like a sunflower in need of water—the constant pounding on pavement had gradually weakened my back, making it incapable of holding my head upright. I was now falling apart quickly. I was at a loss to say how I was going to cover the last five miles, unless I was lying down in the back of an ambulance.

The haunted mile, or Graveyard of Champions, proved its might to me. The course seemed like a boxer landing a variety of punches in a devastating combination: The alternating uphills and downhills were like jabs, hooks and haymakers. Little by little, the course chipped away at every inch of my being, physical and mental.

MILE 23

Uta Pippig: "I look forward to the right turn which moves you down to Cleveland Circle. If you let yourself go just a little bit, and don't push too hard, you can really fly."

– – – –

At the beginning of Mile 23, the runners are treated to a downhill that would be rated Black Diamond if this were a ski resort. After a right turn from Commonwealth Avenue onto Chestnut Hill Street, the runners descend eighty feet closer to sea level as they move past a public pool and skating rink on their right, and the former location of the Bill Rodgers Running Center on their left.

In 1981 Toshihiko Seko used this spot to throw a surge on his competitors: Spotting his old adversary's store, he pushed past Craig Virgin all the way to victory. Later he found great irony in the fact that, en route to breaking Rodgers's course record, he had made his critical move in front of Rodgers's store. The trolley tracks protrude down the middle of the road here, as in Framingham, and must be negotiated with care. The tracks lead the runners down into the gauntlet known as Cleveland Circle.

1971 Sara Mae Berman, unofficial winner of the women's marathon in 1969 and 1970, was passed by Nina Kuscsik near Cleveland Circle. Having lost the lead for the first time, Sara Mae said to herself, "I'm not going to let anyone beat me." Later she recalled: "Seeing her run by was like a kick

RUNNING THE GREATEST DUEL IN THE HISTORY OF THE BOSTON MARATHON, DICK BEARDS-
LEY, FRONT, AND ALEBERTO SALAZAR BATTLE EACH OTHER, THE CROWD, A MOUNTED POLICE-
MAN, AND A NUMBER OF POLICE MOTORCYCLCLES IN 1982. PHOTO COURTESY OF ROBERT
MAHONEY.

in the pants. I knew that there was another level that I could push myself to, and I did it." Berman regained the lead and won the race. Nina Kuscsik won the first officially recognized women's race in 1972.

1981 Elite female runner Patti Catalano was sideswiped by a police horse as she attempted to make her way through Cleveland Circle. Somehow she was able to keep her balance

and finish the race with an American record time of 2:27:51 while finishing second to New Zealander Allison Roe.

The Cleveland Circle five-way intersection is filled with inebriated college students, loose pavement, train tracks, and a sharp left turn onto Beacon Street at the base of the hill. All of those factors make the Circle an ideal location for the spectators and a nightmare for the runners. The sensory overload of the Circle can be overwhelming to the weary runners, who must descend, navigate, and turn all at the same time. It is not unusual for competitors to become disoriented by the mayhem in this multi-branch intersection. In 1976 Jack Fultz turned prematurely onto the wrong side of the road; fortunately a fan yelled at him that he was on the wrong side of Beacon Street. Jack made a ninety-degree turn, worked his way over the train tracks to the eastbound side, and headed off to victory.

The chaos is only magnified for the wheelchair competitors, who may come down the hill at speeds close to thirty-five miles per hour. It is recommended that the racers start braking early so that they can safely cross the raised and sometimes slippery tracks, while at the same time making a left turn. But it's difficult to convince world-class competitors in the middle of a world-class event to slow down for safety's sake. Thus the Circle has claimed many victims, including the leader in the 1980 race, George Murray, who caught his wheel as he attempted to cross the tracks. He worked feverishly to free the tire, but he was unable to repair the damaged wheel in time to hold the lead.

Seventeen years later, the tracks again reached up and changed the outcome of the race. In 1997, Jean Driscoll was in the midst of her run to become the most decorated champion in Boston Marathon history. Locked in one of their classic head-to-head duels, Driscoll and Australian Louise Sauvage raced down the hill into Cleveland Circle, where Driscoll caught a wheel on an exposed track, sending her to the ground with a flat tire and sending Sauvage on to the podium. On that day, Driscoll lost her chance for her eighth laurel wreath but paid the course its due respect after the race: "I had a great race until I met Cleveland Circle."

One year later the two competitors would wage yet another battle. As they approached the fateful tracks together, Louise suggested to her contemporary, "Take it easy here." After crossing over the tracks safely, Sauvage then offered, "Let's go!" Over the next miles, Driscoll built up a significant lead, only to have Sauvage come from behind and heroically beat her at the tape. Both racers recorded the same time, 1:41:19. One year later, in 2000, Jean finally won her record-setting eighth championship before retiring.

The Cleveland Circle area is strictly commercial. Storeowners can pay landlords upward of $40 per square foot for the honor of running a business here. Of course, the college students who frequent the two drinking establishments in the Circle, the famous Maryanne's and City-side, are more interested in the price of a Bud than the owners' overhead. The Cityside is located on the left side of the Circle, with rooftop seating giving patrons a great view and employees a lot of headaches. The manager of the bar describes the profits from Marathon Day as "blood money." He explains: "With two policemen working the door and diners milking their outside table on the roof, the day can be more trouble than the money is worth." But as Mayor Mann of Newton might say, the Cityside has a moral obligation to quench the thirst of those parched spectators.

On the right side of the route after the turn, Maryanne's is hopping as always with shoulder-to-shoulder co-eds from Boston College and cold beers on ice. The manager of Maryanne's (previously known as the Jungle) described the scene at his establishment as a "madhouse."

Many spectators move in and out of the establishments throughout the day as they enjoy the atmosphere of the race. One such fan did more than just enjoy the atmosphere in 1979. Caught up in the excitement of the moment, a well-meaning spectator left the side of the road and fell in next to leader Joan Benoit as she passed through the Circle. In one hand he had a beer, in the other a Red Sox cap. As he ran alongside Benoit, he offered her the following choice: "Either wear the hat or chug the beer." The Maine native chose the hat, which she wore in the closing miles of her victory.

Past the Circle, the course moves to the right side of Beacon Street. If you're in the back of the pack, the temperatures will have dropped significantly by the time you swing onto this thoroughfare into Boston.

Heading east now toward the Atlantic Ocean, the competitors may well be running into the face of a chilly sea breeze rushing down the street from Boston. This road is also split down the middle by the Green Line tracks. These tracks carry the C train at a very deliberate pace. A runner who throws in the towel here and jumps on the train will soon realize that he or she probably would have arrived in Boston faster by running. A local writer once quipped, "A person tied to the Green Line tracks was found dead—he starved to death."

The route works its way straight up Beacon Street with a slight incline. This area is a mix of apartment buildings and businesses. In the first quarter of the mile, the course moves into the seventh municipality of the route, Brookline. Continuing down Beacon Street, many runners realize just how much their pace has slowed when they notice that they are no longer gaining much on competitors who are walking.

> Situated over seven square acres, Brookline is home to 57,107 people who earn just over $87,000 per family and must pay a median house price of $725,000 for the honor of living in this town bordering on the city of Boston.
>
> Not incorporated until 1705, the village known as the "Hamlet of the Muddy River" had to petition the city of Boston in order to win its own identity. After much dispute, the villagers' request was granted, and the new town's boundaries were made to follow the natural line drawn by the Smelt Brook. The waterway (and border) ran through a 350-acre farm owned by the infamous Judge Samuel Sewall, who had inherited the property from his wife. Sewall was the judge who sentenced the Salem witches to death in 1692.

For runners who have something left, this stretch is a prime opportunity. Kathy Switzer found this scenario ideal. "When you are finishing strong, you can pick off as many as a hundred people in a very short distance. The people who are struggling seem like they are going backwards, while you feel like the course is coming to you."

Accompanied by the Green Line on their right, the 1996 leaders take another step toward the finish line in Boston. Photo courtesy of Victah Sailer.

In 1968, Amby Burfoot ran down Beacon Street with the lead and a side cramp, assuming that he would soon be reeled in by his pursuers (as he fought the stitch, Burfoot thought he was slowing down substantially). He didn't care to look over his shoulder because he feared the entire marathon field was closing on him. Burfoot spent the greatest five miles of his life in a state of panic, waiting to be passed. Finally, just yards from the finish line, he turned and, to his great relief, no one was there. He went on to win the race.

Up an incline and down the other side, the runners move toward the end of the mile near the Washington Street intersection, where the crowds continue to pull them forward. Uta Pippig found the crowds here to be very well informed: "Running down Beacon Street is pretty cool. The people are so knowledgeable about the race and the sport. Many of them have radios and are aware of who is leading and are ready for the leaders as they pass."

On the corner is the Hammond Bar. One year, bartender and part-owner Don Connors was amazed to look up from the taps to find a runner dressed as Kermit the Frog who had bypassed the water stops for a cold draft. Donny obliged and sent the runner away a satisfied Muppet.

The runners are now just a short distance from Coolidge Corner, which is about two miles from the finish.

1948 Running stride for stride throughout the race, leaders Gerard Cote and Ted Vogel waged a duel that almost turned into a street brawl. Cote, a four-time champion from Canada who was also a great snowshoe racer, had spent a significant amount of energy attempting to distract Vogel from his game plan. Cote started by stepping on the back of Vogel's sneakers early in the race. On the Newton Hills, Cote continuously cut in front of Vogel in an attempt to break his stride. After coming down the hills, Cote took a glass of water and tossed it over his head, hitting Vogel and sending him over the edge. Finally, after passing through Cleveland Circle, Vogel ran up along Cote and offered the Canadian runner the opportunity to settle their problem in the middle of Beacon Street. Cote ignored the offer and ran onto victory.

— — — —

Despite the fact that Boston was drawing closer, I ran down Beacon Street engulfed in pain and pessimism. By now, I couldn't hold my head up at all, forcing me to rely on my brother to be my eyes. As I ran with my chin fixed to my chest and my vision locked on the pavement below, my brother would give me radar alerts of any walkers on the road ahead. My attempts at drinking were futile: Gatorade or water hit the back of my mouth and came right back out. The sea breeze was picking up, and the temperature seemed to have dropped by at least ten degrees. Mylar blankets, given to the runners on the course, were blowing in the wind and snapping me in the face.

As the elements swirled around me, and Kevin vigilantly inquired about my condition, my mind started to wander, almost as if it wanted to distance itself from my pathetic physical state. I would later find out that disorientation, and even out-of-body experiences of some degree, are not uncommon among marathoners in the last miles. Even elite runners sometimes find themselves running on automatic pilot while their mind vacates the premises. In 1976, Jack Fultz suffered through this condition. With temperatures exceeding 90 degrees, he felt giddy as he soldiered down Beacon Street. First he started to giggle when he realized that he had a shot at achieving his greatest dream. Next, he found himself watching himself run from above, like a sports commentator analyzing his run. Finally, Fultz caught himself rehearsing answers for the post-race press conference. He later explained, "If I was going to win it"—which he did—"I didn't want to be full of clichés and one-liners. I wanted to sound intelligent."

My delirium also came on Beacon Street. In my vision, I traveled back to a blizzard that hit Boston in mid-February. The winter before the race was the worst Boston winter of the century, with over 100 inches of snow. As a result, I was often forced to run in blizzard conditions in order to stay on pace to run in April. My regular route was often impassable due to snowbanks and slippery streets, so I would run around my block over and over, like a gerbil in a wheel. With visibility virtually nil, I ran with my eyes set on the ground directly in front of me, placing each step with care. On each lap I would follow my footprints from the previous lap. If I lost sight of the tracks, it meant I had wandered off the sidewalk into the street and was in jeopardy of being crushed by a snowplow.

Now, some two months later, I again found myself staring at the ground, blindly following the footprints laid by Clarence DeMar, William Kennedy, John McDermott, Roberta Gibb, and hundreds of thousands of others who sought private glory in the streets that lead to Boston.

205

MILE 24

Uta Pippig: "For the first time in the race, you can feel the closeness of the finish line."

— — — —

With the shadows of Boston's skyscrapers drawing nearer, the runners move through Cleveland Circle and down Beacon Street. Riding up and down small inclines and declines that rise and fall like waves, the runners are led into Coolidge Corner, which sits on a plateau following a slight uphill.

Commercial businesses, apartments, and condo-ized buildings surround the Coolidge Corner area. Commercial space can cost upwards of $35 per square foot. A two-bedroom condo sells for approximately $350,000, and apartments rent for more than $1,800 a month—plus $125 a month more for a parking spot. Despite the prices, Coolidge Corner is a melting pot. Visitors here are exposed to a great diversity of religions, cultures, and lifestyles. This is reflected in the variety of delicatessens, movie theaters, and ethnic specialty shops.

Coolidge Corner was named after a local storeowner, David Sullivan Coolidge. His general store, which was named Coolidge & Bros, was located on the corner of Harvard and Beacon Streets, a major throughway from the city to the country. In 1888 the street was widened to 200 feet at the Corner to accommodate an electric train, at the time the longest continuous electric train route in the world.

The aristocrats of Brookline, who could afford to arrange their own transportation, had long been opponents of the train. Said one blue blood: "Unpleasant mechanism of unproven worth. Vulgar common

MAKING THEIR WAY DOWN BEACON STREET, FRIENDS MICHAEL RADLEY AND RICH TWOMBLY
MOVE YET ANOTHER STEP CLOSER TO THE FINISH LINE. PHOTO COURTESY OF CAITLIN RADLEY.

carrier." One wonders whether those aristocrats of Coolidge Corner
would have turned up their noses at their latter-day neighbor John Fitzger-
ald Kennedy, who introduced the world to space travel 80 years later.

After the runners work their way by the Corner at the intersection of
Harvard and Beacon, the course moves downhill toward the end of the

mile. In the early years of the race, the affluent inhabitants of the Coolidge Corner brownstones used to sit in their windows and acknowledge the runners by waving lacy handkerchiefs. Not to be outdone by the upper class, laborers working on these urban estates used to take time from their honest day's work to cheer their favorite runner—William "Bricklayer Bill" Kennedy.

Kennedy, in fact a bricklayer, won the 1917 race and was a consistent top-ten finisher during the 1920s. In the midst of his championship run, Kennedy was overcome by emotion as he ran through Coolidge Corner and was saluted by his brothers-in-trade, who took a quick break from their toil in order to clap their bricks together in an appropriate salute.

Kennedy was applauded not only for his championship run but also for his pre-race call to arms. With the "war to end all wars" being waged across the sea, Kennedy urged all American runners to run the race of their lives. This, he said, would prove to the whole world that Americans were superior in every branch of life. With a handkerchief embroidered with a miniature American flag draped across his head, Kennedy went on to win the marathon in a victory that one official called, "the greatest athletic victory of this country and of any country."

Falling just over two miles from the finish line, the crowds and chaotic atmosphere of Coolidge Corner have made this point an important benchmark in the race and also an obstacle that must be survived. At times, runners have been forced to run single file through the onslaught of well-wishers. Greg Meyer compared the zeal of the populace to a hungry reptile. As he ran toward his championship in 1983, the crowds from each side of the street seemed to meet in the middle of the road. When he approached them, he recalled, "they seemed to open up in front of me like a snake eating." As passed through, he realized he could no longer see the competitors behind him because "the crowd reunited like a snake swallowing."

For many runners this wild environment can be frustrating. As far back as 1920, lead runner Clarence DeMar fell victim to the craziness when a car drove over his foot at Coolidge Corner, ripping open his shoe. Others feed off the passion of the masses, as Gayle Barron did during her run to the wreath in 1978. "Back when I won the race, the marathon was a personal event between the runners and the fans. I ran the last miles in 1978 on a route with just enough space for one runner to squeeze through. Every step had a fan, on each side, just inches from my ear yelling encouragement."

While the fans of Coolidge Corner may inadvertently pose a danger, Bill Rodgers faced a deliberate threat in 1980: Just days before the race Rodgers was the target of a death threat. In the weeks prior to the marathon, Bill Rodgers had publicly castigated President Jimmy Carter for his decision to boycott the 1980 Olympics in Moscow, which was taken to protest the Russians' invasion of Afghanistan. Rodgers, who had been a conscientious objector during the Vietnam War, announced that he would advertise his position by wearing a black armband during his run in the 1980 Boston Marathon, drawing the ire of many who felt that he was tainting the race by using it as his personal political forum.

While most voiced their displeasure through normal channels, one "patriot" called the Bill Rodgers Running Center days before the race vowing that Rodgers would never run through Coolidge Corner alive. The threat was taken seriously, but there was only so much the police could do when more than a million people were waiting to see Rodgers run along a twenty-six-mile course.

Rodgers ran the race, won the race, and survived. He didn't wear the black armband and apparently moved quickly enough to avoid any would-be assassins. But he had a tough time staying focused with the yelling of the boobirds and the fists that were shaken in his face.

At the end of the mile, the runners move past Coolidge Corner and down a hill with the Holiday Inn on their left. One year hotel workers threatened to blockade the race route to protest what they felt were deficient benefits. When Tommy Leonard of the Eliot Lounge heard of the planned demonstration he remarked, "Stopping the marathon is like shooting the Easter Bunny." Within a day of the marathon, the hotel is fully booked for the following year's race.

1898 Running through Coolidge Corner with a substantial lead, Larry Brignolia slipped on a rock and twisted his ankle. As he attempted to get up, medics held him down for five minutes to make sure he was capable of continuing the race. The delay cost Brignolia the world record and nearly cost him the race—popular Harvard runner Dick Grant closed in on Brignolia but never passed him.

1919 At the starting line, Chicago runner Frank Gillespie tried on his new sneakers for the first time. Discovering that they were too tight, he cut a slit in the front of each, exposing the five toes of each foot. Incredibly, he ran into Coolidge Corner with the lead, but was eventually forced to slow down with blisters and cuts, allowing three other runners to overtake him.

1963 Running past Coolidge Corner, Aurel Vandendriessche of Belgium passed Ethiopian runner Abebe Bikila for good. Bikila was an international star after winning the 1960 Olympic Marathon in Rome in his bare feet. Four years later he repeated his Olympic victory, this time with sneakers.

— — — —

By the time my brother and I made it through Coolidge Corner, it was close to 4:30 P.M. I had been running for four hours and only had two and a half miles to go. For the first time since the six-mile mark, I started to think that I had a *chance* of finishing.

Although the crowd had thinned by this point in the late afternoon, there were still plenty of spectators cheering us on. I wondered whether I looked as bad as I felt. Suffering from a bout of paranoia, I listened intently for any disparaging comments in the crowd that might have confirmed my misery—even though I couldn't pick my head up to see the onlookers.

Instead from the side of the road, I heard someone yell. "Hey it's Michael Connelly—All right!" I moved my head to the side just enough to spot Joe and Kevin Radley, the brothers of Michael and Jack. Joe held a video camera as he yelled. Although it was great to hear the bighearted cheer, it was too late in the race to improve my spirits. I wondered if the other guys had passed and hoped they had. The thought provided some extra motivation to push on. I didn't want to be the only one of the four who didn't conquer the Boston Marathon.

By this point Pat Williams keeps saying to himself, "Just get me to Boston."

MILE 25

Three-time winner Sara Mae Berman: "Citgo Hill feels like Mt. Washington. When you get to the base of the hill and look up, your body tells you that it doesn't want to go."

— — — —

After Coolidge Corner the runners are still escorted by the C train, which runs along their left. Halfway through the mile, the train goes underground, and the runners are left to their own means to find the finish line. On the left side of the submerging train sits the local Irish pub, O'Leary's. The owner, Aengus O'Leary, is used to his steady customers throwing down a cold one and zipping out to see the leaders run by. He's also accustomed to having runners stop by the bar for some late carbo-loading. One year he had two Irish priests running the race pull up a couple of stools and fuel up for the last mile and a bit, compliments of a properly poured Guinness. The owner had one thing to say about the state of their condition: "They were thirsty."

1915 Leader Clifton Horne was beginning to sway back and forth as his lead faded. Attendants raced to a local store and bought two raw eggs for Horne, who reluctantly consumed them. He eventually lost the lead but finished second.

The twenty-fifth mile, which starts on a downhill, flattens out for about a quarter of the mile. With less than two miles to go, the runners finally enter the city limits of Boston.

Boston was founded in 1630 and named after Saint Botolph, a town in Lincolnshire, England. It had previously been known by the name of "Shawmut," the Native American word for "living waters." The city was originally dominated by three hills with water on three sides. The hills were eventually scaled down and used as landfill to create the Back Bay and Copley Square out of the Charles River marsh.

Boston was the site of many important events in American history, including the Boston Massacre, the Boston Tea Party, and the Battle of Bunker Hill. In the first half of the nineteenth century, Boston was a center of the abolition movement, and many runaway slaves headed to Boston for refuge. The first all-black regiment, the 54th Massachusetts, came from Boston and fought valiantly during the Civil War.

Boston has always been known for its prominent citizens and affluent families, including Benjamin Franklin, Samuel Adams, the Cabots, Lodges, and Saltonstalls, all of whom figured in the molding of this international city. Luckily for them, they didn't live long enough to have to commute through the Big Dig.

Today Boston is one of the world's greatest college towns and the largest city in New England, with a population of almost 600,000 people spread across an area of ninety acres. The present mayor of Boston, Thomas Menino, looks forward each year to the running of the Boston Marathon: "No tradition quite captures the spirit of Boston like the Boston Marathon. Boston is a world-class city, yet it's also a city of neighborhoods. As runners from all over the world run through the city's streets, spectators from all over rally together to welcome them and spur them on. It's incredible to me how, year after year, the Boston Marathon brings people together like that. The crowds aren't rooting for anyone in particular—they're rooting for everyone. Because on marathon day, everyone is a Bostonian!"

1981 As Ron Hill ran in the final miles of the race, he spied Canadian runner Jerome Drayton, who had stopped running and was sitting by the side of the course. Hill offered him some advice: "Get up and walk if you have to. But finish the damn race!"

Now the runners move through an open intersection at Park and Beacon Streets only to be confronted by the sometimes unexpected and never welcome obstacle called "Citgo Hill." This unpleasant bump in the course takes its name from the large neon sign advertising Citgo Fuel that shines high in Kenmore Square up ahead. The Citgo sign has dominated Kenmore Square since 1965. Shut down during the energy crisis in the early 1970s, it was soon relit and eventually listed as a historical landmark.

Citgo Hill comes at a bad time on the course and has a surprisingly negative effect on the athletes. At this point, most runners are beginning to shut down. Peripheral vision narrows to about two yards on either side, and the runners' hearing may be greatly impaired. That out-of-body experience is starting to sound good. This one last incline rises for a grueling two hundred yards, giving the fresher runners an opportunity and the worn runners an excuse.

Two-time winner Geoff Smith covered this final hill in contrasting states during his consecutive championships. "In 1984, I didn't even know it was there. I felt great at the time, and just breezed over it. In 1985, when I struggled to make it to the finish line with cramps, I was shocked to find this hill in the middle of Mile 25. I wondered if it was always there, or if it was new."

In 1996 the hill was the site of a dramatic turn in the race. It was at this protrusion that thirty-year-old Uta Pippig of Germany chose to stage one of the most courageous comeback victories in Boston Marathon history. Battling cramps and multiple internal ailments, Pippig was chasing Tegla Loroupe from Kenya as they approached the hill. As she closed in on the front-runner, Pippig ran to the side of the road and grabbed a water bottle. She returned to the middle of the route, ripped the top of the container off with her teeth, slugged the water, spiked the bottle down on the ground, and then proceeded to pass Loroupe for good on her way to her third straight Boston Marathon victory.

"Four different times during the race, the pain was so bad that I contemplated dropping out of the race all together." Pippig recounted, "Somehow I kept going and pushed myself. As I approached Citgo Hill, I saw Tegla up ahead and I said to myself, 'Come on Uta, this is your chance!' Somehow I caught her. I don't know how I did it. I replay that part of the race in my mind and I still can't explain how I did it. I guess I won't figure it out until I run the race again and pass that spot. In retrospect I would say this was my greatest victory with respect to overcoming mental and physical adversity."

— — — —

To me Citgo Hill, like Heartbreak Hill, wasn't any harder than any other step on the course. Every step was an effort now. When I reached the hill's peak, I was no more confident than I had been at the bottom. Surprisingly, my mind filled with negative thoughts as I approached the end of the mile. Instead of thinking "Just one mile to go!" I was consumed with the thought that one more mile equaled to four trips around my high school football field. The same distance had defeated me just seven months before the race.

But despite the cloud of negativity that darkened my psyche, I moved forward—not by intention but through a sheer will that seemed beyond my control, as if the end of this warped journey had already been determined. I ran with purpose and pain, knowing that every step brought me closer to Kenmore Square, which would in turn get me closer to the finish line.

Thankfully, three quarters of the way through the mile, I was granted the blessing of distraction. Situated on the right side of Citgo Hill is the world's most magical athletic arena: Fenway Park. As a lifelong Red Sox fan, it was impossible for me to pass this temple of baseball and not be overcome by passion.

Since 1918, Fenway Park has been the home of the team that is guilty of more improbable, impossible, and incredible moments of futility than

WITH THE CITGO FUEL SIGN IN THE BACKGROUND, RUNNERS STRUGGLE UP THE LAST REAL TOPOGRAPHICAL CHALLENGE OF THE RACE. PHOTO COURTESY OF FAYFOTO.

any club in the history of team sports. From Bucky Dent's three-run home run in 1978, to Bill Lee's misconceived pitch to Tony Perez in 1975, to the sale of Babe Ruth to the Yankees, the Red Sox have annually provoked cries of "Wait till next year!" from generations of New Englanders. Being a Red Sox fan is like being the victim in an abusive relationship: Oblivious to the inevitable pain, we return to the scene of the crime each year in hopes of an aberration. Like mice lured into a

216

cheese-filled trap, we pour into this green edifice by the millions, year after year, in the hope that one day the trap won't slam shut on us.

So as I ran over Citgo Hill, embattled in my love-hate relationship with the Sox, I suddenly realized that the Fenway was sliding out of my field of vision, meaning the last quarter of the mile was complete. Finally my affiliation with that team had had a positive effect on my life.

Up ahead in Kenmore Square the crowds will gather ten deep, filled with furloughed fans from the annual Patriot's Day Red Sox game, which started at 11:00 A.M. It's not uncommon for the baseball players to hustle out to the route in order to marvel at their fellow athletes.

In the days of Clarence DeMar, the Boston Braves (now the Atlanta Braves) and the Red Sox used to take turns hosting doubleheaders on Marathon Day. The first game was played in the morning, followed by a break so that the fans and players could watch the race. The second game was played later in the afternoon.

Today I'll need all 33,000 fans of Red Sox Nation to pull me through Kenmore Square.

MILE 26

Craig Virgin, world-class marathoner, on the run through Kenmore Square: "The crowd can suffocate you here and make you become claustrophobic."

— — — —

Halfway over the bridge at Citgo Hill, which runs over train tracks and the Mass Turnpike, the runners pass into the last full mile of the race. Those who have survived to this point begin to curse King Edward VII of England, who ordered the race to be lengthened (from twenty-four-and-one-half miles to twenty-six miles, three hundred and eighty-five yards) so that the 1908 Olympic Marathon would end in front of his royal box. The King could not have foreseen, almost a century ago, the ramifications of his decision. For decades runners have suffered the consequences his selfish proclamation.

Like a battered boxer forced to go extra rounds, the runners now have to traverse the last mile-plus with the burden of bankrupt legs and weakened resolve. The downhill into Kenmore Square is the last real chance for this sadistic course to wreak havoc on those who challenge her. Runners who wrote checks on the hills of Newton are paying dearly now.

No race better illustrates the consequences of running hard early than on John "Elder" Kelley's run for the wreath in 1935. When Kelley entered Kenmore Square he had a five-hundred-yard lead over Pat Dengis. Kelley, who had gobbled chocolate glucose pills along the route, had been struggling with his stomach ever since Coolidge Corner. As he made his way over Citgo Hill, his intestinal pains brought him to an abrupt halt—

Morrison

Jas Henigan

Leading Boston aa marathon led for 16 miles

the press car had to slam on its brakes to avoid hitting the now-stationary runner.

With Kelley bent over at the waist in pain, the crowd urged on the hometown favorite. Kelley unfolded himself and ran two steps before stopping again, sending the crowd into a frenzy. Behind him, Pat Dengis was closing the gap: Kelley had to move or lose. According to the following day's *Boston Globe*, a desperate Kelley applied the "Roman Cure," sticking his fingers down his throat to relieve himself. The trick worked,

With Kenmore Square in the foreground and Boston's skyline in the background, runners are relieved to hear the crowd yell "One more mile!" Photo courtesy of the Boston Athletic Association.

and Kelley ran on to the first of two championships. Later he said, "I overdosed on glucose pills."

Like Kelley, most runners plunge into Kenmore Square in some form of mental or physical free fall. By this stage the legs may no longer have the ability to brake; many runners let gravity throw their bodies down the hill, praying they regain their balance without crashing. Glycogen is a distant memory, and the fuel light is on.

When the course finally leads the runners into Kenmore Square at the end of Beacon Street, the athletes arrive back on Commonwealth Avenue, the home of the hills. The route continues, on a level grade, through the square just a mile from the finish line. Years ago, when beef stew was served at the finish line (to a far smaller field), the runners probably began to salivate here, as they could almost smell the finish. In truth, by this point in the race, most runners are more interested in finishing than eating.

Kenmore Square has long been compared to Times Square in New York City because of the intersecting streets (Beacon, Commonwealth, and Brookline) and the odd angles they make. Like Times Square, this location is ideal for billboard advertisements. Best known for its proximity to Fenway Park and the Boston Red Sox, Kenmore Square is also a bustling gathering spot for the thousands of downtown college students from Boston University and the colleges Simmons, Emmanuel, and Wheelock. It was once known as Governor Square and was the center of Boston's hotel district: Hotels such as the Somerset, Braemore, Sheraton, Buckminster, and Kenmore all stood here, only to give way to condominiums, nightclubs, and Boston University dormitories. The square takes its modern name from the Green Line train stop set in the middle. Thronged with students lugging schoolbooks, girls with purple hair, and commuters hustling to the T, Kenmore Square is a distinctive section of the marathon and the city.

1931 As local favorite Jim Henigan ran through Mile 25, his oldest son saw him and reported to other family members who were gathered in Kenmore Square, "Pa's in front, but gosh he's going awfully slow." After Henigan slowed to a walk, a fan, alarmed by his poor appearance, showered

the runner with cold water from a milk bottle. The press vehicle, which usually sped ahead of the runners to the finish
line, decided to hover around the leader in the hope of capturing his inevitable collapse on film. Henigan, who had
dropped out of his first seven races, eventually made his
way to the finish line to break the tape and ruin the hopes
of the sadistic photographers.

1936 A physically spent and mentally exhausted Tarzan
Brown entered Kenmore Square with the lead. As he attempted to navigate the square, he swerved left and right
drunkenly and was almost hit by a passing car. Brown
somehow regained enough strength to finish the race and
claim the championship.

1991 As Peter Zimmerman, the lead American runner,
worked his way into Boston, his sneaker began to fill with
blood from broken blisters. From Coolidge Corner through
Kenmore Square, he prayed for another American to pass
him so that he could drop out of the race. Zimmerman was
never passed by one of his countrymen, so he felt obligated
to continue on to the finish line, where he completed the race
in bloody sneakers in fourteenth place with a time of 2:15:32.

The bars in Kenmore Square, like bars all along the route, take advantage of Marathon Day to attract customers. The black-leather patrons of the bar the Rath Skelter are annually entertained by a band
called the Bristols comprised of beautiful young girls. ("They can play
too," says the manager.) Another Kenmore bar, Cornwall's Pub, hangs a
sign ROSIE RUIZ STARTED HERE in reference to the infamous "runner"
from New York who jumped into the 1980 race at Kenmore Square and
went on to record the third-fastest time in the history of the race, until
her ruse was uncovered.

Rosie Ruiz, who was born Maria Rosales in Havana, Cuba, before
resettling in New York City, chose "marathoning" as a vehicle to bring

ROBERTA GIBB RUNS THROUGH KENMORE SQUARE DURING HER LANDMARK FINISH IN 1966.
PHOTO COURTESY OF THE BOSTON ATHLETIC ASSOCIATION.

attention to herself. After obtaining fake New York City Marathon credentials through fraudulent means, she convinced her boss to pay her
way to Boston to run the famous marathon. Then she applied for and obtained an official number from the B.A.A.

In Hopkinton, she started the race with the other competitors only
to peel off the course soon after. She reentered the race just past Kenmore
Square and dashed to the finish line, crossing with a time of 2:31.

BILL RODGERS RUNS UP HEREFORD STREET TOWARD BOYLSTON STREET AND THE 1975 CHAMPIONSHIP. PHOTO COURTESY OF FAYPHOTO.

All along the course, people told Canadian runner Jacqueline Gareau that she was running in first. Even television commentator Kathy Switzer, who was following the women's race in a vehicle, yelled to Gareau close to the twenty-two-mile mark, "You're in the lead." When Gareau turned onto Boylston Street, just yards from her greatest moment, she was shocked to hear the announcer refer to her over the PA system as the second-place female runner.

224

But how could this be? No one had ever heard of Rosie Ruiz. Bill Rodgers asked her on the podium, "How are you? Who are you?" Rodgers later would say, "Think of the most famous marathon runners—Pheidippides and Rosie Ruiz—one dropped dead and the other was crazy."

Her scam was eventually exposed: Ruiz had not been spotted at any of the checkpoints, her shirt was almost dry at the finish, and her knowledge of running was elementary. At the press conference, Kathy Switzer, an analyst for a local television station that year, grilled her on topics such as intervals and training. Ruiz was vague and unresponsive. She was eventually stripped of the championship, but she refused to return the winner's medal.

Gareau, who had been cheated of her championship glory, flew in from Canada a week later and ran the final two hundred yards in a pair of jeans. Two hundred people cheered her on while Bill Rodgers held her arm up in victory. Later, she visited the Eliot Lounge where Tommy Leonard was ready for her with a bottle of Dom Perignon on ice and the Canadian flag flying solo over the bar. When she walked in, one of the bar patrons got on the piano and played "Oh Canada." Leonard later said, "There wasn't a dry eye in the house."

1961 John "Younger" Kelley continued his stretch of frustrating runs when three-time winner Eino Oksanen passed him for the lead as they ran past Charlesgate West. (Over his career, Kelley finished second five times and in the top ten no fewer than ten times. He won in 1957, becoming the only runner from the Boston Athletic Association ever to win the Boston Marathon.) Kelley was a favorite with the fans and the press, although his "close but no cigar" finishes frustrated the often temperamental Boston media. After one of Kelley's second-place finishes, the press ripped the Connecticut schoolteacher. Colin Heard of the *Boston Herald* wrote, "How stupid can a schoolteacher be?" John Gihooley, of the *Boston Herald* wrote, "If our schoolteachers are like that, it's no wonder our school system is in trouble."

THE CROWD BENDS IN AN APPROPRIATE QUESTION MARK TO ALLOW RUNNERS TO TURN FROM HEREFORD STREET ONTO BOYLSTON. PHOTO COURTESY FAYPHOTO.

After surviving Kenmore Square, the runners are greeted by the hysterical crowd in the Back Bay. Some line the streets, some hang out of apartment windows, and still others dangle from the rooftops of the connected condominiums. The athletes, who looked like kids on Christmas morning back at the starting line, now look more like deserters from the French Foreign Legion. The screams of "one more mile" are finally accurate.

226

The runners move past the intersection of Charlesgate West, under an overpass, and then past Charlesgate East, where a statue of the Norse explorer Leif Ericsson greets them and inspires them to finish their journey. Like the doughboy in Hopkinton, he faces away from the finish line.

1999 Forced to walk by constricting cramps, Matt Curtner-Smith heard a fan yell at him, "Number 3902, you're looking great." The runner responded with, "Oh really?" to which the fan replied, "No, I lied." Curtner-Smith immediately broke into a gallop all the way to the finish line.

After the statue the runners bear right at the fork and move past a small public park on their left. On the right stands the old Somerset Hotel and the Harvard Club. Here the members of the club used to cheer from a temporary grandstand set up in front of the brick home of Harvard alumni and faculty. Now they watch the race from inside on a big-screen television with the bar and grill open for the day.

Next door to the Harvard Club is the Eliot Hotel, the old home of the legendary (and now extinct) Eliot Lounge. This watering hole became famous in 1975 when a victorious Bill Rodgers told a national audience while being interviewed, "I'm going to the Eliot Lounge." I'm sure Tom Leonard made Rodgers his favorite Blue Whale drink. In 1996, the lounge was sadly closed. Crossing in front of the Eliot Hotel, the runners move over Massachusetts Avenue on their way toward the big right turn off Commonwealth Avenue.

1897 John McDermott, the winner of the first marathon, ran into a little more traffic than he expected at the intersection of Massachusetts Avenue and Commonwealth Avenue. With less than a mile to go, McDermott found himself running in front of a funeral procession and two trolleys, bringing all of them to a halt on his way to the finish line at the Irvington Oval, which hosted the finish for the first two years.

When McDermott entered the oval the crowd was still wild with excitement after the boys from Boston College

upset the favored Fordham College runners in the 100-yard
dash in the annual B.A.A. track and field handicap event. As
McDermott circled the oval, he was said to finish with the
speed and strength of a half-miler.

From 1897 to 1964, the competitors used to continue down Commonwealth Avenue and take a sharp right four blocks from Massachusetts Avenue onto Exeter Street. After the turn onto Exeter, the runners
proceeded straight up the street, passing over Newbury Street and then
through Boylston Street to the finish line, which was situated outside of
the B.A.A. clubhouse

1925 At the turn onto Exeter Street, leader Chuck Mellor
spat out his wad of tobacco, which he had been chewing
throughout the race, so he wouldn't have a protruding cheek
as he was pictured crossing the finishing line.

1939 Running up Exeter Street with the lead, the eccentric
and sometimes hard-to-explain Tarzan Brown stopped short,
took in the scene, looked around at the crowd, and then
moved on to the finish line.

By this juncture, the race is reaching its crescendo. Throughout the
day, the waiting fans have been updated on the race as they struggle to
hold on to their viewing positions. Stacked sometimes *thirty* deep,
these last-mile crowds are known for their intensity and fervor. During
the 1935 race, the excitement and jostling of the crowd overwhelmed
a seventy-five-year-old spectator named Edward Redman: He collapsed
with a heart attack, badly cutting his chin in the process. The Wellesley native was taken to a nearby hospital where he was nursed back to
health.

A hazardous crowd inevitably becomes a hazard for the runners. Sidewalks lined with spectators may become streets crowded with mobs. In
1901, runners lost vital minutes off their times after they were forced to
snake through the Exeter Street crowd. In 1905, eventual winner Fred

Lorz had to leap over a bike in the closing yards and then repeat the feat
at the finish line. While leaping for the line, he caught his foot and
crashed through the tape onto Exeter Street. Efforts to control the chaos
over the years have sometimes only added to it. In the tenth year of the
race, police almost ran over the leader, Tom Longboat, in their zeal to
control the crowd.

1942 Local favorite Fred McGlone collapsed to the ground
as he ran up Exeter Street in sixth place. To avoid being disqualified, he frantically waved away people who approached to help him. Finally a policeman who could no
longer stand the pathetic sight picked up McGlone and carried him across the finish line.

In 1965, the finish of the race was moved to the shadow of the brand-new fifty-story Prudential Center. On Easter Sunday of that year, the Prudential Center welcomed the public to an open house, and on Monday they welcomed the runners of the Boston Marathon. The new finish line on Boylston Street forced the B.A.A. to adjust the route in Hopkinton and at the turn from Commonwealth Avenue. The starting point was moved to the Ashland side of the town green in Hopkinton, and the finish line was now reached after taking a right turn onto Hereford Street from Commonwealth Avenue, one block up from Massachusetts Avenue and the old Eliot Lounge.

As with all the turns on the course, the runners must position themselves correctly here to "run the tangent" and make the turn in the least amount of distance. In 1971, Alvaro Mejia and Pat McMahon were running shoulder to shoulder around this corner when McMahon was sent bouncing into the crowd. Race Director Jock Semple swore that Mejia had elbowed the other runner off the course on his way to a five-second victory.

Past the corner, the runners proceed slightly uphill toward the intersection with Newbury Street. The sight of certain streets and landmarks provoked random thoughts in me throughout the race. As I passed over Newbury Street, I couldn't help noticing that business wasn't as usual. Normally the sidewalks here are filled with college kids with trust funds and the bourgeois of Boston with shopping bags, who come to Newbury Street to spend and to be seen 364 days of the year. I was grateful to be running and not driving, because parking is insane down here.

After crossing the intersection, the road takes an unexpected and nasty little climb. At the top of Hereford Street, the route turns left onto Boylston Street. Most runners have a difficult time negotiating the tight turn. Their spent legs force them to round off the corner on the far right side of the street. At this point, an uphill grade undetectable to the eye, but registered by the legs, leads you to the twenty-six-mile mark—385 yards from the finish line.

1987 In an effort to catch lead runner Toshihiko Seko, British runners Steve Jones and Geoff Smith teamed up in the last quarter of the race to close the gap. As they turned off

Hereford Street and onto Boylston Street, Seko was approaching the finish line. So the team of Jones and Smith shook hands and wished each other well in their battle for second place, which Jones won by five seconds.

The thrill of turning from Hereford Street onto Boylston Street was mind-boggling. For the first time since I stepped on the course in Hopkinton, I knew that I would conquer the route that had destroyed so many. For a century, hundreds of thousands of runners had lined up in Hopkinton with the dream of somehow defeating twenty-six miles, eight towns, multiple hills, and the madness of a vengeful course. Now I ran (albeit slowly) with the blue and yellow banner of the B.A.A. finish line in my sights. In minutes I would realize my dream.

The needle in the knee, the catheters in my heart, the countless ice bags—all had contributed to this moment. To be given this opportunity meant that God had deemed me worthy, for some reason, of his intercession. Over the last fifteen miles, I ran with his grace and with the love of friends and family.

I needed to run the closing yards to honor their commitment to my cause and me.

Ron Hill: "I wasn't certain of winning until I made the last turn. . . . This is a good fear—it keeps you moving."

385 YARDS

Dr. George Sheehan: "Everyone who finishes the Boston Marathon has their own great moment in sports. Each one of us, on this day, has achieved greatness."

— — — —

Three hundred and eighty-five yards—1,155 feet—13,860 inches—that's all that's left. The competitors move down Boylston Street past the Prudential Building and its fountain, where runners cool themselves on summer days. Continuing past the Boston skyscraper, the runners cross in front of the Lenox Hotel at the corner of the Exeter Street intersection.

The Lenox Hotel has long been associated with the Boston Marathon because of its proximity to the finish line. When the race finished outside of the B.A.A. clubhouse, the hotel's side door on Exeter Street was often prominently displayed in newspaper photos of the winners breaking the tape. The hotel has 214 rooms and throws a barbecue party on the rooftop for their top clients on race day.

On the left side of the route, bars are filled with fans or private parties. Local hot spots like Whiskey's are overflowing with race fans, while top steakhouse Abe and Louie's opens its doors for race sponsor Mercedes and their private party.

In 1986 the start and finish of the race were rearranged to accommodate the new sponsor of the race, John Hancock Financial Services. The starting line was moved back to the east side of the Hopkinton town green, while the finish was moved down Boylston Street about a quarter of a mile to the Boston Public Library.

GERARD COTE WINS ONE OF HIS FOUR BOSTON MARATHONS AS HE CROSSES THE FINISH LINE IN 1944. PHOTO COURTESY OF THE BOSTON PUBLIC LIBRARY PRINT DEPARTMENT.

The Boston Public Library opened in 1854 and was the first publicly supported library in the world, the first library to lend out books, and the first to open branch sites throughout the city.

Architect Charles Follen McKim based his design on the plans of a building in Paris, Henri Labrouste's Bibliotheque Ste. Genevieve, but the library was customized to fit in with the neighboring buildings: the Romanesque Trinity Church and the Italian Gothic Old South Church. In 1965, the library added the Johnson Building where the B.A.A. clubhouse once stood in the first third of the century.

The library acts as a depository for Massachusetts and regional federal government documents, United States government patents, and United Nations documents. It receives more than two million visitors a year and holds over six million books, three million government documents, and ten millions patents.

There is no greater finishing stretch in the marathoning world than the 385 yards of Boylston Street. It is here that dreams are realized and runners are rewarded with what eight-time champion Jean Driscoll describes as a goosebump-raising experience that causes all the stress of the journey to disappear: "It's a euphoric feeling whenever anyone achieves a goal, whether it's winning, beating a time, or just finishing the race."

No one would concur with that opinion more than Uta Pippig, who overcame a plethora of obstacles on the way to her third championship in 1996. As she ran down Boylston Street and into history, she turned to the crowd and shared the moment with screams of conquest. "Some people feel that I'm too emotional, but that's me," she says. "I feel a special connection with the people who line the streets to cheer, and I want to show these people who are sharing in the moment that I appreciate them and the race."

With one hundred yards to go, runners who are packed in among the masses may use the Old South Church Steeple behind the finish as a reference point. For the lead runners, the street is wide open, making the final yards an ideal stage for the dramas that sometimes occur when rivals reach the home stretch together. After twenty-six miles of racing, their fates will be determined by yards or feet or even inches. It almost seems unfair that a runner could fight the good fight and persevere against all the internal and external obstacles, only to lose the victory in the closing steps.

In 1906, eighteen-year-old Tim Ford, the youngest runner ever to win the race, broke the tape on Exeter Street only six seconds ahead of his challenger, David Kneeland, in the first dramatic duel in the marathon's history. (Clarence DeMar was the oldest competitor to break the tape when he ran to victory in 1930 at the age of forty-one, an amazing nineteen years after his first victory.)

In 1978, Bill Rodgers and Jeff Wells matched strides throughout the course while the pace car and press bus were trapped behind them, leaving the runners on their own to calculate their splits. In the end Rodgers won the classic battle by two seconds (with the pace car and press bus finishing sixth and seventh, respectively).

Nobody knows what motivates a great runner to push past the limits that stop the rest of humanity. Is it the heart or the mind or the body? Is it the prize money or the pride of accomplishment? Is the glory for the runner, or family, or country? The great champions have raced toward the finish line with a spirit not recognizable in mere mortals. In 1988 and again in 2000, runners from Kenya and Ethiopia staged breathtaking finishes. In 1988 Ibrahim Hussein beat Juma Ikangaa by one second for his first of three championships. In 2000, marathon fans were treated to a once-in-a-lifetime battle in both the men's and women's races. In the men's race, Kenyan Elijah Lagat nosed out Ethiopian Gezahenge Abera; both finished with a time of 2:09:47. Finishing three seconds behind in third place was Kenyan Moses Tanui. Soon the women took the stage, with the three leaders racing down Boylston together. When the dust settled, Katherine Ndereba of Kenya (2:26:11) had outkicked second-place finisher Irena Bogacheva of Kyrgyzstan (2:26:27) and Fatuma Roba of Ethiopia in third (2:26:27).

To participate in an event such as the Boston Marathon, to reach beyond his or her normal abilities, an athlete must have vision. To reach for the brass ring is difficult enough when it is simply personal. But for those runners who carry the hopes of an entire nation on their backs, the pressure to succeed is monumental. Most return home unsuccessful. Those who return with a laurel wreath from the Boston Marathon become national heroes.

In 1926, Johnny Miles returned with his parents to their home in Sydney Mines, Nova Scotia, after winning his first of two Boston Marathon championships. As he stepped off the train, he was taken from the station to the local hotel on the shoulders of the townspeople. Later he appeared on the balcony of his hotel room to greet the people.

Twenty years later, Stylianos Kyriakides, a citizen of Greece, ran to honor his people. Kyriakides, who a few years earlier had barely avoided being executed by the occupying Nazis, carried a handwritten note in each hand. He read the first note before the starter's gun was shot: "Do or die." Upon winning the 1946 race, he opened up his other fist and read the second note: "We are victorious."

Like Johnny Miles, Boston-area champions Johnny Kelley and Clarence DeMar also stirred up great feelings of pride upon their victories. In 1927, winner Clarence DeMar returned to his hometown of Melrose, Massachusetts, to find the bells in the town center in full chime. The town turned out to greet its hero and shake the hand of the man who put them on the map. (When he was through with the greetings, he went home and had supper with his mother. He then changed and went out and played a baseball game, two hours after finishing the race.)

Almost a decade later in 1935, winner John Kelley was driven to his parents' home in Arlington, Massachusetts, compliments of the local police forces, with sirens blaring. The fire station rang its bells thirty-nine times in recognition of Kelley's winning the thirty-ninth Boston Marathon.

— — — —

Twenty-six miles and 385 yards. The start in Hopkinton seems as though it took place weeks ago. The runners lived each yard one at a time. As each step was completed, it became a distant memory while each yard in front seemed to stretch farther away. The cold, the heat, the rain, the snow, the traffic, the spilled beers, the car fumes—all for this euphoric feeling of crossing a simple line. The runs in the morning, at lunch, in the dark, past the chasing dogs, the puddle-splashing cars, the cars that pull out onto the crosswalk, the cars that played chicken with you—all for this euphoric feeling of crossing a simple line.

Of course it's not a simple line. It's a mental and physical barrier that, when conquered, offers a feeling of exaltation that is incomparable. During my training runs and physical therapy sessions, I used to envision myself running down Boylston Street in an effort to convince myself that this all would be worth it. I wondered and dreamed how special the moment would be. The commitment and the agony would be worth it—every step, every bead of sweat, and every twinge of pain.

As I worked my way down Boylston Street, I was bewildered to find that the finish line was still so far away. I decided to keep my head down and just work each step. My brother, fighting hard to slow his pace to stay with me, started to get excited. "Pick them up and put 'em back down. You're doing it! You're gonna do it! Listen to the crowd—they're all yelling for you. Keep it going!"

With about a hundred yards to go and tears swelling in my eyes, a burst of wind hit me in the face, which almost knocked me over. As I continued toward the finish line, I realized that I was living the dream I had dreamed so often: I was running the last hundred yards of the Boston Marathon. It was one of those rare moments in life when dreams and reality become one.

As I crossed the finish line four and a half hours after leaping over the starting line, I pumped my fist in the air twice with the last bit of strength I had left, and then leaned on my brother. Kevin simply said, "You did it."

PART

III

REJOICE! WE CONQUER!

CROSSING THE LINE

Sara Mae Berman: "The wonderful thing about athletic achievement is that it is finite. There is no ambiguity. You did it and no one can ever take that away from you."

— — — —

"The race was a big success. There is assurance that this event will be an annual fixture." So announced a B.A.A. official after the 1897 running of the American Marathon of the Boston Athletic Association.

And it has been an annual fixture. For more than a century, runners have worked their way through Hopkinton, Ashland, Framingham, Natick, Wellesley, Newton, Boston, Brookline, and back into Boston in order to fulfill a dream held by runners throughout the world: to run Boston.

For those who have crossed the finish line, the accomplishment is both physically exhilarating and psychologically uplifting. A destiny has been found and a goal has been met. Although most runners go unheralded, their willingness to accept the challenge and conquer it is enough of a laurel wreath. For over a century, the competitors of the Boston Marathon have exemplified physical and mental strength. Their many acts of courage and feats of greatness continue to add to the allure of the world's greatest race. Their determination and bravado help to inspire others to reach for greatness.

1971 Eight-year-old Tom Bassler of Palace Verdes, California, ran twenty-six miles and finished the race alongside his father.

CHAMPION JOHN "ELDER" KELLY CROSSES THE FINISH LINE IN 1935. NOTE THAT OFFICIALS NEVER PUT THE TAPE UP AND THAT KELLY DROPPED HIS AUNT'S HANDKERCHIEF JUST YARDS BEFORE CROSSING THE LINE. PHOTO COURTESY OF THE BOSTON PUBLIC LIBRARY PRINT DEPARTMENT.

IN AN EFFORT THAT EXEMPLIFIES THE BATTLE OF THE BOSTON MARATHON, A 1992 COMPETITOR REFUSES TO BE DENIED. PHOTO COURTESY OF THE *BOSTON HERALD*/JIM MAHONEY.

1972 Sylvia Weiner ran the marathon in a time of 3:47. Throughout the struggle, she called upon her survival instincts to meet the challenge. Weiner had spent her youth trapped in the terror of a Nazi concentration camp. "I always wanted to live. I always had the will for it. Now I have victory."

1974 Dr. Hing Hua Chun of Honolulu, his wife Connie, and their six children—Jerry, Hinky, Daven, May Lee, June, and Joy—ranging in age from nine to fifteen, all ran and completed the twenty-six-mile journey to Boston.

1975 Bob Hall was the first wheelchair competitor recognized by the B.A.A. Race Director Will Cloney promised Hall that if he finished the race within three hours, he would be presented with a finisher's certificate. Hall's time was 2:58.

1980 After finishing her first marathon, 48-year-old Ruth Bortz called her four kids and told them not to wait until reaching her age to run a marathon, because once you conquer those twenty-six miles you realize you can do anything in life. In 2002 Ruth and her husband, Dr. Walter Bortz, became the first senior couple of 70 years to complete the Boston Marathon.

The goal is met. The satisfaction is eternal. For the average marathoner, the medal is the tangible confirmation of victory. A ribbon with its attached pendant provides the runner validation for the blood, sweat, and tears that have been shed in order to participate in this event. Each year after receiving his medal, Pat Williams ponders how a fifty-cent medal could be worth a million dollars.

1996 Swedish runner Humphrey Siesage died of a massive heat attack while crossing the finish line. His medal was sent to his family in Stockholm. Their sadness must be somewhat softened by the fact that their loved one died achieving his dream and what few humans ever accomplish.

While the average runner is ecstatic with his medal, elite runners are more appropriately rewarded for their superhuman skills. Up until 1986, the winners were presented with non-monetary symbols of victory. In 1986, the marathon joined the world of professional sports to assure that the finest runners would keep lining up in Hopkinton each year. The compromise was difficult but necessary. Since then the B.A.A. has awarded over $8 million in prize money, including $600,000 for the 100th running. For the 2002 edition, the purse was $525,000, allotted as follows:

WILL CLONEY, DIRECTOR OF THE BAA, IS DETERMINED NOT TO LET A COLLEGE PRANKSTER CROSS THE 1959 FINISH LINE. PHOTO COURTESY OF THE BOSTON PUBLIC LIBRARY PRINT DEPARTMENT.

	OPEN DIVISION MEN/WOMEN	MASTERS	WHEELCHAIR
1st place	$80,000	$10,000	$10,000
2nd place	$40,000	$5,000	$5,000
3rd place	$22,500	$2,500	$2,500

The setting of new world and course records can add up to $80,000 to the pot. Along with the money, the victors have been the recipients of

accompanying gifts, which have included a Mercedes, a punch bowl, a bronze statue, a gold medal studded with diamonds, and pewter goblets.

1993 In an effort to provide the most hospitable environment possible for top athletes, B.A.A. officials presented three-time champion Ibrahim Hussein with a waffle-maker and several boxes of waffle mix when he mentioned that he couldn't get waffles back home in Kenya.

While the prize money and the related gifts draw the athletes to the race, no symbol of victory is more desired than the laurel wreath. For over a century, the elite have run Boston for the opportunity to be crowned king or queen of that year's Boston Marathon.

Since 1897 the laurel wreath has been fashioned from branches specially cut from a Kotinos (wild olive) tree just outside of Marathon, Greece, and then flown to Boston for the awards ceremony. Over the years, representatives of Greece have frequently been chosen to crown the winner, strengthening the link between the 1896 Olympic Games in Athens and the Boston Marathon. The wreath also serves as a link to the race's origin—Pheidippides's run of conquest.

From the first race to the most recent, the wreath has invoked mixed feelings of maliciousness, possessive ownership, and even sometimes indifference.

Both in 1909 and in 1939, the wreath was stolen from the deserving winners. Henri Renaud had his wreath and trophy stolen by a traveling circus, which had "borrowed" the awards; three decades later, Tarzan Brown's wreath was stolen from his bag in the Boston University locker room.

Some six years later, with the country finishing up the European campaign of World War II and mourning the death of President Franklin D. Roosevelt, runners and members of the media tried to convince winner John "Elder" Kelley to send his laurel wreath to Eleanor Roosevelt as a sign of sympathy for the passing of her husband. Kelley retorted, "I think the wreath has more significance to me than it would for Mrs. Roosevelt."

While Kelley appreciated the emblem and what it reminded him of, five-time wheelchair champion Jim Knaub looked at the wreath and related trophies in another light. "Admiring my trophies or daydreaming of past accomplishments is an act of looking backwards. For me, I have to continue to move forward. I'm afraid if I look back I might stop moving forward. It's like running a race—just concern yourself with what's ahead—anything behind you doesn't matter." After each of his triumphs, Knaub would immediately leave the winners' stand and seek out a young child to give the youth his laurel wreath as a memento of the race.

After the winner crosses the finish line, the post-race activities attempt to move according to plan, but sometimes it's better to let things flow at their own speed. After the 1907 marathon, race officials had to delay the post-race ceremonies while they tried to get the winner to stop running. Tom Longboat, of Hamilton, Ontario, finished the race outside the B.A.A. headquarters in great shape. From there, he proceeded to enter the B.A.A. gym and run laps around the indoor track. Finally, officials convinced Longboat to slow down to a walk, fearing he might drop dead of a heart attack.

Half a century later in 1963, B.A.A. officials attempted to whisk the winner, Aurele Vandendriessche of Belgium, away from the crowd to give him a post-race physical. Instead he pushed the officials away, discarded his blanket, and proceeded to mingle with the crowd like a presidential candidate disobeying his secret service agents.

Eventually the winners fall into line and the activities related with victory take their course. Following various ceremonies, the runners are then paraded in front of the media for their annual Q&A session. Usually the press conference is a monotonous affair, although the repetition provides a common thread from race to race. Each year the media ask the same questions and the runners reply with the same answers. Only the faces change. The media say, "How do you feel? When did you know you had it won? Are you happy?" The runners say, "I feel great. I could run another marathon! I knew I had it won when I crossed the finish line. Yes, I'm happy."

In 1976, after running through one of the hottest races in the history of the event (40% of the starters dropped out), overheated champion Jack Fultz was hurried into the press conference without an opportunity to cool down or stretch out. There he was thrown into a barber's chair and peppered with questions for over an hour. When he finally got up, he could barely keep his feet.

1948 After winning his fourth championship in 1948, Gerard Cote of Quebec told the press, "Gentlemen, Gentlemen! One beer! One cigar! Then we can talk about the race."

1975 Women's Champion Liane Winter of West Germany graciously accepted the accolades of the press but finally said, through her translator, "Thank you. Could you get me a beer? I would really like a beer."

The press conference also provides the victors the opportunity to verbalize what was an intensely private war. For the first time since making history, they sit in front of the assorted scribes and cameras and tell the story of their conquest.

In 1968 Amby Burfoot recounted his run as the perfect run. "From the moment the gun sounded, I ran with an ease that I had never experienced. I felt like I was running beyond my means while at the same time staying within myself. I can only explain my run as one of supreme effortlessness."

Jack Fultz told a similar story of a free and fluid race: "My run was so relaxed and comfortable that I was concerned that I wasn't pushing myself enough. But when I finally came upon a clock I was on the exact pace that I had hoped."

Likewise Gayle Barron saw her 1978 run as the race where everything came together. "I had run a number of marathons previous to 1978. In each of those races, I always would be afflicted with some type of ailment, whether it be blisters, cramps, or something worse. This year everything worked perfectly. I ran like I had never run before. Each mile was quicker than I had ever run, but I felt like I was in a light jog. I remember being on the winner's podium and being shocked. I could have kept going. I felt perfect. The day was perfect."

Then there was John "Younger" Kelley, the 1957 winner, expressing a sentiment that more of us might echo: "I had to prove something to myself. I never figured out what the hell it was, but I did it."

Of course, the most memorable post-race speech ever delivered came from the lips of Pheidippides himself when he shouted to the assembled Athenians "Rejoice! We conquer!" and then dropped dead.

— — — —

I didn't have to deal with the press at the end of my race, but I was summarily quizzed by friends and family. Of course, I was all too happy to discuss the race and revel in my unprecedented accomplishment— often my answers were more detailed than the questioner might have liked. Having conquered the world's greatest race only six months after struggling to finish a mile, I was more than willing to tell my tale to anyone kind enough to listen.

TRIALS AND TRIBULATIONS

Frank Shorter: "You can't think of your next marathon until you've forgotten your last one."

— — — —

Over the years, the race has delivered many dramatic events and fabulous finishes. But, as with any institution that has been around for over a century, there have also been infamous moments that have fastened themselves like ivy to the history of the race. The Boston Marathon has been shaped by both the good and the bad, sometimes by forces from within the race and sometime by uncontrollable outside forces.

Maintaining order from Hopkinton to Boston is a huge task. Since 1897, press buses, cars, trains, dogs, horses, rain, snow, heat, police, and millions of spectators have all played a role in the race and its outcome. And the malevolent race seems happy to co-opt these outside forces in its effort to inflict as much pain and madness as possible upon those who dare to challenge it. Throughout its history, these peripheral elements have often had a direct impact on the race and its outcome. Certain notorious moments have shined a spotlight on the race's deficiencies, such as in 1907, when a freight train dissected the course in Framingham, and in 1956, when the lead pack was stalked by a dog which eventually galloped onto the course and knocked down John "Younger" Kelley.

Such happenings have caused much concern among the runners. Following the 1929 race, champion Johnny Miles was so troubled with the condition of the race and the impact of outside elements that he penned an article in the next day's *Boston Globe*. In an editorial he wrote, "It was not only a battle against a great runner, but a battle against fumes of gasoline, automobiles, motorcycles which were often too close for comfort and a dog who jumped me before Coolidge Corner and scared me."

Even Johnny "Elder" Kelley voiced a complaint following his forty-seventh Boston Marathon in 1978 at the age of seventy-nine. He felt that the crowd had hurt his run. "If I weren't bunched up, I could have broken 3:30. I love this race and the people, but the runners need to be able to run."

For decades the Boston Marathon was the only world-class marathon available to runners apart from the Olympics. If runners wanted to challenge themselves against the sport's most enduring competition, then they had to come to Boston. Over time this status created arrogance and complacency at the B.A.A., and the quality of the race suffered.

1977 Jerome Drayton of Canada, who had just moments before won the Boston Marathon, crossed the finish line, stopped, and looked back at the race route with disgust. He briefly wore the laurel wreath before taking it off, as if his family name would be tainted by association with the race. He moved from the finish line to the press conference, where he vented his frustration with the course, the spectators, and the B.A.A.

He complained that the start was disorganized and people grabbed his shirt and kicked him in the calf. Throughout the route, he said, water stops were sporadic and unmarked, and mileage signs were small and inconspicuous. Checkpoints were located at odd spots, making it hard for the runners to calculate their splits.

He scoffed at, mocked, and ridiculed a race that was much more than just a race to the people of Boston and Massachusetts. How dare he come into our home, run our race, take our championship, and turn his nose up at us? He had a nerve.

(He turned out to be right.)

With the running boom in the 1970s, the need to conduct the marathon in a safe and responsible fashion became a growing concern. A laurel wreath, some gauze on the bottom of some feet, and a shake of the hand wasn't going to do it anymore. Runners were waiting for the B.A.A. to grow the race into a first-class international event. That meant bringing professionalism to the greatest amateur event in the world next to the Olympics. This type of change didn't sit well with the Boston community.

Boston was built on Swan Boats, Irish politicians, baked beans, the losing Red Sox, and a number of men running a race in April for the thrill of competition. Boston was built on tradition, and thus variations were discouraged.

Still, there was no doubt that the race was in dire need of a tune-up. The complaints from top runners like Jerome Drayton and even Massachusetts's own Greg Meyer were a wakeup call to the B.A.A., as was the growing competition from marathons in Chicago and London.

Even Race Director Guy Morse had to acknowledge that the race had deficiencies: "The situations involving Jerome Drayton and Rosie Ruiz caught our attention." Fortunately the B.A.A. did respond to these gaffes: Over time the organization pruned and cultivated the race into the first-class operation it is today. Besides increasing budgets and raising standards, the B.A.A. also adopted more vigilant checkpoint monitoring to prevent pseudo-athletes from stealing glory. Although Rosie Ruiz publicized the issue of cheating, throughout the race's history there were always runners who attempted to cut corners in their effort to conquer Boston.

1909 Howard Pearce of New Bedford was rushing toward the tape to the cheers of thousands of spectators when a police sergeant tackled him moments before he crossed the line. Pearce, the apparent leader, had jumped into a car in Wellesley and rode to Kenmore Square, where he reentered the race. Many policemen, unaware that he had cheated, cheered the runner on as they held back the crowd. Luckily, the alert sergeant prevented Pearce from experiencing the thrill that he didn't deserve.

1916 The fifth-place finisher, A.F. Merchant, was seen by a race volunteer getting into a car on Beacon Street. Merchant denied the boy's accusation.

1927 Several runners who had earlier dropped out of the race jumped back onto the course between the second- and third-place runners after being transported by an unknown vehicle. Their actions spoiled the finish of the real third-place runner (and past champion) William Kennedy.

1997 John and Suzanne Murphy, a husband and wife team who had apparently won their respective age categories, were disqualified after they failed to show up on videotapes shot at checkpoints along the course. Despite a constant headwind, John and Suzanne Murphy recorded finishing times in 1997 that were, respectively, eleven and twelve minutes faster than their 1996 Boston Marathon times. Anthony Cerminaro and Susan Gustafson were eventually recognized as the rightful winners of the men's senior category and the women's veteran's group.

Advances in technology, such as the shoelace microchips used since the 1996 race, have allowed the B.A.A. to assure the fairness of the competition and to deter future swindlers from attempting a "Rosie Ruiz."

The responsibility of administering the race is massive. The B.A.A. attempts to control whatever they humanly can, and continue to make adjustments. Thanks to their efforts, the race in Boston every April has remained the finest venue in the running world.

ELLISON "TARZAN" BROWN PROUDLY FASHIONS HIS LAUREL WREATH AFTER WINNING THE SEC-
OND OF HIS TWO BOSTON MARATHONS IN 1939. PHOTO COURTESY OF THE BOSTON PUBLIC
LIBRARY PRINT DEPARTMENT.

ICE BAGS AND COLD BEERS

Dr. Marvin Adner, medical director for the marathon: "The last thing you should do to be healthy is run a marathon."

— — — —

After the race is over, the runners are reminded by their bodies that running twenty-six-plus miles is not what the human body was intended to do. After crossing the finish line, each competitor undergoes a physical. Feet, knees, mind, and the rest are all evaluated in order to ascertain whether the runner should head for the showers and the post-race parties or over to the medical tent.

Up until the 1960s, competitors were examined by a physician prior to the race. During the event, the doctors would be chauffeured by train or car to the finish, where they would again poke and prod the athletes in order to declare each in good health. The post-race exam included: a listen to the heart and the lungs; a jump on the scale to see how much weight the runner lost during the race; and, in some years, a heart x-ray so that the doctors could study whether marathon running had a negative impact on the body. Usually, the doctors would smile and declare to the press, "All are healthy other than some loss of weight and blisters on the feet."

When there were five hundred runners, a quick listen with a stethoscope and a jump on the scale was feasible. But ever since Bill Rodgers triggered the running craze, the post-race medical check has been obliged to mature into a full-scale triage area that closely resembles a MASH unit after a violent battle. The runners are in good hands—if not good feet—

after the Boston Marathon of today: There are cots, medical nurses, IV nurses, intravenous therapists, podiatrists, cardiologists, intensive care personnel, drug test officials, even psychiatrists. Below is a list of supplies that are stocked for each race, according to *The Boston Globe*:

500 bags of ice	1,000 adhesive bandages
380 stretchers	500 towels
1,500 blankets	1,500 intravenous bags
500 tongue depressors	500 tourniquets
200 sick bags	150 blood-pressure cuffs
175 ace bandages	and stethoscopes
1,500 gauze pads	80 thermometers
2,000 adhesive bandages	2,000 pairs of medical gloves
250 rolls of moleskin	35,000 gallons of spring water
500 surgical soaps	200 bottles of antiseptic hand-wash
500 tubes of petroleum jelly	2,000 tubes of antibiotic ointment

— — — —

After I crossed the finish line, I felt an overwhelming desire to fall asleep. Medical personnel recommended that I take a detour into the medical tent and regain my faculties. With a drained body, a stiff knee, blisters on my feet, and chills, I concurred with their diagnosis. I entered the tent and was led over to an open cot. A nurse kindly attended to me while my brother Kevin went in search of some dry clothes. As the nurse completed her due diligence she went through her litany of questions including, "Any known medical problems?" That was when I realized that, for the first time in two decades, I didn't have to respond, "I have the heart disease WPW."

What a win-win-win the entire event had been. Not only had I conquered the Boston Marathon, I had also formed a lifetime bond with my three friends Rad, Richie, and Jackie, and best of all, I had rid myself of the disease that had saddled me for all too long. Lying on the cot in disarray, I realized that the last six months had earned me invaluable long-term benefits. Running the marathon would pay me dividends for the rest of my life.

Back in the short term, the job of putting me back together was in the able hands of the medical tent team. They bundled me up with blankets and moved a portable heater over to my side, allowing my system to slowly return to normal. Before being allowed to depart, I was required to drink twenty-four ounces of Gatorade, twelve ounces of water, and twelve ounces of cold chicken soup. After I had consumed enough fluid to tip me over, two physical therapists made me take a lap around the tent to satisfy them that I was capable of walking. As I circled the tent, I noticed that there was a news camera, with its red light on, filming the scene. Back at my parents' house, my mother called into the kitchen to let my father know that I was on TV. When he ran into the den, he found the sight of his son being walked around the medical tent like some patient from the movie *One Flew Over the Cuckoo's Nest*.

Eventually I completed my last lap of the day and was allowed to leave the tent and find my family at the Boston Common a mile down Boylston Street. As I walked down the street, with two Mylar blankets taped around me like capes, a well-meaning girl offered me a PowerBar. I felt like saying, "I don't need a PowerBar. I need to be read my last rites!"

It was almost 6:00 P.M. and the sun was down. The temperature had plummeted into the low forties, and the wind was howling. The thought of doing another mile was out of the question. Luckily a volunteer assessed my state and offered me a ride to the Boston Common in a wheelchair. Once there I found my wife, son, and brother—and the loneliness of the marathon was over.

Dr. Lyle Micheli, captain of the finish line medical team warns, "Marathon running is a very special sport; it's something you don't play games with. You have to really respect that event."

The consequences of disrespecting so great a physical effort can be severe. Even those who train properly expose themselves to the hazards of the race. It's only when the adrenaline subsides that most competitors start to realize how much they have just overextended their bodies. Many a marathoner has sat on a medical cot or in a hotel room and thought: "Never again will I do this to myself."

1897 John McDermott, the winner of the first race, told the press that this would be his last long-distance race. He said: "I hope you don't think I'm a coward or a quitter, but look at my blistered feet." McDermott lost eight pounds over the course.

1905 After the usual post-marathon physicals, Dr. Blake bemoaned that a number of the runners finished in a bad way. He continued, "They can blame their handlers for this. These men were given whiskey on their journey, which is a bad thing. The men who didn't take alcoholic stimulants fared much better."

1976 Kim Merritt, winner of the women's race, was reported to have said after the race, "I don't know if I'll do it over again." She was later taken to the hospital for observation.

After witnessing the carnage in the medical tent, Tony Chamberlain, a writer from *The Boston Globe*, reported in 1989, "There were cries of pain, shoes full of blood, gaunt mummies walking around—it resembled a scene from a war."

In 1982 no casualty was more worthy of attention than Alberto Salazar, who had pushed himself to the limit winning the race. Second-place finisher Dick Beardsley kept whispering "I took him to the finish." Salazar was whispering, "I don't feel too good."

Salazar ended up in the garage of the Prudential Center, which acted as the makeshift infirmary for the walking wounded of the marathon that year. Suffering from hypothermia, Salazar's body temperature dropped to 88 degrees. Doctors and IV nurses injected three liters of 5% dextrose/saline solution into each of Salazar's arms in the effort to bring his temperature back to normal.

Physical punishment was not unusual for Salazar. During the Falmouth Road Race the previous August, Salazar was taken off the course with a temperature of 108 degrees. He was quickly placed in a rubber raft with a hundred pounds of ice to bring down his body temperature. Suffering from hyperthermia, Salazar slipped into a coma and was given the last rites. Salazar lived to run again, but after Boston he was never the same.

There are two rules of thumb that predict what kind of traffic the medical tent will see after a marathon. The first is what *Boston Globe* sportswriter Dan Shaughnessy referred to as the inverted rule of finish theory: "The longer you wait, the worse shape the runners are in." In other words, four-hour marathoners tend to look worse than three-hour marathoners. The second factor is heat: The number of competitors in need of medical care is usually a function of the weather more than anything else. A hot day for the marathon is a nightmare, not only for the runners but also for the doctors, attendants, and nurses who are responsible for providing care along the route.

1909 When the temperature hit 97 degrees, 91 runners dropped out from a starting field of 164.

1927 Runners throughout the route dropped out as thermometers registered more than 80 degrees. At the end, doctors reported several cases of heat stroke and three cases of heart dilation. Johnny Miles was a "pitiful sight," reported *The Boston Globe*, as the defending champion was carried to the finish in a motor car.

1985 Almost 2,000 runners were treated by medical personnel as a result of the 70-degree temperatures.

1993 With the temperature approaching 80, medical personnel were forced to use almost 800 IV bags to revitalize spent runners.

As Ray Hosler put it, "After twenty-six miles of running, you either feel like a conquering hero, or a defeated and bludgeoned victim."

For many, of course, blister care and rehydration is simply a pit stop on their way to the many celebrations held throughout Boston. Micky Lawrence of Image Impact, the post-race coordinator, calls the proceedings after the race a necessary element of the day. "This type of post-event party gives the experience some closure. Psychologists have told us that an endeavor of this magnitude demands some type of forum for competitors to ease their emotions with other individuals who shared their experience."

Modern-day activities start around 6:00 P.M., thus giving the runners the opportunity to cool down and relax. Winners and celebrities stay busy answering to the press and well-wishers. For some, the time lapse poses a problem because of the need to check out of hotel rooms. Others have to keep moving after the race or their bodies will not regenerate the energy needed to get dressed and go out some three hours later.

The brotherhood and sisterhood of runners is a close community. On the course the runners are separated only by time; the goal and the distance traveled are the same for all. Following the race, the field rejoices together if only for the fact that they all faced a common foe—the course.

Uta Pippig used to revel in the post-race events. "After the marathon is over, I like to stop by a couple of parties and enjoy the other competitors. I really respect all of the runners. Like a woman who breaks 4:20 for the first time—she might have a full-time job and a family, but she met and defeated a challenge. This is a great accomplishment."

Prior to the Eliot Lounge's closing, the bar used to host THE post-marathon party. If you came in with your bib number, Tommy Leonard would reward you with a free beer. The winners were presented with seats of honor while the piano serenaded them with their national anthems. Ricky and Dick Hoyt always visited the bar, where Ricky was given his annual victor's ride on the patrons' shoulders to a comfortable seat.

At the Copley Plaza, the awards dinner is held in the Grand Ballroom while out in Hopkinton, Race Director Dave McGillivray is just starting his run from Hopkinton to Boston so that he can keep his Boston Marathon streak alive. His run is a little more difficult because of his hectic day and because cars have now been allowed back on the route.

Following the awards ceremony at the Copley, there are parties at the local dance clubs and hotels for those who can still move their legs. Following the 100th running, Lansdown Street, just outside of Kenmore Square, was turned into a miniature version of Bourbon Street in New Orleans.

Over the years, athletes have finished out this day of challenge in various ways. Here is how some of the athletes "experienced closure."

1927 After winning his fifth championship, Clarence DeMar was brought to a Melrose movie theater in order to greet his Boy Scout troop. When Demar walked in, the boys almost tore off the roof.

1929 Eddie Mack, from the Boston Garden, invited and hosted the runners at boxing matches that were held the night of the race.

1946 After finishing the marathon in ragged shape, Harvard first baseman Bill Fitz hustled over to Cambridge where his team was locked in an extra innings game against the University of Connecticut. In need of a big hit, Fitz's coach asked him if he could pinch hit. Fitz responded, "Yes, but if I get on I need a pinch runner."

1959 Eino Oksanen from Finland was spotted doing polka at 12:30 A.M. in a Quincy, Massachusetts, social club ten hours after winning his first championship.

1979 Bill Rodgers and Joan Benoit were invited to the White House to have dinner with President Jimmy Carter. Depending on the interests of the sitting president, runners are now customarily invited to run with the president.

After winning her races, Uta Pippig has felt great relief: "I feel good for myself and for the people who gave up so much to support me. In training, you have shut yourself off from so many people who are important in your life. Now I know I'll have the opportunity to reunite with them."

For me the finish brought liberation. The long training runs, the hustle to find a baby-sitter, the ice bags—all would now be a memory. Only

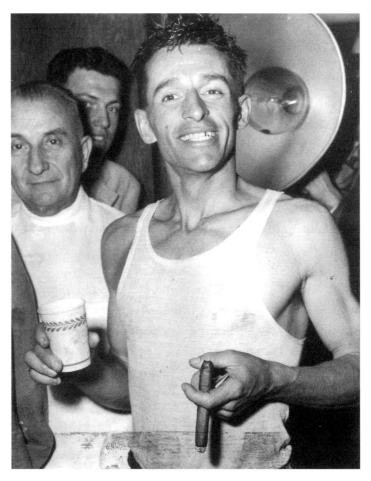

Four-time winner Gerard Cote indulges in the fruits of victory after winning the 1948 Boston Marathon. Photo courtesy of the Boston Public Library Print Department.

the spirit of conquest would remain. Like a battered boxer, I said to myself, "I will never again wage war with the twenty-six miles from Hopkinton to Boston." I had satisfied the wild curiosity that had held me for years.

After arriving home from a stiff thirty-minute cab ride, I was in no condition to party or dance into the night. As I unfolded from the taxi, I faced one more obstacle in my long day: the six steps of my front porch. For six months I had hopped down these steps en route to my training runs; now I was presented with the task of scaling up them. I clutched

260

the banister, but my legs refused to cooperate. So I turned around and mounted the steps backwards. Whatever it takes.

Shuffling across the porch where I always did my stretching, I eased myself over the threshold as my wife held the door for me. I had arrived home safe and sound. Twenty-four hours before, I had walked out that door a different man. Now I was the proud owner of a Boston Marathon medal and all the physical and mental benefits that come with it.

Later in the night, I sat at my kitchen table, barely in one piece, to have dinner with my family. My wife placed a delicious meal in front of me, which I struggled to keep down. When I had gathered enough strength, I made my way to the bathroom and sank into a nice hot tub where I discovered that I had suffered a bad sunburn on the backs of my legs during my four-and-a-half-hour trek.

Around 8:00 P.M., Richie called to see how I had done. We were both excited to hear that all four of us had been successful in reaching the finish line. If one of us had dropped out, the overall experience would have been tarnished. On this day the four of us ran in our own little private running club and thankfully shared in the exhilaration of finishing.

Before Richie hung up, he reminded me of the pledge we had made to each other some six months earlier. We had put our hands together like the Three Musketeers and vowed to each other to run the Boston Marathon. We were true to our vow.

Five minutes later Michael and Jack Radley came by to make sure I still had a pulse. They were sore and tired but smiling. I was glad they had come by: I needed some closure to the event, and I wanted to see and hear from my three comrades. Later as they headed out the door to settle in their own homes, Rad turned and said, "We did it." I echoed his sentiment with my own "We did it," as if I was saying it to myself in disbelief. Again we shook hands and congratulated each other, parting with a special bond that would last a lifetime.

Fifteen minutes later I settled into bed with a sunburn, an injured knee, and a spent body. Staring at the ceiling, I couldn't help but revel in my day's accomplishment. Over and over, I replayed the race in my head and got goose bumps every time I crossed the finish line. Even months later, when I passed over the marathon course, I found myself saying "I did it." The race was over, but the benefits would last forever.

EPILOGUE

Amby Burfoot: "Boston was everything in my eyes. Boston was, to me, more important than the Olympics. Boston was in my blood. It had to be Boston."

— — — —

Where does the race go from here? What country will turn out the next generation of world-class marathoners? Will the African nations continue their mastery of the roads from Hopkinton to Boston? Will John Hancock Financial Services keep supporting the race? Will there ever be another Johnny "Elder" Kelley? What will the next hundred years hold for the modern world's oldest race?

Change means new and uncharted waters. Change is scary to New Englanders. We like to know where we're going and how we're going to get there. Electric scoreboards at Fenway Park, the implosion of the Boston Garden, and the demolition of the elevated train system didn't come about without a fight. But somehow we survive and even sometimes privately admit that change can be for the better. Women runners, wheelchair competitors, regular checkpoints, frequent water stops, prize money, the B.A.A. unicorn on the face of the commercial products, and adjustments to the route—these are all changes that have greatly improved the Boston Marathon.

When asked about the race, Guy Morse of the B.A.A. quotes the bylaws of the 115-year-old club, which state that the "exclusive purposes of the Association shall be the promotion of the common good and health and welfare of the general public and the encouragement of the general public to improve their physical condition by the promotion and regulation of amateur sports competition, with particular emphasis on the sponsorship of long distance running events (especially the traditional annual Boston Athletic Association Marathon) and of the track and field teams and meets and similar athletic exercises."

Morse goes on: "As with most events that have withstood the test of time, the Boston Marathon's success has been the result of a combination of factors. We have been innovative in the race's technical support. The support of our communities and dedication of runners together with the durability of the Boston Athletic Association through changing times and sometimes criticism have brought about strong leadership and organization. Of course we have benefited from certain intangibles such as a fair amount of good luck and fate, as well."

For over a century, the race has kept its mantle as the world's greatest race. Like the New England seasons, the race changes but always stays the same. Runners still venture west of Boston to compete in an endurance event that pushes the limits of the mind and body.

For 364 days of the year, the route from Hopkinton to Boston is simply a twenty-six-mile stretch of pavement, not much different from any other road. But on the day of the Boston Marathon, the road from Hopkinton to Boston comes alive with a pounding pulse and a passionate heart. Referred to by some as alluring and seductive, and by others as heartbreaking, this course has a romantic enchantment for both the competitors and the spectators.

For more than 100 years, images from the Boston Marathon have been ingrained in the souls of those who come to challenge, conquer, or cheer. The memories endure: Clarence DeMar's proud chest breaking the tape, Uta Pippig's radiant Boylston Street smile, Bill Rodgers's gloved hands, John "Elder" Kelley's immortal stride, and the sight of a small boy on his father's shoulders.

For the competitors, the race is more than just a road race—it is a love affair. It is a link to our past. It represents tradition and innocence. It is the one day of the year when representatives from every corner of the world share a bond. From every walk of life, individuals come to run, to watch, and to follow a dream here on the 365th day.

For six months, I ventured outside of my element in search of a sublime pot of gold at the end of an unknown rainbow. At age thirty-two, I knew that the world offered opportunities that I had yet to explore. Little did I know that my journey would become a metaphor for my life. Little did I know that the intangible benefits of running twenty-six miles would serve me in all aspects of my life.

Back in October, I elected to take a trip. I wrote down the destination and piece by piece created the path that would deliver me. When I arrived, I was introduced to myself. I looked in the mirror and now knew that my spirit possessed endless possibilities. I ran in order to answer the questions. After crossing the finish line, I unveiled layers of potential that will allow me to run any race.

Fulfillment comes in many shapes and colors. Running the Boston Marathon produced in me a profound sense of accomplishment. I ran from Hopkinton to Boston that day unaware that my inner soul would be tested and rewarded.

In November my heart had stopped, in April my heart had soared. I had run Boston.

A SIMPLE MEDAL THAT MEANS THE WORLD. PHOTO COURTESY OF FAYFOTO.

MEN'S OPEN CHAMPIONS

1897	John J. McDermott, New York City, NY	2:55:10
1898	Ronald J. McDonald, Cambridge, Ma	2:42:00
1899	Lawrence J. Brignolia, Cambridge, Ma	2:54:38
1900	James Caffrey, Hamilton, Ontario	2:39:44
1901	James Caffrey, Hamilton, Ontario	2:29:23
1902	Sammy Mellor, Yonkers, New York	2:43:12
1903	John C. Lorden, Cambridge, Ma	2:41:29
1904	Michael Spring, New York City, NY	2:38:04
1905	Fred Lorz, New York City, NY	2:38:25
1906	Timothy Ford, Cambridge, Ma	2:45:45
1907	Tom Longboat, Hamilton, Ontario	2:24:24
1908	Thomas Morrissey, New York City, NY	2:25:43
1909	Henri Renaud, Nashua, New Hampshire	2:53:36
1910	Fred Cameron, Amherst, Novia Scotia	2:28:52
1911	Clarence DeMar, Melrose, Ma	2:24:39
1912	Mike Ryan, New York City, NY	2:21:18
1913	Fritz Carlson, Minneapolis, Mn	2:25:14
1914	James Duffy, Hamilton, Ontario	2:25:01
1915	Edouard Fabre, Montreal, Quebec	2:31:41
1916	Arthur Roth, Roxbury, Ma	2:27:16
1917	William Kennedy, Port Chester, NY	2:28:37
1918	Armed Services relay, Camp Devens	2:29:53
1919	Carl Lidner, Quincy, Ma	2:29:13
1920	Peter Trivoulidas, Greece	2:29:31
1921	Frank Zuna, Newark, NJ	2:18:57
1922	Clarence DeMar, Melrose, Ma	2:18:10
1923	Clarence DeMar, Melrose, Ma	2:23:37
1924	Clarence DeMar, Melrose, Ma	2:29:40
1925	Charles Mellor, Chicago, Ill	2:33:00

1926	John Miles, Sydney Mines, Nova Scotia	2:25:40
1927	Clarence DeMar, Melrose, Ma	2:40:22
1928	Clarence DeMar, Melrose, Ma	2:37:07
1929	John Miles, Sidney Mines, Novia Scotia	2:33:08
1930	Clarence DeMar, Melrose, Ma	2:34:48
1931	James Hennigan, Medford, Ma	2:46:45
1932	Paul de Bruyn, Germany	2:33:36
1933	Leslie Pawson, Pawtucket, RI	2:31:01
1934	Dave Komonen, Ontario, Canada	2:32:53
1935	John Kelley, Arlington, Ma	2:32:07
1936	Ellison Brown, Alton, RI	2:33:40
1937	Walter Young, Verdun, Quebec	2:33:20
1938	Leslie Pawson, Pawtucket, RI	2:35:34
1939	Ellison Brown, Alton, RI	2:28:51
1940	Gerard Cote, Hyacinthe, Quebec	2:28:28
1941	Leslie Pawson, Pawtucket, RI	2:30:38
1942	Bernard Joseph Smith, Medford, Ma	2:26:51
1943	Gerard Cote, Hyacinthe, Quebec	2:28:25
1944	Gerard Cote, Hyacinthe, Quebec	2:31:50
1945	John Kelley, Arlington, Ma	2:30:40
1946	Stylianos Kyriakides, Greece	2:29:27
1947	Yun Bok Suh, South Korea	2:25:39
1948	Gerard Cote, Hyacinthe, Quebec	2:31:02
1949	Karl Gosta Leandersson, Sweden	2:31:50
1950	Ki Yong Ham, South Korea	2:32:39
1951	Shigeki Tanaka, Hiroshima, Japan	2:24:45
1952	Doroteo Flores, Guatemala	2:31:53
1953	Keizo Yamada, Japan	2:18:51
1954	Veikko Karvonen, Finland	2:20:39
1955	Hideo Hamamura, Japan	2:18:22
1956	Antti Viskari, Finland	2:14:14
1957	John Kelley, Groton, Ct	2:20:05
1958	Franjo Mihalic, Yugoslavia	2:25:54
1959	Eino Oksanen, Helsinki, Finland	2:22:42
1960	Paavo Kotila, Finland	2:20:54

1961	Eino Oksanen, Helsinki, Finland	2:23:39
1962	Eino Oksanen, Helsinki, Finland	2:23:48
1963	Aurele Vandendrissche, Belgium	2:18:58
1964	Aurele Vandendrissche, Belgium	2:19:59
1965	Morio Shigematsu, Japan	2:16:33
1966	Kenji Kimihara, Japan	2:17:11
1967	David McKenzie, New Zealand	2:15:45
1968	Ambrose (Amby) Burfoot, Groton, Ct	2:22:17
1969	Yoshiaki Unetani, Japan	2:13:49
1970	Ron Hill, Chesire, England	2:10:30
1971	Alvaro Mejia, Columbia	2:18:45
1972	Olavi Suomalainen, Otaniemi, Finland	2:15:39
1973	Jon Anderson, Eugene, Oregon	2:16:03
1974	Neil Cusack, Ireland	2:13:39
1975	Bill Rodgers, Melrose, Ma	2:09:55
1976	Jack Fultz, Arlington, Va	2:20:19
1977	Jerome Drayton, Toronto, Canada	2:14:46
1978	Bill Rodgers, Melrose, Ma	2:10:13
1979	Bill Rodgers, Melrose, Ma	2:09:27
1980	Bill Rodgers, Melrose, Ma	2:12:11
1981	Toshihiko Seko, Japan	2:09:26
1982	Alberto Salazar, Wayland, Ma	2:08:52
1983	Gregory Meyer, Wellesley, Ma	2:09:00
1984	Geoff Smith, Liverpool, England	2:10:34
1985	Geoff Smith, Liverpool, England	2:14:05
1986	Rob de Castella, Canberra, Australia	2:07:51
1987	Toshihiko Seko, Japan	2:11:50
1988	Ibrahim Hussein, Kenya	2:08:43
1989	Abebe Mekonnen, Ethiopia	2:09:06
1990	Gelindo Bordin, Milan, Italy	2:08:19
1991	Ibrahim Hussein, Kenya	2:11:06
1992	Ibrahim Hussein, Kenya	2:08:14
1993	Cosmas Ndeti, Kenya	2:09:33
1994	Cosmas Ndeti, Kenya	2:07:15
1995	Cosmas Ndeti, Kenya	2:09:22

1996	Moses Tanui, Kenya	2:09:26
1997	Lameck Aguta, Kenya	2:10:34
1998	Moses Tanui, Kenya	2:07:34
1999	Lameck Aguta, Kenya	2:09:47
2000	Elijah Lagat, Kenya	2:09:47
2001	Lee Bong-Ju, South Korea	2:09:43
2002	Rodgers Rob, Kenya	2:09:02

WOMEN'S OPEN CHAMPIONS

1966	Roberta Gibb, Winchester, Ma	3:21:40 *
1967	Roberta Gibb, San Diego, Ca	3:27:17 *
1968	Roberta Gibb, San Diego, Ca	3:30:00 *
1969	Sara Mae Berman, Cambridge, Ma	3:22:46 *
1970	Sara Mae Berman, Cambridge, Ma	3:05:07 *
1971	Sara Mae Berman, Cambridge, Ma	3:08:30 *
1972	Nina Kusick, South Huntington, Ny	3:10:26
1973	Jacqueline Hansen, Granada Hills, Ca	3:05:59
1974	Michiko Gorman, Los Angeles, Ca	2:47:11
1975	Liane Winter, Wolfsburg, West Germany	2:42:24
1976	Kim Merritt, Kenosha, Wi	2:47:10
1977	Michiko Gorman, Los Angeles, Ca	2:48:33
1978	Gayle Barron, Atlanta, Ga	2:44:52
1979	Joan Benoit, Cape Elizabeth, Me	2:35:15
1980	Jacqueline Gareau, Montreal, Quebec	2:34:28
1981	Allison Roe, Takatuna, New Zealand	2:26:46
1982	Charlotte Teske, Darmstadt, West Germany	2:29:33
1983	Joan Benoit, Watertown, Ma	2:22:43
1984	Lorraine Moeller, Putaruru, New Zealand	2:29:28
1985	Lisa Larsen Weidenback, Battle Creek, Mi	2:34:06
1986	Ingrid Kristiansen, Oslo, Norway	2:24:55
1987	Rosa Mota, Porto, Portugal	2:25:21
1988	Rosa Mota, Porto, Portugal	2:24:30
1989	Ingrid Kristiansen, Oslo, Norway	2:24:33
1990	Roas Mota, Porto, Portugal	2:25:24
1991	Wanda Panfil, Poland	2:24:18
1992	Olga Markova, Russia	2:23:43
1993	Olga Markova, Russia	2:25:27
1994	Uta Pippig, West Berlin, Germany	2:21:45

1995	Uta Pippig, West Berlin, Germany	2:25:11
1996	Uta Pippig, West Berlin, Germany	2:27:12
1997	Fatuma Roba, Ethiopia	2:26:23
1998	Fatuma Roba, Ethiopia	2:23:21
1999	Fatuma Roba, Ethiopia	2:23:25
2000	Catherine Ndereba, Kenya	2:26:11
2001	Catherine Ndereba, Kenya	2:23:53
2002	Margaret Okayo, Kenya	2:20:43

*unofficial

MEN'S WHEELCHAIR CHAMPIONS

1975	Robert Hall, Belmont, Ma	2:58:00
1976	No contestants	
1977	Robert Hall, Belmont, Ma	2:40:10
1978	George Murray, Tampa, Fl	2:26:57
1979	Kenneth Archer, Akron, Oh	2:38:59
1980	Curt Brinkman, Orem, Ut	1:55:00
1981	Jim Martinson, Puyallup, Wa	2:00:41
1982	Jim Knaub, Long Beach, Ca	1:51:31
1983	Jim Knaub, Long Beach Ca	1:47:10
1984	Andre Viger, Quebec, Canada	2:05:20
1985	George Murray, Tampan, Fl	1:45:34
1986	Andre Viger, Quebec, Canada	1:43:25
1987	Andre Viger, Quebec, Canada	1:55:42
1988	Mustapha Badid, Pontoise, France	1:43:19
1989	Philippe Couprie, Pontoise, France	1:36:04
1990	Mustapha Badid, St. Denis, France	1:29:53
1991	Jim Knaub, Long Beach, Ca	1:30:44
1992	Jim Knaub, Long Beach, Ca	1:26:28
1993	Jim Knaub, Long Beach, Ca	1:22:17
1994	Heinz Frei, Switzerland	1:21:23
1995	Franz Nietlispach, Switzerland	1:25:59
1996	Heinz Frei, Switzerland	1:30:14
1997	Franz Nietlispach, Switzerland	1:28:14
1998	Franz Nietlispach, Switzerland	1:21:52
1999	Franz Nietlispach, Switzerland	1:21:36
2000	Franz Nietlispach, Switzerland	1:33:32
2001	Ernst Van Dyk, South Africa	1:25:12
2002	Ernst Van Dyk, South Africa	1:23:19

WOMEN'S WHEELCHAIR CHAMPIONS

1977	Sharon Rahn, Champaign, Il	3:48:51
1978	Susan Shapiro, Berkeley, Ca	3:52:35
1979	Sheryl Blair, Sacramento, Ca	3:27:56
1980	Sharon Limpert, Minneapolis, Mn	2:49:04
1981	Candace Cable, Las Vegas, Nv	2:38:41
1982	Candace Cable-Brookes, Las Vegas, Nv	2:12:43
1983	Sherry Ramsey, Arvada, Co	2:27:07
1984	Sherry Ramsey, Arvada, Co	2:56:51
1985	Candace Cable-Brookes, Long Beach, Ca	2:05:26
1986	Candace Cable-Brookes, Long Beach, Ca	2:09:28
1987	Candace Cable-Brookes, Long Beach, Ca	2:19:55
1988	Candace Cable-Brookes, Long Beach, Ca	2:10:44
1989	Connie Hansen, Denmark	1:50:06
1990	Jeanne Driscoll, Champaign, Il	1:43:17
1991	Jeanne Driscoll, Champaign, Il	1:42:42
1992	Jeanne Driscoll, Champaign, Il	1:36:52
1993	Jeanne Driscoll, Champaign, Il	1:34:50
1994	Jeanne Driscoll, Champaign, Il	1:34:22
1995	Jeanne Driscoll, Champaign, Il	1:40:42
1996	Jeanne Driscoll, Champaign, Il	1:52:56
1997	Louise Sauvage, Australia	1:54:28
1998	Louise Sauvage, Australia	1:41:19
1999	Louise Sauvage, Australia	1:42:23
2000	Jeanne Driscoll, Champaign, Il	2:00:52
2001	Louise Sauvage, Australia	1:53:54
2002	Edith Hunkeler, Switzerland	1:45:57

INDEX

275

Nichol, Bob, 29
Nick's, 122
Nike Corporation, 32, 136
Nocella, Debbie, xv,
Noe, Mark, 92
Norris, Fred, 163
Northwest Airlines, 19

O

O'Brien, Dick, 190
Ocean Spray Cranberries, Inc, 19
Offtech, Inc., 19
Oksanen, Eino, 163, 225, 259
Old South Church (Boston, MA), 234
O'Leary, Aengus, 212
O'Leary's, 212
Olympic Marathon, 26, 86, 0108, 152,
    193, 210, 218
Olympics, vii, 5, 6, 16, 141, 209, 245,
    249, 250, 263
Olympic Stadium, 6
One Flew Over the Cuckoo's Nest, 255
O'Neil, Louise, 133
O'Neil, Tip, 191
Orlando Magic, 61
Orr, Bobby, 147
Oskam, Os & Bev, 44, 47
Oslo, Norway, 47
Out Lady of Victories, 32

P

Palace Verdes, CA, 239
Palka, Fred & Paula, 121
Paris, 233
Parker, Jay, 182
Parker, Ken, 100, 171
Patriot's Day, 7, 23, 38, 98, 111, 181, 217
Pawson, Les, 128, 132
Pearce, Howard, 250
Perez, Tony, 216
Perini (Family), 78
Perini Construction, 78
Persians, 5
Petch, Charles, 166
Pheideppides, 5, 6, 178, 225, 245, 247
Philadelphia, PA, 34, 100
Philippines, 140

Phipps, Rob, 41
Pillar House, 156
Pippig, Uta, xi, xv, 37, 39, 46, 72, 86,
    114, 115, 129, 132, 133, 138, 150,
    168, 198, 204, 206, 214, 215, 234,
    242, 258, 259, 264
Pontiac, 19
Portugal, 86
Powerbar/Power Food, Inc., 19, 118,
    145, 255
"Praying Indians," 104
Preservagi, Dick, 69
Proctor, George, 172
Prosperous Gardens, 69
Providence College, 180
Prudential Center, 229 230, 232, 256
Public Broadcasting System (PBS), 20

Q

Quebec, 246
Quansigomog Indians, 64
Quincy, MA, 259

R

R.H. Long Auto Sales, 93, 94
Radley, Joe, 211
Radley, John "Jack" or "Jackie", xvi, 34,
    49, 96, 97, 98, 121, 173, 193, 211,
    254, 262
Radley, Kevin, 211
Radley, Michael "Rad", 7, 34, 49, 54, 61,
    86, 96, 97, 98, 121, 165, 173, 193,
    207, 211, 254, 262
Radiofrequency Catheter Ablation, 10
Rainear, Dennis, 22
Ratcliffe, Tom, xvi,
Rath Skelter, 222
Ratti, Gloria, vii, xv
Ray, Joie, 136
Red Cross, 66, 77
Redman, Edward, 228
Red Sox Nation, 217
Renaud, Henri, 245
Revere, Paul, 5, 38
Rhode Island, 108
Ribicoff, Charles, 106
Road Runner, 9

283

Roba, Fatuma, 31, 32, 86, 116, 175
Roberts, Eugene, 189
Rocky, 61
Rodgers, Bill "Boston Billy," ix, xv, 18,
    56, 58, 115, 119, 146, 148, 150,
    166, 170, 185, 198, 209, 224, 225,
    227, 235, 244, 253, 259, 264
Rodgers, Charlie, 147
Roe, Allison, 200
Roger Maris Asterisk,"60
Rolling Stones, 54
Rome, Italy, 210
Ronzoni/Hershey Pasta, 19
Roosevelt, Eleanor, 245
Roosevelt, President Franklin "FDR",
    168, 245
Rosales, Maria, See Rosie Ruiz
Rose, Tim & Mary Kate, 192
Ross, Donald, 160
Roxbury, MA, 101
Ruiz, Rosie, 222, 223, 225, 250
Rummakko, Pentto, 150
Russia (Russian), 32, 133
Ruth, Babe, 216

S

Sabinal, Jacinto, 194
Saint Botolph, 213
Salazar, Alberto, 37, 138, 140, 151, 180,
    199, 256, 257
Salem Witches, 202
Saletan, Becky, xvi,
Saltonstall (family), 213
Sapp, Warren, 67, 68
Sauvage, Louise, 141, 200, 201
Sawyer, Diane, 131
Scandinavia (Scandinavian), 150
Schmidt, Aaron, xvi,
Schwabb, Denise, 144
Scituate, MA, 86
Scottish, 100
Segal, Erich, 84
Seko, Toshihiko, 166, 174, 198, 230
Semple, John "Jock," 13, 59, 80, 81, 82,
    83, 84, 87, 89, 90, 100, 101, 121,
    146, 230
Sewall, Judge Samuel, 202

Sharon, MA, 29
Shaughnessy, Dan, xvi, 257
Shaw, Bruce, xv,
Shawmut, 213
Sheehan, George Doctor, 232
Shelly, Lyle, 178
Sheraton Hotel (Boston, MA), 221
Sherpas, 8
Shorter, Frank, 26, 152, 178, 247
Sidney Mines, Nova Scotia, 295
Siesage, Humphrey, 241
Silva, German, 73, 74, 166
Simmons College, 221
Ski & Tennis Chalet, 178
Smith, Geoff, 31, 65, 88, 134, 155,171,
    174, 178, 179, 180, 214, 230
Socrates, 4
Somerset Hotel (Boston, MA), 221, 227
Song, Ki Yoon, 102
Sony Walkman, 87
Souder, Edmund,
South Africa, 29, 30
South Korea (Korean), 102, 116, 126
Southworth, Sandra, xvi
Spanish American War, 122
Speen, John, 106
Sports & Fitness Expo, 29, 31, 32
Sri Lakshemi Temple (Framingham,
    MA), 82
St. Ignatius Church, 192, 195, 197
St. John's Seminary, 195
St. Peter, 38
Stanley, Francis, 172
Stanley, Freelan, 172
Stanley Brothers, 172
Stanley Steamer, 172
"Star Spangled Banner," 46, 49
Steve Miller Band, 50
Steven's Corner, 69
Stockholm, Sweden, 241
Stockdale, James, Admiral, 39
Suh, Yun Bok, 172
Sullivan, Bob, xvi
Sunshine Biscuits, 19
Suomalainen, Olavi, 167, 194
"Superman," 121
Swan & Stuart, 140